T0328986

Antiquity Now

Written in a lively and accessible style, *Antiquity Now* opens our gaze to the myriad uses and abuses of classical antiquity in contemporary fiction, film, comics, drama, television—and even internet forums. With every chapter focusing on a different aspect of classical reception—including sexuality, politics, gender, and ethnicity—this book explores the ideological motivations behind contemporary American allusions to the classical world. Ultimately, this kaleidoscope of receptions—from calls for marriage equality to examinations of gang violence to passionate pleas for peace (or war)—reveals a "classical antiquity" that reconfigures itself daily, as modernity explains itself to itself through ever-expanding technologies and media. *Antiquity Now* thus examines the often-surprising redeployment of the art and literature of the ancient world, a geography charged with especial value in the contemporary imagination.

THOMAS E. JENKINS holds a Ph.D. in classical philology from Harvard University and is Professor and Chair of the Department of Classical Studies at Trinity University in San Antonio, Texas. He has published widely on classical texts, including his book *Intercepted Letters: Epistolarity and Narrative in Greek and Roman Literature* (2006), as well as articles on Ovid, Euripides, Homer, and especially classical reception. He has been a Fellow of the Center for Hellenic Studies in Washington, DC, and winner of the inaugural Paul Rehak Award for his article on Lucian's *Dialogues of the Courtesans*. In 2013, Jenkins premiered a new stage version of Plautus' *The Haunted House* at the Overtime Theater in San Antonio, Texas.

Antiquity Now

The Classical World in the Contemporary
American Imagination

———

THOMAS E. JENKINS

CAMBRIDGE
UNIVERSITY PRESS

University Printing House, Cambridge CB2 8BS, United Kingdom

One Liberty Plaza, 20th Floor, New York, NY 10006, USA

477 Williamstown Road, Port Melbourne, VIC 3207, Australia

4843/24, 2nd Floor, Ansari Road, Daryaganj, Delhi - 110002, India

79 Anson Road, #06-04/06, Singapore 079906

Cambridge University Press is part of the University of Cambridge.

It furthers the University's mission by disseminating knowledge in the pursuit of
education, learning and research at the highest international levels of excellence.

www.cambridge.org
Information on this title: www.cambridge.org/9780521154345

© Thomas E. Jenkins 2015

First published 2015
First paperback edition 2017

A catalogue record for this publication is available from the British Library

Library of Congress Cataloging in Publication data
Jenkins, Thomas E., 1971–
Antiquity now : the classical world in the contemporary American imagination / Thomas Jenkins.
    pages   cm
Includes bibliographical references and index.
ISBN 978-0-521-19626-0 (Hardback)
1. United States–Civilization–Classical influences.   I. Title.
E169.12.J47 2015
973–dc23   2014044737

ISBN 978-0-521-19626-0 Hardback
ISBN 978-0-521-15434-5 Paperback

Contents

Illustrations

Acknowledgements

It is a pleasure to record my many debts during the gestation of this book. *Antiquity Now* was first supported by a fellowship at Harvard University's Center for Hellenic Studies in Washington, D.C. and further aided by a term of research support at Trinity University; it has been improved immeasurably by the astute questions and responses of audiences and students at Washington and Lee University, the University of Houston, The Open University, the University of Iowa, Uppsala University, Northwestern University, Harvard University, and Bryn Mawr College. For support and advice, I especially thank "The Writing Group" at Trinity University—Nicolle Hirschfeld, Shannon Mariotti, Tim O'Sullivan, Corinne Pache, and David Rando—and other colleagues who have commented generously on various chapters or drafts, including Richard Armstrong, Erwin Cook, Anne Duncan, Rachel Joseph, Gregory Nagy, Bladimir Ruiz, Richard Tarrant, and Richard Thomas. The anonymous readers for Cambridge University Press provided much needed (and often witty) encouragement along the way, and have spared me from many a blooper. Commissioning Editor Michael Sharp provided crucial and timely feedback as the shape of the project inevitably morphed over time, and Elizabeth Hanlon guided the manuscript through its final production. I also thank Susan Cohen for preparing the index—the first ever to feature Beyoncé and Cato the Elder on the same page—and to the eagle-eyed Anna Hodson for copy-editing. Needless to say, all errors are my own.

I owe a special debt of gratitude to several cohorts of Trinity University undergraduates who have survived sprints through the seminar *Antiquity and Modernity*, where much of this material was first introduced. They have challenged my assumptions, encouraged my boldness, and have uncovered surprising new examples of classical reception, some of which feature in the following pages. These students' freshness, exuberance, and good humor have made it an especial pleasure to ponder the intersections of antiquity and now.

1 | Introduction

On May 23, 2000, millions of Americans pondered an ancient Greek poem—in the *original* Greek. Certainty is impossible, but this was likely the greatest *en masse* reading of ancient Greek *ever*. The reason? That evening witnessed the season four finale of *Buffy the Vampire Slayer*, Joss Whedon's cult television series about an unlikely posse of monster-killers. At the beginning of this particular episode ("Restless"), Willow (a young American sorceress) has just finished tattooing Greek on a fellow witch's back (that of Tara, her lover); the Greek—excepting perhaps an errant iota—is epigraphic and absolutely legible (to those, of course, who know Greek). For about six seconds, the camera travels the length of Tara's back, in effect, "reading" the Greek for the audience, and allowing the viewer a moment's rumination on the text (see Figure 1.1). After the camera—and Willow—finishes the poem, the camera cuts away to an extended conversation between Tara and Willow, and soon the episode leaps into the wider "Buffyverse" of Watchers, and Slayers, and slithering Lovecraftian horrors from alternate dimensions. In a moment or two, the Greek is gone.

But not forgotten. For most audience members, a "naïve" reading of the poem—that is to say, of the legible but unfathomable Greek—would focus precisely on the "deadness" of the language: an ancient tongue used to summon, it seems, ancient and unfathomable powers. The *content* of the poem would be immaterial: its *form* is the thing, such as *abracadabra* or other incantatory utterances. For most readers, then, the Greek poem is a signifier of magic, setting the scene for that particular episode's heavily oneiric and fantastic story arc. Yet the Greek is assuredly not content-less, but is rather an *authentically* ancient poem, calculatedly included by series creator Whedon in this most postmodern of narratives. Indeed, *Buffy*—as the booming scholarship on Buffy has proven—constitutes a quintessentially postmodern text, a series that mimics in form the lowly genre of "teen dramady," while juggling startling explorations of sexuality, metaphysics, desire, and even eschatology.[1]

---

[1] Jowett 2005: 2 describes *Buffy* "an ideologically and formally ambiguous postfeminist artifact, one that is characteristic of postmodern cultural production." For Jowett, postmodernism is the crucial critical mode for the interrogation of cultural change.

Figure 1.1. Willow paints Sappho's poem 1 on Tara's back, in the episode "Restless" of *Buffy the Vampire Slayer.*

(In its broader narrative aspects, *Buffy* absolutely invites comparison to established patterns of heroic saga; Buffy even undergoes a shocking *katabasis*—a descent to the underworld—and a triumphant, practically messianic return.) Although the show makes fun of its cartoony, monster-dispatching archetypes (indeed, the characters refer to themselves as "The Scooby Gang," a nod to the syndicated 1970s *Scooby-Doo* cartoon serial), true Buffyphiles appreciate that the show is as literary and knowingly allusive as the best of American fiction. A season finale penned by the show's creator is not apt to feature meaningless Greek.[2]

Immediately after the finale, therefore, curious Buffyphiles harnessed the power of the internet to discover what a few erudite viewers had already grasped on a first "reading": that Willow was not inscribing just *any* poem on Tara's back, but the most extensive fragment we possess of Sappho, the famous poet of Lesbos from the early sixth century BCE. And here we begin our exploration of what happens when contemporary artists appropriate, or "receive," a classical text: in other words, here we begin our examination of how (and why) ancient literature continues to be inspiration for contemporary social agitation. Even as late as the turn of the millennium, a lesbian story arc on television ran afoul of both popular attitudes towards sexuality as well as network censors, who allowed the erotic storyline of Tara and Willow only as long as there was no "kissing" (or worse!): that is, as long as Tara and Willow's homosexuality remained notional rather than physical. After all, it had been only been three years since Ellen Degeneres' controversial "coming-out" episode on ABC's *Ellen*, which cost the network two corporate sponsors (Chrysler and J. C. Penney) and which generated angry and impassioned editorials across the country (including Reverend Jerry Falwell's timeless denunciation of "Ellen Degenerate").[3] Other networks, as well, remained skittish about including openly homosexual characters in their programming.[4] At the highest levels of televised media, homosexuality was still a controversial—and therefore unwelcome—theme.

---

[2] For a reading of Buffy's fifth season through the lens of Virgil's *Aeneid*, see Marshall 2003. (As Marshall notes, at least one other character in the show—Giles the Librarian—could be expected to possess some level of classical education.)

[3] For an overview of the fallout from Ellen's "coming-out" episode, see Lacey Rose's "The Booming Business of Ellen DeGeneres: From Broke and Banished to Daytime's Top Earner," www.hollywoodreporter.com/news/ellen-degeneres-show-oprah-winfrey-jay-leno-364373?page=1. Accessed April 21, 2014.

[4] Hubert 1999: 609.

As Joss Whedon noted on the show's blog in May 2000,[5] the WB network's restrictions on open displays of same-sex desire forced him to be "creative" as an artist: in season four's sixteenth episode, which prefigures the finale, a magical spell, mutually performed by Tara and Willow, "substitutes" for sex, thereby enabling the show's creators to explore the characters' relationship through the symbols of another discourse entirely: the sisterhood of witchcraft.[6] As so often, then, homosexuality, denied the opportunity for transparent discourse, operates only metaphorically, with its themes, priorities, and contradictions mapped onto another symbolic system. In this way, American television seems to be mirroring—at a remove of some fifty years—the arc of American stage drama, which too had its efflorescence of "closeted" theater of the type penned by mid-century authors Edward Albee and Tennessee Williams. Tony Kushner's 1993 opus *Angels in America: A Gay Fantasia on American Themes* neatly reversed America's "closeting" of homosexuals by "closeting" America within an unabashedly gay and sweeping epic, and one would be hard pressed today to locate systematized censorship of homosexuality in the production of New York theater.[7]

In the same period, however, television remained an unwelcome space for openly homosexual characters and themes. Ellen's "coming-out" episode notwithstanding, the appearance of homosexuality on American television was uncommon, if not outright taboo; homosexuality thus remained metaphorically displaced and "closeted." In the May finale of the fourth season of Buffy, then, Whedon complicates this metaphorical displacement of homosexuality by including a love spell that's not only erotic, but *specifically* (even, in a sense, punningly) lesbian/Lesbian: the two operating planes of *Buffy*'s discourse on Tara and Willow—the textually magical and the subtextually homosexual—thus mirror and reify each other.[8] In the poem inscribed on Tara's back, the narrator—who, for

<hr/>

[5] The original blog for *Buffy*—named *The Bronze*, after a featured bar within the show—remains archived and searchable; the URL for Joss Whedon's May 4, 2000 comments is currently: www.cise.ufl.edu/cgi-bin/cgiwrap/hsiao/buffy/get-archive?date=20000504.

[6] Jowett 2005: 50.

[7] For a notorious and homophobic exposé of "disguised" homosexuality, see Kaufmann 1966, a contemporary indictment of both Williams and Albee.

[8] For Mendlesohn 2002: 69, such a displacement "actually undercuts a queer reading of Willow at all, first by neutralizing her sexuality and then by rechanneling thoughts of lesbian relationships in a safe direction." I disagree; queerness necessarily displaces more straightforward patterns of sexual discourse, and the inclusion of Sappho 1 absolutely reinscribes Willow into the framework of modern sexual desire. Mendlesohn concedes that the inclusion of Sappho helps halt the "deeroticization" of Willow, but is generally disappointed by Whedon's gesture.

simplicity's sake, we shall call Sappho—calls out to the goddess Aphrodite after her lover has spurned her:

> Iridescent-throned and immortal Aphrodite,
> Wile-weaving daughter of Zeus: I implore you!
> Do not crush my spirit with curses or torments,
>> O reverend one,
>
> But approach here! If ever you have heard
> My pleadings, then return: for once before
> Having left your father's golden
>> House...
>
> [you said...]
>
> "Whom should Persuasion again
> force into affection for you? Who,
> O Sappho, is doing you wrong?"
>
> "For even if she flees; quickly she shall pursue;
> Even if she spurns gifts, she shall give them;
> Even if she does not love, soon she will love,
>> Though entirely unwilling."

As scholars such as Segal and Faraone have observed, this first poem of Sappho includes all the hallmarks of a literary love spell: the invocation to a deity; the indignant expression of injustice; and, most chillingly perhaps, the unwilling subjugation of the object of desire.[9] (Left unsaid, but implicit, are the punishments inflicted upon the unwilling, including sleep deprivation, fever, and physical pain. There is little that is sentimental about an Ancient Greek love spell.[10]) Sappho thus witnesses a theophany in which Aphrodite promises to restore Sappho's girlfriend: however troubled the relationship, Sappho's lover will return to her, if only through magic. While many of Sappho's fragmentary poems glance at potentially homo-erotic themes—such as fragment 16's praise of Anactoria's "lovely walk and bright visage," or the suggestively ripening apple of fragment 105—Sappho's "Hymn to Aphrodite" tackles the issue head-on. The poem's

---

[9] Segal 1974; Faraone 1999: 136–7.

[10] For the general category of ancient Greek *agogê*, or 'charm' spells, see Faraone 1999: 41–95; a fine comparandum to the Sappho poem is PGM XIXa.50–54: "Aye, lord demon, attract, inflame, destroy, burn, cause her to swoon from love as she is being burnt, inflamed. Goad the tortured soul, the heart of Karosa, whom Thelo bore, until she leaps forth and comes to Apalos... Do not allow Karosa herself ... to think of her own husband, her child, drink, food, but let her come melting for passion and love and intercourse...."

passionate, urgent evocation of same-sex desire dovetails exactly with Whedon's subtextual drive to "out" Willow and Tara as passionate, physical lovers; frustrated and stonewalled by modern network censors, Whedon turns to antiquity in order to criticize and interrogate modern sexual mores, however obliquely. Artistically, the poem even prefigures the eventual break-up of Willow and Tara in season six, and Willow's transformation—after Tara's shocking death—into "Dark Willow," a witch who only uses magic for self-serving, ultimately destructive ends. In this respect, she is not unlike the Sapphic narrator of poem 1: an erotic being who channels supernatural energy for morally dubious purposes. (Fragment 1 may be a "love" poem in some senses, but it's hardly a cheery gloss on same-sex attachments.)

So what seems a throwaway moment in *Buffy*—a Greek tattoo on a sinuous back—in fact permits a bifocal examination of the poetics of modern homosexual discourse, compelled (as so often) to swerve into other poetic and semiotic systems, this time into the classical. But, intriguingly, the discourse of such a reception works both ways; at the same time that the inclusion of Sappho's poem "queers" the relationship between Willow and Sappho—thereby evading network censors—*Buffy* is indubitably and assuredly queering Sappho.[11] For there is nothing *necessarily* gay or homosexual about Sappho's poetry; indeed, for most readers in most times, Sappho has been assuredly, even aggressively, heterosexual. Even in antiquity, Sappho's name was attached to a beautiful young man named Phaon—"the bright one"—out of despair for whom the poetess hurls herself from a cliff.[12] This sorry affair finds reflections in traditions both ancient and modern. The (pseudo-Ovidian) epistle from Sappho to Phaon pitifully laments "Phaon, even as you frequent the faraway fields of Sicily's Aetna, a flame burns in me no less than Aetna's own!" (*Heroides* 15.11–12), while Mary Robinson's 1796 Sapphic sonnet cycle includes the following ecstatic reflection on Phaon's powers of attraction:

> Why, when I gaze on Phaon's beauteous eyes,
> Why does each thought in wild disorder stray?
> Why does each fainting faculty decay,
> And my chill'd breast in throbbing tumults rise?
> (4.1–4)[13]

---

[11] For a sociological analysis of the queering of Willow in terms of fan response, see Driver 2007: 57–90. For Driver, the inscription of Sappho on Tara marks the exchange as "one of the most sensual scenes in the show... fluid yet flesh-bound, this [is] a corporeally luscious scene..." (68).

[12] Knox 1995: 278–9.   [13] Robinson 1796.

Sappho's shadowy *historical* presence has allowed—perhaps encouraged— a parallel *artistic* and *fictional* presence, one far more powerful and influential than, paradoxically, the "real" Sappho. As Dimitrios Yatromanolakis has demonstrated, such a semiotic diffusion took place almost immediately after Sappho's death: "Sappho" thus proliferated as a nexus of *ideas*—ideas that often blossomed into long-running traditions (such as the torrid Phaon/Sappho affair), or which languished after their original social contexts no longer applied. In her afterlife, "Sappho" was thus remolded into a staggering number of shapes and forms: from a heterosexual vixen; to a female symposiast; to a lustful courtesan (one who opted to *lesbiazein*, or, in Ancient Greek, 'to perform oral sex'); and even (in a notorious comparison) to a prim and virginal schoolmistress.[14] This last maneuver was a desperate bid by nineteenth-century Prussian classicist Ulrich von Wilamowitz-Moellendorff to sanitize a recent and troubling trend: the Victorian equation of Sappho's biography and lyrics with contemporary same-sex impulses and desires. Only among the Victorians, then, did Sappho finally emerge as a "modern" homosexual, or lesbian;[15] and it was this "idea" of Sappho that American lesbians in the 1950s adopted as a sort of calling card, a password, a code.[16]

When Whedon introduced Sappho's poem into *Buffy The Vampire Slayer*, he inserted "Sappho," not Sappho: he placed himself at a long line of artists who have appropriated Sappho's work for contemporary ideological ends. Indeed, as Whedon has himself remarked, he considers himself a feminist: the underlying generic assumption of *Buffy the Vampire Slayer* is that the naïve female "victim" in prototypical slasher films—say, from the *Halloween* series, or its brethren—constitutes a misogynistic projection of female insecurity, ineptitude, and impotence. As a general rule, women in such horror films rarely defeat their (masculine, sadistic)

---

[14] For Sappho-as-symposiast, see Yatromanolakis 2007: 197–220; for the sexual fetishes of Lesbian women, see Yatromanolakis 2007: 183–9; for the early twentieth-century reception of Sappho as a virginal proto-gym teacher, see Parker 1993. See especially Parker's important formulation: "Every age creates its own Sappho. Her position as *the* woman poet (as Homer is the male poet), the first female voice heard in the West, elevates her to a status where she is forced to be a metonym for all women. Sappho ceases to become an author and becomes a symbol" (Parker 1993: 149–50).

[15] See especially Prins 1997: 94: "Although questions about Sappho have persisted for many centuries, her association with lesbian identity is a particularly Victorian phenomenon, and a legacy that persists in modern lesbian studies." Wood 1994 explores the "queering" of Sappho in *fin-de-siècle* Europe, including its musical subcultures (especially opera). Goldhill 2006: 250–74 examines the similar destabilization of Sappho's sexuality in the visual arts.

[16] Richlin 2005.

attackers: the vanquishing of the enemy is thus left to the male hero, and the pretty heroines must make do with virtual arias of screaming. (A particularly unattractive corollary is that sexually active heroines—those who flaunt or otherwise exercise their sexuality in ways that could be considered threatening or transgressive—are sure to meet particularly grisly ends.) The postmodern *Buffy*, by contrast, posits a universe in which the notional epitome of slasher-victimhood—a blue-eyed, blonde minx with a Valley Girl moniker—is, ironically, a being of immense power, savvy, and smarts: the eternal savior instead of the eternally saved. While *Buffy* scholars are split on the range and impact of Whedon's feminism, the inclusion of Sappho's poem 1 helps to skew—even "queer"—*Buffy* as a site of contested feminine identities, lesbian and otherwise.[17] In his bid to subvert the dominant discourses of gender in American horror and action films, Whedon turns to antiquity, however briefly, to support the construction of a controlling, even awesome feminine subject.

In Whedon's season finale, Sappho's poem thus functions in at least two different discursive modes: one, entirely as form (an ancient Greek poem or spell), the other, as content (the inscription of same-sex desire). There is, perhaps, a third mode here as well: readers who intuit that the Greek must have *some* homoerotic implication, but cannot actually read the Greek, thereby inscribing or constructing "Sapphic" lesbianism as unknowable or inscrutable. Depending on the narrative "frame," the text thus yields multiple meanings, including a controversial one: the reformulation of Willow and Tara as modern, American lesbians. I turn now to similar collision of form and content, of antiquity and modernity, with an even stronger bent towards the postmodern: what happens when we launch an ancient Roman poet—for example, Horace—into cyberspace? What happens when a poem concerning first-century BCE Augustan social reform finds itself commenting—by accident or design—on Clinton-era social devolution? As so often, the result is a semiotic maelstrom, and a glimpse into the continuing negotiation of classical antiquity as a precursor—or metaphor—for American society itself.

Horace's *Odes*—a series of lyric poems published in three books in 23 BCE, with a fourth added in 13 BCE—remain one of the cornerstones of Augustan literature.[18] Taken as a unit, they cover an impressive swath of

---

[17] For the ongoing debates on the extent of Whedon's feminism, see Levine 2007. For an impassioned diatribe against the self-importance of Buffy studies, see Jenkyns 2002.

[18] For the date of 23 BCE, see Nisbet and Rudd 2004: xix; Hutchinson 2002 argues for separately published volumes.

human experience—from meditations on erotic experience, with both
women and boys; to philosophical ruminations on time, death, and aging;
to social inquiry and commentary on contemporary events. In terms of
technique, they remain a tour de force: for the most part, Horace adopts
complex Greek meters—Alcaics, Sapphics, Glyconics, Asclepiads, among
them—and wrestles his Latin into these graceful, albeit non-native, forms.
Consonant with Roman toleration for self-admiration, Horace is happy
to offer that as a collection, these odes constitute a *monumentum aere
perennius*, "a monument more lasting than bronze" (3.30.1).

But not all parts of the *Odes* have earned an equal immortality. While
Odes 1.5—concerning the traumatizing lass Pyrrha—has been so popular
that Ronald Storrs could assemble a book consisting *entirely* of translations
of this single ode—Horace's so-called *Roman Odes* (the first six odes of
the third book) have resisted continued appropriation.[19] Poems on love,
death, aging, and the evanescence of youth: such aperçus possess universal
appeal and are easily adaptable.[20] The *Roman Odes'* emphasis on morality,
coupled with far-flung allusions to myth and to contemporary foreign
policy, sits less comfortably with modern artists, and the poems seem far
less amenable to creative adaptation. The *Odes'* increasing cynicism about
the morals of contemporary Romans features an illustrative fable in *Odes*
3.5, in which the Roman hero Regulus, captured in Africa by the Cartha-
ginians in 255 BCE, receives a parole to Rome in which to argue for
prisoner exchange. Instead, Regulus persuades the Roman Senate to reject
the proposal; he then (honorably) returns to Carthage, where he is re-
imprisoned, hideously tortured, and executed.[21] Horace's point is that men
of old were made of sterner stuff, happy to die for cause and country (in
contradistinction, perhaps, to the effete and nervous populace of Horace's
contemporary cityscape). In fact, the poem ends (3.5.53–56) with Regulus
returning to Carthage as if merely concluding a day in court—as if about to
retire to an estate in Venafrum (a rural town south-east of Rome) or

---

[19] Storrs 1959.

[20] Theodore Ziolkowski 2005 notes that mid-century American receptions of Horace's poetry
tend to be emphatically a-political. He cites, for example, a portion of Lawrence Durrell's 1944
"On First Looking into Loeb's Horace": "This lover of vines and slave to quietness/ Walking like
a figure of smoke here, musing/ Among his high and lovely Tuscan pines" (196). Here, Horace's
political poetry is ignored in favor of his more reflective pastoral musings. Later adaptations—
such as Robert Lowell's adaptation of *Odes* 2.7 (1967)—could indeed espouse a political
viewpoint (in this case, pardon for conscientious objectors of the Vietnam war (204)). As we
will see, Mezey's *To the Americans* continues this interpretative vein of politicizing Horace.

[21] For Cicero's version of events, see *De Off.* 3.99 and *In Pisonem* 43; Blätter 1944/5 is a useful
compendium of the variants of the Regulus tale.

perhaps to Tarentum, a resort town and place of relaxation. Horace thus juxtaposes the mundane (and implicitly contemporary) life of *otium*, 'leisure,' to the perils faced by the heroes of the past.

The following poem is even bleaker in its portrayal of contemporary (Roman) society and thus leads us to a curious collision of Augustus and Clinton, of papyrus and the blogosphere, of Roman defeat and terrorism's ascension. If *Odes* 3.5 features an implicit warning about the deterioration of the Roman stock, 3.6 pulls no punches in its uninviting assessment of current and future Roman depravity. It begins with a crisis in Roman religion: "Though guiltless, you will continue to pay for the sins of your forefathers, Roman, until you repair the crumbling temples and shrines of the gods, and the statues that are begrimed with black smoke."[22] Only because Romans have traditionally held themselves humble before the gods (*dis te minorem quod geris,* 3.6.5) have they been able to rule; Horace further argues that Roman impiety is to blame for the recent military disasters in the Eastern provinces. Because of Roman irreverence, "Monaeses and the troops of Pacorus have twice squashed our ill-omened attacks"—once in 40 BCE when the Parthians destroyed the army of Marc Antony's legate Decidius Saxa, and again in 36 BCE during Antony's disastrous invasion of the same province.[23] Worse yet, these setbacks left Rome vulnerable to "The Ethiopian" (3.6.14), a thinly veiled reference to the much-reviled Egyptian queen Cleopatra.

And this is just the beginning. From martial affairs Horace turns to marital ones, as generations fertile in sin (*fecunda culpae*) defile marriage, the home, and the populace in general. First, Horace focuses on the family. A young Roman girl takes up the art of dancing – and as if this action weren't sufficiently alarming, she learns *Ionian* dancing: the most effeminate and most raunchy type, tainted as it is with the luxuriance of the East. Hand in hand with dancing go the family's "incestuous loves" (*incestos amores*): as soon as the husband and *pater familias* reels with wine, the wife seeks out young adulterers. Worse yet—could it get any worse?—the husband doesn't care, and to be frank, it's good money when the wife lands a high-paying Spanish captain for a trick (3.6.29). It may be degrading (*dedecorum*), but it's also lucrative. In contrast, Horace juxtaposes these incarnations of iniquity with the nobler stuff of yesteryear: "Not from parents like these came the young men who stained the sea with Punic blood … No, they were the manly children of peasant soldiers" (3.6.33–38), able to plough the earth with Sabellian mattocks, while hauling

---

[22] Translation from Nisbet and Rudd 2004: 163.

[23] For the historical background see Nisbet and Rudd 2004: 103; West 2002: 67.

timber under the watchful eye of their harsh mother. The ode concludes with some of Horace's most famous, but also most controversial, lines:

> Damnosa quid non imminuit dies?
> Aetas parentem peior avis tulit.
> Nos nequiores, mox daturos
> Progeniem vitiosiorem.
>
> (3.6.45–48)

> Iniquitous time! What does it not impair? Our fathers' age, worse than our grandfathers', gave birth to us, an inferior breed, who will in due course produce still more degenerate offspring.

And so the poem, and the cycle, ends: the poet gazes into the pit of Roman degeneracy and searches fruitlessly for the bottom. It's a disconcerting way to end the series, and at least one scholar has attempted to arrest the nihilism by appealing to the rather more hopeful invocation to the children at the beginning of the "Roman Odes" cycle (*Odes* 3.1): "Just as resolve to restore the ruined dwellings of the gods in the City reverses the effects of time, so too can the relentless deterioration of Roman virtue be arrested if Horace's call to moral re-armament is heeded."[24] David Schenker reviews this and other spirited attempts at alleviating the tone of nihilism and despair; he concludes that "while the impulse to look for some moderating quality is understandable, there is no moderation at the end of the Sixth Roman Ode," and that it is "only through considerable special pleading ... that the final pessimistic stanza can be made to yield reminders of the beginning of the poem, much less the whole series."[25] In other words, a reader is stuck with taking that final stanza at face value: we are worse than our forefathers and doomed to produce children even more wicked than we.

This might seem a surprising, even phony, sentiment coming from Horace, who elsewhere extols a life of fancy-free bachelor living and who never actually produced children, worse or not. If the *Roman Odes* are, in some sense, a poetic buttress for the emperor Augustus' proposed moral and marital legislation—designed to encourage remarriage and procreation—Horace isn't exactly doing his part for the effort.[26] A modern

---

[24] Witke 1983: 75. This is more or less the interpretative stance taken up by David West in his commentary (2002: 71): "The last stanza of the ode would then contain an implied condition. '(*If* we do not accept a reform of sexual behaviour supported by marriage laws) the degeneration of the Roman state (and consequent disasters) will continue.' Horace here avoids such explicit preaching ...."

[25] Schenker 1993: 164.

[26] For a brief overview of Augustus' marital and moral legislation see Frank 1975: the laws were intended to curb celibacy; aid in the procreation of children; and discourage intermarriage

commentator tries to exculpate Horace from such hypocrisy: "R[.G.M.] N[isbet] would rather not be drawn into speculations about the poet's sincerity; it was not [Horace's] business to formulate social policy but to write an effective poem."[27] This is a crisp (if not ultimately convincing) rebuke: i.e. that poets produce poetry, not progeny. Or, one can, with David Armstrong, confront directly the tastelessness of the moralizing: that only Horace's poetic skill rescues these verses from being "the low point of all Roman poetry."[28] In any case, Ode 3.6 segues abruptly—even disconcertingly —to Ode 3.7, a comparatively sunny ode of erotic consolation. The *Roman Odes* may conclude with the inevitable dissolution of mankind into a morass of wickedness, but at least there's always sex in the offing.

Though none of Horace's Odes have titles per se, *Odes* 3.6 has been traditionally glossed as "To the Romans," which, if a bit bland, at least takes into account the intended audience for the poem, as well as the poem's didactic tone. In 2004, on the online poetry forum *Eratosphere*, an eager blogger posted a late 1990s adaptation of the poem by acclaimed Californian poet Robert Mezey; Mezey is now professor emeritus at Pomona College and his *Collected Poems 1952–1999* was awarded the 2001 Poets Prize for American Poetry. Mezey's own version of *Odes* 3.6 was intriguingly titled "To the Americans," and the resulting controversy speaks volumes about what happens when a classical work—like *Buffy's* Sapphic ode—is suddenly reinterpreted in light of contemporary social trends.

The hullabaloo over "To the Americans" was an accidental firestorm, which makes the episode all the richer. The website *Eratosphere* is mostly dedicated to the finer points of metrical analysis and criticism; separate forums exist for the discussion of established and emerging poets, and more specialized forums are established for poets who wish to submit works-in-progress for criticism. Potential posters are urged to self-select their level of poetic craft and accomplishment, which is just one indication how seriously the site takes its role as watchdog and defender of all things metrical, and how learned and biting the criticisms might be. A budding poet should be prepared for some hard-hitting responses (e.g., from a commentator to a neophyte artist: "Your principal stresses run 3,5,5 in the tercets, but sometimes your lines are accentual syllabic and sometimes

between social classes. For more extended analyses see Treggiari 1991: 60–80 and 277–98.
Fowler 1992: 273 considers Horace's *Odes* 4.5, with its extended panegyric of Augustus, the "easiest to read as straightforwardly fascist," and indeed Horace's (at least superficial) support of the régime has been read against the rise of Hitler and Mussolini in the 1930s.
[27] Nisbet and Rudd 2004: 99.   [28] Armstrong 1989: 101.

only accentual. I have not read you before, so I can't judge whether this is an intentional effect, or the ineptitude of a metrical novice.")[29] A moderator is also happy to offer comments about larger themes: "Sure this [poem] sounds nice, but sound does not suffice to counter the want of apprehensible content . . . [Except for one stanza] the rest is dross."[30] Even those who diligently revise a poem might receive some *extremely* curt criticism from members of the community: "This thing in both its incarnations is execrable, and I mourn the expense of spirit expended by . . . others in trying to correct the irremediable."[31] (The aggrieved poet responds: "Both of your last two posts on this site have been the type of facile ditties that a Hallmark poet would write.")

It is in this sort of cozy, nurturing atmosphere that one reads with interest the thread on "Classical Meters in English," a mode of poetic expression that has been something of a parlor trick for English poets for centuries. The difficulties involved are numerous. Greek and Roman poetry was based on quantitative meters, in which syllables are considered long or short depending on vowel length. Traditional English prosody, by contrast, is usually regulated by accent and line length; syllable length is at best a tertiary consideration. The least effective way to duplicate classical meters, then, is to compose English poetry by counting the vowel length of individual syllables. In his devastating review of W. J. Stone's *On the Use of Classical Metres in English*, the distinguished classicist and poet A. E. Housman declared that Stone's method (of counting English "long" and "short" syllables) created "verses of no sort, but prose in ribands"; he further demonstrated the folly of Stone's *vade mecum* on "classical metres" by hilariously imposing a weakly accented native French meter—the Alexandrine—onto ordinarily strongly accented English words:

> Why does not a lobster ever climb trees or fly?
> Can he not? Or does he think it would look silly?
> I have made these verses as well as I am able:
> You must be to blame if they sound disagreeable.[32]

---

[29] www.ablemuse.com/erato/ubbhtml/Forum17/HTML/003739.html. Accessed July 5, 2006.

[30] www.ablemuse.com/erato/ubbhtml/Forum17/HTML/003727.html. Accessed July 5, 2006. Lest I be accused of focusing on moderator Alan Sullivan, here's some pointed criticism from Clive Watkins: "The imagery is jumbled, the thought incoherent, the fit of sense to metre clumsy, the sentences unwieldy and sometimes ungrammatical, the punctuation often odd. As a result, the overall effect is turgid."www.ablemuse.com/erato/ubbhtml/Forum17/HTML/003721.html. Accessed July 5, 2006.

[31] www.ablemuse.com/erato/ubbhtml/Forum17/HTML/003721.html. Accessed July 5, 2006.

[32] Housman 1972: 486–7.

But Stone's method was also extreme: most practitioners of classical verse in English have instead steered a middle road by taking the ancient metrical scheme, based on quantity, and transferring it, intact, to the English accentual system. This results in a curious, hybrid metrical system in which English words are poured into a complete foreign stanzaic structure (for instance, Sapphics or elegiac couplets).

In July 2004, one discussion on *Eratosphere*—frequented by self-proclaimed "Spheroids"—centered on the possible uses of the Sapphic stanza in English (a stanza with three longer lines, and ending with a shorter *adoneus*). It is the same meter employed by Willow on Tara's back, in her inscription of Sappho 1. The discussion then segued to a longer, more involved debate about classical meters, including Alcaics, a complicated stanzaic form imputed to the Greek lyricist Alcaeus and occasionally adopted by Roman lyric writers as well. In purely technical form, a typical line looks like so: ˘ ˉ | ˉ ˘ ˘ | ˉ ˘ | ˉ ˘ | ˉ X, with occasional metrical substitutions. An English "version" of the Alcaic, then, would replace the longs and shorts with stressed and unstressed syllables, thus approximating the shape of the original Greco-Roman meter. At this point, Paul Lake helpfully offered Robert Mezey's 1990s Alcaic poem, a version of Horace's *Odes* 3.6, "To the Romans." "To the Americans" transplants the original poem to a Clinton-era *Zeitgeist*, and transforms Horace's original charge of Roman impiety into an indictment of American moral laxity:

> Not till every blackened church has been rebuilt,
> and you have repented in dust and ashes—
> of God mocked in the universities,
> blasphemous jokes in the chic galleries,
>
> repented, even though you yourselves be guiltless,
> of covetous hearts, of ears uncircumcised,
> deaf to others' pain, of worshiping
> wealth and filth, of overweening power,—no,
>
> not till you call to mind the ancient mystery:
> only obedience to Him commands obedience,
> will you face your shame, Americans,
> and only then begin to make amends.

This "American-ization" of Horace's poem begins with a bang, and the Latin vocative *Romane*, "o Roman" from *Odes* 3.6.2 is here delayed to the third stanza, "Americans." The begrimed statues and Roman temples of Horace find their parallel in abandoned American churches; the guiltless (*immeritus*, 3.6.1) Roman finds his own parallel in the guiltless American (l. 5), who must nevertheless repent his sins; and the Romans' forgetfulness of their humility before the gods finds a response—but not exactly a parallel—in Mezey's call for "obedience to Him." As we shall see, this is an important interpretative nuance: not only the switch from polytheism to monotheism (reinforced by the allusion to Jeremiah 6.10, "uncircumcised ears"), but from humbleness to religious duty. The swipe at universities and "chic galleries" seems a nod to growing neoconservative dissatisfaction with American higher education and (liberal) cultural elitism, an argument most forcefully propounded by Allan Bloom in his fulminating 1987 work *The Closing of the American Mind*.

The following stanzas continue the radical appropriation of Horace's climate through contemporary American allusions. In the original, Horace demonstrates the gods' disfavor by pointing to the foreign military disasters in Asia Minor. Mezey springs a surprise:

> You have already faced the Lord's fierce anger,
> faced the humiliation of being forced
> to watch one of your sons, a naked
> corpse dragged through the dust of Mogadishu,
>
> all around him the faces of his killers,
> gloating savages, one wearing his dog tags;
> and bombed-out embassies, innocent
> Africans butchered for your fathers' sins;

The Battle of Mogadishu was one of America's most embarrassing military setbacks in the post-Vietnam era. By the early 1990s, Somalia in general and Mogadishu in particular were engulfed in a civil war between rival clans; warlord Mohamed Farrah Aidid was a main perpetrator of the violence, and an obstacle to any lasting peace. On October 3, 1993, United States Army Rangers attempted to capture two of Aidid's henchmen using an air assault; two Black Hawk helicopters were shot down, thereby provoking a desperate rescue attempt and an extended battle. By the end of fighting, about twenty U.S. soldiers and hundreds of Somalis had been killed.[33] The violence helped to cement anti-American sentiment in the region and led to President Clinton's withdrawal of American forces from the area in 1994. A particularly powerful visual expression of the chaos was

---

[33] For a clear-eyed account of the battle of Mogadishu, see Stevenson 1995: 91–5; like Mezey, Stevenson sees America's involvement in Somalia as involving "questions about the moral duties of a nation" (xvi).

the sight of dead American soldiers dragged through the streets, as relayed by CNN and thus to the world. Mezey's reference to the bombed-out embassies appears to be the American ones destroyed by Al-Qaida in Kenya and Tanzania in 1998.

On the one hand, Mezey has set up a sure parallel between Horace's "disasters in Parthia" and the 1993 disaster in Somalia, both of which seem to stem from (1) divine retribution for moral depravity and (2) military overconfidence. The poor easterners—"savages" in Mezey's version—win out because they are, in a sense, less depraved than we are: they may have "paltry necklaces" (*Odes* 3.6.12) but now at least they can claim American "dog tags" (Mezey, 18) as their loot (*praedam, Odes* 3.6.11). At the same time, Mezey has broadened the comparison, and deepened the pathos, by alluding to Achilles' shocking impiety at the end of Homer's *Iliad*. Famously, Achilles, gloating over the death of Trojan hero Hector, drags his enemy's naked corpse three times around the walls of Troy: an appalling act of barbarity both for the Greeks, and it seems, for us.

Just as Horace stressed both the military and social decline of Rome, so too does Mezey turn to the myriad problems of domestic society. The "venom" in our veins has gathered so much strength that:

> . . . today, the nubile preteen reveling
> in hip-hop, her virginity twenty times lost
> (discarded, rather), lies dreaming of
> what new taste-thrill? whips? threesomes? Whatever.

Horace's newly maturing maiden (*matura virgo*, 22) has here morphed into a nubile preteen; her skills in Ionian dancing (*motus Ionicos*, 21–22) are transferred (to my mind, inappropriately and hilariously) to hip-hop; incestuous love-affairs are now S&M-inflected or richly polyamorous. A brief concluding exclamation appropriates this preteen's own nonchalance: "whatever." Mezey then introduces the preteen's sister—or, rather, mother, who "stands ready to open / her scented privacies to stranger, / some stockbroker buddy of her husband's" (30–32)—a clever updating of Horace's salesman (*institor*, 30). Just as in the original Horatian ode, the husband is full partner in this procurement: "he was the go-between!" Sometimes it suits her, however, to ditch her husband and find "her own whoremaster" (as is fitting for "a cunt on the house," l. 34).

If Horace looks back to the Middle Republic as a fount of relative virtue—to the veterans of the Carthaginian war who could stain the sea with Punic blood and then return to fetch the firewood (*recisos/portare fustis*, 40–41)—then Mezey's solution is to laud the American soldiers of

WWII (thus hitting upon the same trope as Tom Brokaw's similarly themed, and contemporaneous, *The Greatest Generation*, 1998). "Not from such unclean loins did the lean farmboys/ the hardbitten wranglers and factory stiffs spring/ who waded ashore at Normandy": here Mezey transmutes the Roman invasion of Carthage into the Allies' invasion of France in 1944. Meanwhile, those who died "in the Solomons, in the Ardennes, in the sky . . . bled for and saved us"; in contrast to present-day Americans, these were "tough, God-fearing young men," who, like Horace's Middle Republic forefathers, were excellent on a farm: who "rode the tractor/ long past sundown . . . or sold windfall fruit on grey sidewalks/thin shirts and sharp faces against winter . . .." All these sentiments lead inexorably to the final two stanzas, which, just as in Horace's version, provoke in the reader either derision or sympathy:

> they came of better stock. May God have mercy.
> Their grandchildren, so licentious, so greedy,
> go on dancing, drinking and snorting,
> lovelessly fucking, all frantic, manic—
>
> Degeneration doesn't come suddenly
> to an end; shrugged at, accepted, it takes over.
> Who will die to save their grandchildren,
> come face to face once more with real evil?

It's worth noting that Mezey has here *expanded* Horace's original ending into two stanzas: the penultimate stanza in particular seems like a riff or a phantasmagoria on degenerate themes: dance, booze, drugs, sex. The vatic voice of the original ode—which sadly predicts our "increasingly vice-ridden" progeny (l. 48)—here anticipates as well the probable twenty-first-century response: a shrug. Having detailed America's social, military, and religious failings in the age of Clinton, Mezey's poem ends with the bleak prediction of America's helplessness in the face of its own annihilation.

"To the Americans" first saw extended circulation in Mezey's *Collected Poems 1952–1999*.[34] When cited on the blogosphere in 2004—at first, simply for its assured command of that tricky, classical Alcaic meter—the poem's metrical considerations turned out to be the least of its commentary-worthy features. Form was ignored. Reaction to the *content*, however, was swift and, in blogospheric fashion, vociferous.[35] Female

---

[34] Mezey 2000.
[35] All three pages of responses are archived by the Internet Wayback Machine, available here: http://web.archive.org/web/20040813113843/www.ablemuse.com/erato/ubbhtml/Forum9/HTML/000943.html. Names are those as listed on the Ablemuse forum.

readers of the blog, especially, condemned the rhetoric of the piece; one of the first responses, by Janet Kenny, deplored its "typical patriarchal militarism," while Kate Benedict pulled few punches: ". . . one can only hope this is purely a persona poem and not indicative of the poet's real views, which appear to match those of terrorists. Perhaps that was the point[,] yet what does the poem achieve? It gives voice to someone who hates Americans but doesn't understand them at all. Nothing he says rings true . . . This poem tests my personal credo that poetry is a place for everything, for here we have bile, misogyny, prudery, a hostile sort of nostalgia . . . yuck." Janet Kenny continues this theme: "I am offended by the possessive and sexist view of women in this poem which probably derives from Horace, which, to my shame I haven't read. Only one step from the Taliban."

In a strange and noteworthy sequence of events, Mezey's defenders and even detractors called upon the *original* Horatian poem to resolve this heated exchange about politics and poetry in the age of Clinton, with several hoping that the Mezey was in fact just adopting the *persona*, 'the mask,' of Horace. This hope turned out to be a frustrated one when Mezey *himself* popped up on a neighboring forum and announced to the Spheroids that he stood by every accusation.[36] (So much for possible hermeneutic aid and succor of *personae*.) The blogger "AE" engages in some philological analysis of the Mezey and Horace, astutely noting that Mezey really changed the meaning of the line concerning humility: "the sentiment, 'only obedience to Him commands obedience,' seems jarringly medieval in a modern context: it is the implicit justification of the 'divine-right' king, or, more generally, of theocracy. To take this seriously as a political principle would indeed, as has been suggested, lead into the lap of the Islamic extremists." Which leads us back, in turn, to Mezey and, implicitly, to Horace as an incendiary proto-terrorist. Clay Stockton notes that the rhetoric of the poem, as typically understood in America, is "associated here in the States with Christian fundamentalism," and indeed the Spheroids tended to take sides depending on their self-professed liberal or conservative leanings. A reader from Portland sadly opined: "Mezey intertwines military might, patriotism, and Christianity in a sickeningly infinite loop," while a Pennsylvanian decried such criticism as "contemptible and dishonorable in every way. [Mezey]'s Horace adaptation is not only superbly crafted, but its argument rings true as a warning bell."

---

[36] http://web.archive.org/web/20070520203937/http://www.ablemuse.com/erato/ubbhtml/ Forum3/HTML/000480.html. "And yes, my accusations are somewhat modeled on Horace's, but I also believe everything I say (as I'm sure he believed what he said)."

Another Spheroid labeled the poem "stunning": "This is a prophetic voice like Jeremiah's or Ezekiel's." Contrariwise, a counterblast from Kevin Andrew Murphy: "[T]he logic of the piece really goes down the crapper when it falls into the cliché of the old man ranting about these kids these days with their newfangled threesomes and whatnot, plus the selective memory, imagining that whorehouses were invented last Tuesday."

This fever-pitched argument over a poem in Alcaics goes on for pages, devolving into all sorts of name-calling ("moralizing bastard," "pitiful ignorance") before being shut down (!) by the list moderator. A surprising, last ditch appeal to stop the mud-slinging arrives in the form of a soothing salve of New Criticism, as formulated by Clay Stockton: "Prof. Mezey is *translating* after all . . . and many of the members who have responded negatively to his work have been far more careful about separating the dancer from the dance. . ." This is an interesting hermeneutic tack: that Mezey is free from culpability because the original poem, however transmogrified, is Horace's; Mezey is merely the midwife of (some revolting) Augustan poetry into a new age. And then there's Mezey's own internet commentary on his poem—which one could obviously never expect from Horace: ". . . I'd guess that most of the grandchildren of the survivors [of WWII] have gone to college and been indoctrinated in their teachers' moral superiority to American imperialism, hegemony, racism etc. etc. That is to say, their idea of 'real evil' is their own country, and that the minority who are now in uniform and risking their lives are poor kids for the most part, and disproportionately black, Hispanic, etc. And I think Horace would have noticed this too." At the end of the thread, Mezey states that he was "a little taken aback by the savagery of the responses to my poem and by the very careless readings."[37]

For all of the hoopla over Horace's anniversary—the volume *Horace 2000: A Celebration - Essays for the Bimillenium* suggests some sort of global gala—I would wager that Horace barely impinges on the consciousness of most Americans, even Americans with a passion for the poetical. The fact that most Spheroids—a self-selected, erudite lot—had never even *heard* of Horace's *Roman Odes* does not bode well for the collected classical knowledge of the man on the street; there may be passing acquaintance with the so-called "greats" of antiquity—of Homer's *Odyssey* or Sophocles' *Oedipus Tyrannus*—but even major authors of antiquity, such as Sappho or Horace, remain merely names, merely ciphers. In a sense, the

[37] www.ablemuse.com/erato/showthread.php?t=555&page=2

disjunction of these authors' reputation and their art—we know *that* they are great, but not *why* they are great—provides a window of opportunity for later artists (Whedon and Mezey, among them) to refashion the *idea* of these ancient authors along distinctly modern lines. Sappho and Horace are now happily (or unhappily) Americanized as a gender-bending Lesbian, or as a kvetching, vaguely threatening religious Fundamentalist, and these new associations are, in part, facilitated by the new medium of the internet, which both facilitates artistic dissemination but also pits interpretative communities against each other. In this way, unfamiliar figures from the antiquity pop up in the strangest of places—indeed, the study of classical reception is a bit like the carnival game Whac-a-Mole—and force a re-evaluation of what is timeless and what is trendy, what is ontological and what is constructed. And the surprise re-emergence of Sappho and Horace in contemporary art—like many other artists from the classical world—are the subject (and object) of this book: how (and why) *modern* artists and thinkers adapt and mold ancient texts to explore contemporary concerns about ethnicity, gender, ideology, and sexuality. (In the conclusion, we'll also explore why this subsequent picture of the ancient world is quite nearly self-contradictory, splintered into mutually exclusive shards.)

The relationship between ancient and modern literature has been long recognized; the parameters of that relationship, however, have been forever in dispute. Jonathan Swift's cheeky satire, *The Battle of the Books: A Full and True Account of the Battle Fought Last Friday Between the Ancient and the Modern Books in St. James' Library* (1697, pub. 1704) outlines (and wholly rejects) an antagonistic relationship: for Swift (as for many English authors), modern literature largely *depended* on ancient literature for inspiration and for guidance. This relationship became known, in both classical studies and in the academy more widely, as "the classical tradition," or the "influence" of earlier (and implicitly) greater minds on subsequent artists. This influence might seem direct and bold—say, Richard Strauss' operatic version of Sophocles' *Elektra*—or rather more opaque and obscure (Alexander Pope's loopy, parodic *Duncaid*, a skewering of Virgil's staid *Aeneid*). Such influence remained, however, a one-way street: knowledge of the classical world (particularly its literature) was assumed by both modern artist and modern viewer/reader. In this way, the classics provided a sure basis for the continuing examination of human society and its myriad foibles; ultimately, the classics allowed—if only through modern descendants—a window onto the human condition.

"The classical tradition" was and is an unashamedly humanistic notion, indicating a belief in antiquity's transcendental powers of inspiration and influence concerning the very idea of humanity.[38] Indeed, the most impassioned defense of the classical tradition was penned by none other than Gilbert Highet, the scholar most closely associated with Columbia University's "Literature Humanities" course, a great books sequence from Homer to Shakespeare and beyond. Entitled *The Classical Tradition: Greek and Roman Influences on Western Literature*, Highet's *magnum opus* is a sprawling, intoxicating romp through two millennia of classical "influence," from the darkest of Europe's benighted ages to the modernist journeys of James Joyce's *Ulysses*. In one sense, Highet is exceptionally sanguine about antiquity's power to improve the modern human condition: "Without [the Greco-Roman strain] our civilization would not merely be different. It would be much thinner, more fragmentary, less thoughtful, more materialistic—in fact . . . it would be less worthy to be called a civilization, because its spiritual achievements would be less great."[39] For Highet, the "gift" of antiquity is the possibility—but only the possibility—of a modernity tolerable in its spiritual aspects; written shortly after WWII, *The Classical Tradition*, for all of its sunny rhetoric concerning Sophocles and Virgil, nevertheless betrays a deep pessimism about the opportunities for cultural evolution: "We are so accustomed to contemplating the spectacle of human progress that we assume modern culture to be better than anything that preceded it." We forget, Highet continues, "how many forces of barbarism remain, like volcanoes on a cultivated island, still powerfully alive, capable of not only injuring civilization but of putting a burning desert in its place."[40] Here, Highet grafts a popular, schematic view of antiquity—of Greeks and Romans against the "barbarian" other—onto modernity: in the wake of the German (and Italian) incursions on the continent, we must remain—like the Greeks and Romans before us—alert to the forces of savagery. Highet even includes a glance at the recent Holocaust and the creation of The Bomb: "But now, around us, have appeared the first ruins of what may be a new Dark Age." Desperately, then, Highet clings to antiquity as a bulwark against a future frightening in its moral ambiguity, or even moral nihilism: "The true relation between the modern world and the classical world is the same, on a larger scale, as the relation between Rome and Greece. It is an educational relationship."[41] We must *learn* from antiquity: after all, through their immortal art, they defeated the barbarians, and thus barbarism. So might we.

---

[38] Jan Ziolkowski 2007: 18. "[The classical tradition] may be linked to conservatism, not so much of an overtly political as of a cultural brand . . ." See also Kallendorf 2007: 2 on the movement from "tradition" to "reception."

[39] Highet 1949: 1.   [40] Highet 1949: 4.   [41] Highet 1949: 548.

This is inspiring stuff, and the rhetoric of "the classical tradition" is not to be lightly discounted: it's a term still widely in use within the profession of classics (the Society for Classical Studies—an umbrella organization of classical scholars—long had a standing committee devoted to it). But while Mezey's "To the Americans" might, with some pleading, be included under the rubric of "the classical tradition," it's harder to see how *Buffy's* Sappho might be profitably included as well, or at least without hoots of derision. Two recent volumes published back-to-back indicate some fault lines in contemporary approaches to the classical tradition: one is the straightforwardly entitled *A Companion to the Classical Tradition* (2007), with twenty-eight chapters dedicated to the "impact of the classics on postclassical culture," worldwide.[42] The next year saw the publication of *A Companion to Classical Receptions*, in chapters that explore "ancient and modern reception concepts and practice." Both tomes cover roughly the same subject area: the transformation of classical texts, myths, and ideas into their modern counterparts. Why not, then, employ the same term?

The difference, very roughly speaking, is in each approach's underlying theoretical basis, with "classical tradition" theorists continuing the line of inquiry begun with the likes of T. S. Eliot and Gilbert Highet, and "classical reception" theorists generally drawing on the work of the German Hans-Robert Jauss, along with Jacques Derrida.[43] In his seminal essay "What is a classic?," first delivered in 1944 to the Virgilian Society, Eliot proffered the now (in)famous definition: "If there is one word on which we can fix, which will suggest the maximum of what I mean by the term 'a classic', it is the word maturity. ... A classic can only occur when a civilization is mature; when a language and a literature are mature; and it must be the work of a mature mind. ... To define maturity without assuming that the hearer already knows what it means, is almost impossible: let us say then, that if we are properly mature, as well as educated persons, we can recognize maturity in a civilization and in a literature, as we do in the other human beings whom we encounter."[44] This definition veers dangerously close to Justice Potter Stewart's equally infamous definition of pornography: "I know it when I see it."[45] For Eliot, a classic—say, Virgil's *Aeneid*—is a classic when a properly trained mind (say, Eliot's) recognizes it as such. For Eliot, the *Aeneid* or Sophocles' *Oedipus Tyrannus* is

---

[42] Kallendorf 2007: 1.
[43] For an elegant introduction to classical reception studies, see Hardwick 2003.
[44] Eliot 1944/1975: 116–7.   [45] Jacobellis v. Ohio, 378 U.S. 184, 197 (1964).

"classical" because *immanently* classical: its sublimity of thought and expression boasts a maturity of diction that elevates it above its peers, and even its original era of composition. It becomes then an exemplar of all that is majestic about art—and becomes too an object of emulation by later poets and artists (for instance, Milton or Pope). These artists then continue the "tradition" of the past into the present and (barbarians notwithstanding) the future.

The problem with such a definition—besides its inherent subjectivity—is its implicit reliance on the unflagging admiration of a particular classical artist. Eliot's choice of Virgil is a shrewd one: Virgil's critical fortunes have rarely waned. He has *always* been a classic, even when his (seemingly) pro-imperialist stance is at odds with anti-royalist sentiment.[46] But what happens if an ancient author's popularity receives periodic revivals? Or flourishes only in a strictly circumscribed set of circumstances? Does that make him "classical" or influential in Eliot's sense of the term?[47] Simon Goldhill has neatly catalogued the ways in which Lucian, a Greek-speaking Syrian working on the periphery of empire in the second century CE, influenced or inspired early Humanists, including Erasmus; but Goldhill also catalogues Lucian's myriad nineteenth- and twentieth-century detractors (for either his waggish amorality or his perceived Jewishness).[48] Lucian once may have been classical—worthy of emulation as a Greek prose writer or worthy of scorn as a corrupting influence—but few today would argue that Lucian (for all of his charm) is anything like a "classic" in the sense of Homer or Ovid. To the extent that he is read at all, it's as a required text for graduate work in classical studies: a Harvard doctorate in classical literature still requires—in theory—a perusal of Lucian's *The Dream* and *Assembly of the Gods*. Lucian is thus "academically" classical, but not precisely in the way that Eliot envisioned; authors such as Lucian make

---

[46] Caldwell 2008 traces the waning of Virgil's influence in seventeenth- and eighteenth-century England, owing largely to "royalist" readings of the *Aeneid*; contrariwise, Kallendorf 2007 traces the popularity of anti-imperialist readings from the pre-modern period to the mid 1700s. Rees 2004 anthologizes the early reception of Virgil (see especially Shanzer's "Epilogue," 201–213); Baswell 1995 the same for medieval receptions in England; Thomas 2002 for twentieth-century readings, including fascist.

[47] Something of Eliot's influence can be seen in notion of classical "imitation." For instance, Herrick 1966: 559: "the sixteenth-century writers of tragedy did not imitate Seneca exclusively, or Ovid, or Virgil, but were more apt than not to combine Seneca with material from Ovid or Virgil…" For Herrick, early modern tragedy is thus a mash-up of three "canonical" authors from antiquity.

[48] Goldhill 2002: 44–54, on Erasmus' debt to Lucian in *The Praise of Folly*; Goldhill 2002: 93–100 on anxieties concerning Lucian's Semitic origins.

problematic Eliot's assertion that a classical canon is self-evident. Obviously, the idea of a "classic" varies over time.

Which leads us to the other side of the classical tradition/classical reception divide: if studies on the classical tradition concentrate on the immortality of the classical canon, classical reception studies concentrate, rather, on the vicissitudes of individual texts, authors, and myths. Or as Charles Martindale phrased it in his barnstorming "manifesto" on classical reception studies:

> In terms of the hermeneutics which I have been defending, a classic becomes a text whose 'iterability' is a function of its capacity, which includes the authority vested in its reception, for continued re-appropriations by readers. As a result of these appropriations the works so appropriated become richer as they are projected through history, because more 'voices' have made themselves heard within them. In this way reception theory can reconcile tradition and culturalism with progress in an empowering synthesis.[49]

Martindale's definition draws on two different, but complementary, schools of intellectual thought. The first strain is that of Hans Robert Jauss, who in his elucidation of a *Rezeptionsästhetik*, argued for a hermeneutics of "the new" that elevated the status of artists working within an established tradition, a new-ness so powerful and influential, that it could "alter the perspective on the old, and thereby [alter] the canonization of the literary past."[50] In the case of Sappho and Horace, their works find a meaning through a reading/re-reading by the later artists Whedon and Mezey, who, at the same time, alter our conceptions of Horace and Sappho themselves. (The more such ancient artists are contested as an *idea*, the more classical they become; we'll return to that paradox in a moment.) Such an argument "rejects the 'essentialist' conception of literary art," as de Man puts it, and privileges, rather, the diachronic accretion of meaning: Horace's *Roman Odes* mean more—or at least mean *differently*—after a community of readers declares them Fundamentalist, rather than merely fundamental.[51] At the same time, Martindale blends Jauss' aesthetic considerations with the semiotic critique of Jacques Derrida; Derrida's famously controversial method of deconstruction divorces hermeneutic *intent* from hermeneutic *result*: the resulting "play" of signifieds and signifiers does not (as detractors allege) rob an artwork of *any* meaning but rather imbues an artwork

[49] Martindale 2006: 1; Martindale 1993: 28.   [50] Jauss 1982: 35.
[51] de Man p. x, in Jauss 1982.

with a *plenitude* of meanings.[52] All art, like all language, is potentially (even essentially) polyvalent, its meaning(s) constituted at the point of reception or appropriation.

My project then, is to consider the ways in which classical works are continually refashioned as "classical" through—in Martindale's terminology—continued appropriations; in particular, I wish to examine appropriations that dovetail with contemporary ideological concerns. Thus, I will be deliberately skirting what I deem purely aesthetic transformations of classical texts, or instances in which the modern "receiver" is attempting consciously and conspicuously to construct a transparent window onto the author's original intent. For better or worse, this excludes most translations, even celebrated ones. Robert Fagles' 2006 version of the *Aeneid*, for instance, translates the heroine Dido's bitter harangue against Aeneas—who is deserting her for a chance to found Rome—like so:

> I hope, I pray, if the just gods still have any power,
> wrecked on the rocks mid-sea you'll drink your bowl
> of pain to the dregs, crying out the name of Dido,
> over and over, and worlds away I'll hound you even then
> With pitch-black flame. . .
>
> (4.479–483)

A formalist literary critic could say much about this translation of *Aeneid* 4.382–385; for example, how it captures the name of Dido as a line end in both the Latin (4.383) and the English; how it misses the ironic appellation of the gods as *pia* (l. 381), a phrase that hurls Aeneas' usual epithet of *pius*, 'pious,' back in his face; how the phrase "over and over" neatly adds a sense of futility to the phrase *saepe uocaturum*, 'often about-to-shout,' and how the verb "hound" adds a hunting metaphor that may or may not be present in the original verb *sequar* ('I shall follow'). And yet there are certainly operating principles here: in his "translator's postscript" Fagles offers that he was aiming for a (modern) readability, a literary elegance, and the potential for effective performance.[53]

It is true, of course, that even an "aesthetic" translation can be ideologically motivated or informed. Judged from just the tome itself, Sarah Ruden's recent version of the *Aeneid* (2008) seems to be as faithful, and literal, a translation as Fagles' version, produced only a few years before. Indeed, in her own notes, Ruden discusses the technicalities of verse translation: she prefers, for instance, the use of Anglo-Saxon words over their more

---

[52] Derrida 1985: 1–28.   [53] Fagles 2006: 389–405.

flowery, Latinate synonyms (viii) and harbors as well a fondness for the English iambic pentameter (ix). About the poem itself, she expresses a "lowland view" of the controversy over Virgil's (possibly anti-imperialist) political sympathies, preferring to sidestep the issue in favor of more general ruminations concerning the profundity of tragedy in Virgil's world-view (xi).[54] So, on the surface, there don't seem to be any distinctive, contemporary social forces at play here. Yet an interview with *The Chronicle of Higher Education* reveals the influence of gender on the production of this particular *Aeneid*. As a graduate student, Ruden was warned against a dissertation on Ovid because too many women were working on the Roman poet's love poetry; so Ruden chose the famously potty-mouthed Petronius instead. Ruden complains, in fact, that too many female scholars still work on ancient love poetry; they are "talking and writing endlessly about 'gender' in prescribed terms. It's like a seraglio." So for Ruden, the choice of Virgil's martial text is, in a sense, a revolutionary one: she is, as far as I can tell, the first female translator of the entire *Aeneid* into English. In fact, by virtue of her gender, she senses that her publication taps into different Virgilian strains than previous male-translated versions: "I'm going to get killed for voicing this, but I believe women have the right attitude," she says. "Women get more involved. The authors are more real to us. We develop relationships with them."[55] But while the *impulse* to tackle the *Aeneid* might have been motivated by considerations of gender or discrimination, it's difficult to determine the *effect* on Ruden's translation: like Fagles' version, the translation is sober, clear, and lucid, but not appreciably "feminist" in its take on Virgil.[56] Rudens' translation of the identical break-up runs as follows: "I hope that heaven's conscience has the power/ To trap you in the rocks and force your penance/ down your throat, as you call my name…" (4.382–384). This is a lovely translation, but it doesn't seem to further the aims of any particular modern social movement.

To my mind, more interesting—and closer to the central concerns of this book—is how Dido's tragic break-up with Aeneas figures in the modern imagination as an investigation of both ancient and modern sexual systems. We begin with Purcell's opera *Dido and Aeneas* (1689). The initial

---

[54] Quotations from Ruden 2008.

[55] http://chronicle.com/free/v54/i36/36b00901.htm. "Measuring the 'Aeneid' on a Human Scale," by Jennifer Howard. Print edition: May 16, 2008. Volume 54, Issue 36, Page B9.

[56] In his cautionary remarks on translation and reception studies, Rudd 2006: 1–7 notes that just because every translation is an interpretation, it does not follow that every translation is a *different* interpretation. Indeed, Fagles and Rudens seem to me to hold similar views about both Virgilian translation and thought.

placement of Dido's name clearly marks her as the protagonist of the piece, and thus we see (already) in Purcell's adaptation the transformation of the *Aeneid* from a tale of heroic suffering to a distinctly female erotic tragedy. Yes, certainly we see (and hear) plenty of Aeneas in *Dido and Aeneas*, but Dido's story is clearly paramount, including her violent curse of Aeneas (as above), as well as her subsequent, haunting *Totenlied*, "When I am laid in earth." It is a staggeringly beautiful aria that Wayne Koestenbaum naturally includes in his "Pocket Guide to Queer Moments in Opera." Why naturally? Because all of *Dido and Aeneas*, on Koestenbaum's reading, is a type of "coming out" story for Dido: an erotically repressed individual who only gradually gains, through a series of painful encounters, the power of erotic expression.[57] Tragically, she reaches the pinnacle of such expression— a "coming out"—at the same time she reaches an emotional rock bottom: ergo, her grief is "queer" because both awkward and extravagant, both climactic and deeply uncomfortable. Thus Purcell's Dido—like, perhaps, Virgil's Dido—may be read as a cipher for repressed homosexual desire. (A reception-history of the erotics of Dido-obsession would also need to take into account the young Hector Berlioz' reading of Virgil: "How often I have felt my heart throb and my voice quiver and break when construing the fourth book of the *Aeneid* to my father!. . . my lips quivered, I could scarcely stammer out the words; and when I reached the line *Quaesivit coelo lucem, ingemuitque reperta*, the sublime vision of Dido, 'seeking light from heaven and moaning as she found it,' overwhelmed me, and I broke down utterly."[58] Here, Berlioz (unintentionally?) replicates the symptoms of the "pathology of love," as adumbrated in numerous classical works, including Sappho's fragment 16. At the moment a man 're-enacts' Dido, he erotically falls to pieces.)

Mark Morris' dance-theater version of *Dido and Aeneas* (1989), preserved on DVD and still touring the United States, takes Koestenbaum's conceit even further: the role of Dido is danced by none other than Mark Morris. Mark Morris, an out, gay choreographer, not only figures Dido as "queer" in voice, but as queer in body: her flesh is literally embodied by a hulking gay male, who thus destabilizes the erotic situation at the heart of the story (see Figure 1.2).[59] Instead of presenting, through Purcell's music, one of antiquity's most celebrated "heterosexual" romances, Morris translates the relationship to the twentieth century, with a gender-bending, "gay" relationship between the two principals. Though the production is frequently campy—Morris also plays the (non-Virgilian) Sorceress as a deliciously maleficent vamp—Morris' impersonation of Dido isn't, by the

---

[57] Koestenbaum 1993: 233–4.   [58] Berlioz 1966: 7.   [59] Morris 1996: 141–50.

Figure 1.2.   Mark Morris as "Queen" Dido, in his version of Purcell's opera.

same token, effeminate: she is a queen in title, not portrayal. In fact, Morris, a large man, may even come off as threatening: certainly, Dido's slap on the cheek of Aeneas registers like a thunderclap. Though Morris hasn't (to my knowledge) explained *why* he switched the gender of Dido, one can surmise that he is re-inscribing homosexuality back into antiquity; or at least forcing the audience to confront the notion of a "classical romance" that's not, by the same token, a heterosexual romance. Though Rudens' translation of Virgil might indeed be influenced by ideologies of gender or sexuality—how could it not?—Morris' version hits the audience over the head with the artistic equivalent of a two-by-four.

And that is the focus of this book: adaptations of ancient texts and themes that are outrageously, violently, wonderfully un-literal. That means that this project (like others in the field of reception) pushes the boundaries of what might be termed *classical studies*: it's a truism that professional classicists stress the influence and profundity of classical texts, but it's equally true that some classicists get nervous when adaptations stray too far from the source. By training, we classicists prefer our ideologies to be classical ones—of the stresses put on a text by the forces of republic and empire, or the tensions between polytheism and monotheism. Presentism—the imposition of modern concerns and values on the past—makes us understandably uneasy. And yet it's *precisely* in classical texts' ability to remain sites of cultural contestation that the works remain "classical"; it's *precisely* because marginalized (or empowered) groups appeal to classical texts that such texts' authority is thereby reinforced and reconstituted. It's not enough to say, however grandiloquently, that classics remain classics because they appeal to universal concerns; classics remain classics because they appeal to *specific* concerns.

This project thus looks at some *specific* contemporary concerns, and how classical texts are used to mirror or illuminate them, and I am keenly aware that my own cultural contexts may well determine which concerns receive the most attention. Certainly, this is true of L. P. Wilkinson's 1978 volume *Classical Attitudes to Modern Issues*, similarly divided into neat chapters. The *emphases* of his chapters might seem surprising, however: abortion and family planning; women's liberation; homosexuality; and (a bit of a surprise, here) nudism.[60] My own division betrays an early twenty-first-century (and mostly American) bias: for me, the most

---

[60] The research on the history of nudism in Germany—related to national concerns about health and the body—is fairly advanced: see for instance Chad Ross' *Naked Germany: Health, Race and the Nation* (Oxford, 2005). For nudism in Britain, the state of scholarship is more piecemeal: there is, however, Philip Carr-Gomm's *A Brief History of Nakedness* (Reaktion, 2010).

intriguing areas of classical reception lie in gender studies; ethnic studies; and American politics, including eco-criticism.[61] Sometimes, such receptions bubble up through what is popularly termed "popular culture," a discursive matrix that features an especial predilection for "trashing" the classics. More than any other category, pop culture receptions interrogate the notion of "what is a classic" with more savagery (and sometimes bravery) than other modes of discourse. To rewrite T. S. Eliot: a classic is a text that loses something in the trashing.[62]

Finally, it's true that receptions of antiquity often play fast and loose with facts: facts, after all, can be positively irritating when they contradict an otherwise satisfactory argument. For better or worse, Americans have largely inherited the *idea* of antiquity as through osmosis, an idea not necessarily founded on the highest ideals of scholarship or empirical observation. Even writers of the first rank are not immune to the perils of free association when it comes to antiquity. For instance, in his over-the-top memoir of travel in Greece in the 1930s, *The Colossus of Maroussi*, the American novelist Henry Miller muses over the ancient past as he wanders from place to place: "At Mycenae I walked over the incandescent dead; at Epidaurus I felt a stillness so intense that for a fraction of a second I heard the great heart of the world beat and I understood the meaning of pain and sorrow; at Tiryns, I stood in the shadow of the Cyclopean man," and so forth (57).[63] Rarely has a country, and a history, been so romanticized as Miller's fairy-tale Greece, a world in which Miller finally comprehends the truths of "pain and sorrow" and can listen to the world's heart beat; with every new location, this American traveler opens "a new vein of experience, approaching the heart of a star which is not yet extinguished" (57). It's little surprise that Miller's sidereal Greece mostly revolves around Miller: during a trip to Eleusis, an historically sacred spot outside of Athens, he opines:

---

[61] It was with some hand-wringing that the adjective "American" found its way into the title of this study, partly because I didn't, and don't, wish to give the impression that *every* example bears specifically on classical reception in the United States. Clearly, certain authors—such as Ireland's Seamus Heaney or Canada's Margaret Atwood—cannot be easily subsumed under the heading of American, even if their work comments (sometimes pointedly) on the United States' policies or influence. Mass media are even more complicated: a film such as *Troy* can be viewed both as a product of the American film industry but also as the personal project of German filmmaker Wolfgang Petersen. As a native of Ohio, however, I was particularly drawn to American material in elucidating the major trends in contemporary classical reception, and I hope that the occasional non-American examples complement the analysis of receptions specific to the United States.

[62] For the term "trashing," I am indebted to Hawkins' 1990 examination of the phenomenon (*Classics and Trash*), though Hawkins is rather more concerned with English classics than Greco-Roman ones.

[63] All quotations from Miller 1941.

"Here the light penetrates directly to the soul, opens the doors and windows of the heart, makes one naked, exposed, isolated in a metaphysical bliss which makes everything clear without being known ... At Eleusis one becomes adapted to the cosmos" (45). By "one" Miller means Miller, and all of the richness of Greece is reduced to a catalyst for Miller's ruminations on Western metaphysics. The hyperbolic language extends to Greece's people as well: "In Greece one has the conviction that *genius* is the norm, not mediocrity. ... Her art, which goes back fifty centuries, is eternal and incomparable" (83). Another bromide of the Romanticization of Greece: it never changes. It is somehow always *there*.

But even as Miller traipses (and indeed, bums) his way through Greece, he can never leave his American citizenship behind; Miller's vision of Greece is forever informed by his American past, even as he attempts to distinguish the two: "In a way which it is beyond the comprehension of my fellow countrymen to grasp Greece is infinitely larger than the United States. Greece could swallow both the United States and Europe" (49). Miller is particularly keen on the commonalities between the prehistories of Greece and the Americas: "Everything connected with Argos, shimmering now in the distance as in the romantic illustrations for text-books, smacks of the American Indians" (90). Miller's thoughts on Greek women—a source of never-ending fascination for the eternally randy Miller—is also informed by his American roots: "The ordinary Greek girl whom one sees on the street is superior in every way to her American counterpart; above all, she has character and race, a combination ... which forever distinguishes the descendents of ancient peoples from the bastard off-shoots of the New World" (108). Like many who rhapsodize over the ancient world, Miller draws an easy (and not particularly defensible) line of descent between e.g. Minoans and modern Greeks, in contradistinction to the nomadic European colonizers of the New World.

But the beauty part is that Miller's experience of this "archetype of the miracle wrought by the human spirit" (84), of his "veritable re-birth" (237) while standing in King Agamemnon's tomb, of an "earth flamy with spirit as if it were an invisible compass" (92), is predicated on, indeed even *enabled by*, ignorance of elementary fact. In one of the most amazing passages of the travelogue, Miller makes an astounding confession: "Beyond Knossos my mind pictured nothing ... That Homer had sung of the hundred cities of Crete I didn't know because I could never bring myself to read Homer..." (154).[64] Let us take a moment to reflect on

---

[64] It might be that Miller's ignorance of ancient Greek (or even *translations* of ancient Greek) is the curious end result of nineteenth-century educational debates in both Britain and America,

that last admission. Miller has no problem—in fact, takes great joy in—proclaiming all sorts of verities concerning the history, genealogies, and mythology of Greece; but when actually journeying to Crete he not only admits his ignorance of Homer but confesses an *aversion* to Homer. The reason is not hard to fathom. It's because Miller suspects that Homer, a complex and authentic artifact of the ancient world, might challenge his *preconceived* notion of Greece as the ur-navel of the universe, in which one's soul expands and shrinks with the cosmos, etc. Instead of reading and analysis, then, Miller relies on intuition: ". . . I felt, as I have seldom felt before the ruins of the past, that here [at Knossos] throughout long centuries there reigned an era of peace" (121). No proof needed for this American: he just *feels*. It's a trait that Miller attributes to all Americans contemplating the ancient world: "Greece is what everybody knows, even *in absentia*, even as a child or as an idiot or as a not-yet-born. It is what you expect the earth to look like given a fair chance" (152). Even American *fetuses* understand Greece! For Miller, Greece is an integral part in the intellectual, or at least spiritual, formation of every American.

But in a strange, roundabout way, Miller, in spite of (or perhaps because of) his lyrical rhapsodizing, anticipates modern reception studies by a few decades: "To-day as of old Greece is of the utmost importance to every man who is seeking to find himself. My experience is not unique. And perhaps I should add that no people in the world are as much in need of what Greece has to offer as the American people. Greece is not merely the antithesis of America, but more, the solution to the ills which plague us" (211). Miller here situates Greece as squarely antithetical to America; for him, America is the anti-Greece, and forms its identity in contradistinction to this ancient conglomeration of islands and city–states. The implicit metaphor—sickness from plague—also constructs America as diseased or polluted, and thus Greece as a purifying medicine. This will be an important theme of this book: that ideological appropriations of antiquity transpire because of antiquity's (perceived) powers of salvation.

Can we cure America by appealing to the past? Perhaps not; but as we shall see, in manifold and wondrous ways, we Americans try.

---

strands of which de-emphasized philological skills even while advocating a broader understanding of *Altertumswissenschaft*, 'Science of Antiquity.' Goldhill 2002: 223–4 traces, for instance, Matthew Arnold's promotion of a specifically Greek "spirit" even while Arnold himself seems to have an incomplete grasp of Greek grammar. As Goldhill puts it: "Scholarship is secondary to spirit. Arnold doesn't mind admitting that he has to look up words when he reads the Greek anthology." Henry Miller does not even bother to look up words!

2 | It's Greek to them: Gay and lesbian receptions of the ancient world

In the Western mind, gay identity and historical metanarratives have been inextricably linked, up to and including the 'ancient' Greco-Roman past. Though some influential analyses of gay identity posit a relatively recent genesis for the construction of homosexuality (for John D'Emilio, the industrial revolution and subsequent urbanization; for Foucault, the medical discourses of the nineteenth century),[1] they differ, crucially, from gay and lesbian narrators of their *own* history. Lesbian and gay representations of the past—including the classical world—are potentially "political and cultural interventions in(to) the present," and thus offer alternative narratives to traditional chronologies and tropes of the ancient and pre-modern world.[2] Even the application of the notion "homosexuality" is fraught with ideological implications: inscribing "homosexuality" within the sexual practices of the Romans and Greeks provides a past to a community that often appears past-less and therefore frighteningly revolutionary. Such practices also carry a racial charge, as appeals to the ancient Greek past also reify the notion of homosexuality as a primarily white, European phenomenon, a rhetorical maneuver obviously problematic for gays and lesbians of color.[3] Though reference to the "love that dare not speak its name" had been code since at least Victorian times, appropriations of antiquity became both increasingly more open and more varied in the Edwardian, and post-Edwardian eras. Edward Carpenter's 1902 tract *Ioläus: An Anthology of Friendship* is a diachronic (and synthesizing) catalogue of what we would now term "same-sex relationships" rather than mere "friendship"; it figures Greco-Roman antiquity as the natural fount of enlightened social thought from Plato to Walt Whitman. Classically themed "Uranist" poetry, which explored same-sex desire under the guise of Greco-Roman translations and allusions, continued even through the 1920s: it's one way in which Hellenophilia masked a *philia*

---

[1] D'Emilio 1983; Foucault 1980, and as below.   [2] Bravmann 1997: 28.
[3] Bravmann 1997: 67. "The racially limited 'access' to Ancient Greece, whose genealogy is itself a retrospectively fabricated historical fiction, works simultaneously to determine the substance and significance of racial categories and to reiterate historically embedded racial meanings."

of quite a different sort.[4] Post-WWII receptions include the classically grounded and pathbreaking journal from the One Institute;[5] mid-century and contemporary receptions feature any number of "queer" or gender-bending productions of classical tragedy, including Richard Schechner's *Dionysus in 69*. A specialized mode of reception concerns classics and AIDS, as Greco-Roman texts concerning pestilence and illness are refigured as commentaries on this most contemporary of plagues. Thus the gay and lesbian reception of antiquity continues to inform modern sensibilities concerning the interplay of gender, history, and desire, even as we careen well into the twenty-first century.

As we shall see, gay and lesbian appropriations of antiquity nearly always represent ancient homosexuality as a phenomenon analogous to modern homosexuality; this is in contradistinction to more recent academic discussions, which (with some spectacular exceptions) emphasize the *discontinuity* of sexual practices from ancient to modern times. For example, the American philosopher Martha Nussbaum cites a letter from the Greek philosopher Epicurus, a passage that, she claims, "always occasions gasps and embarrassed giggles" from undergraduates:[6]

> "The truly pleasant life is not produced by an unbroken succession of drinking bouts and revels; not by the enjoyment of boys and women and fish and other things that a luxurious table presents. It is produced by sober reasoning ..." (*Letter to Menoeceus*, 132).

What discomfits the undergraduates (and, presumably, post- and pre-graduates) is how clearly Epicurus structures two important aspects of ancient male desire: (1) boys and women obviously fit into the same sexual category (which implies that biological sex is less important than position or sexual action) and (2) that sex is itself lumped together with fish and food (implying that sexual desire is little different than other types of appetite, and certainly not indicative of self-fashioning or sexual identity).[7]

---

[4] For a book-length overview of the Uranists, see Smith 1970.   [5] Richlin 2005.
[6] Nussbaum 1990: 46.
[7] The same sort of startling structural alignment is present also in Cato's "On Farming," in which the author urges the savvy landowner to catalogue year-end inventory and then sell-off any superfluous property: "[the farmer should sell] his olive oil, if it can fetch a good price, and any leftover wine and grain; sell also old oxen, blemished sheep, blemished cattle, wool, hides, an old wagon, old tools, an aged slave (*servus*), an ailing slave (*servus*), and whatever else might be left over" (*De Re Rustica*, 2). Here, we see that for at least one Roman landowner—and presumably for many—slaves (*servi*) inhabit the same structural position as other exportable or fragile agricultural property, include wine-jars and hoes. The fact that slaves are *human* is here less important than their *function*: viewed through the eyes of Cato, the catalogue is entirely of-a-

In addition, there is the implicit commercial aspect: women, boys, and fish are all goods to be purchased for money and consumed at the proper social occasion. There's nothing sentimental or "Hallmark" about Epicurus' list of standard bourgeois pleasures.

Now, Epicurus' catalogue is startling (and giggle-worthy) to most Americans because our own sexual and commercial matrices do not lump together women, boys, and trout in the same categories, to the extent to which we can generalize. (A predilection for e.g., flounder does not, for instance, occasion social opprobrium or legislation.) Until the past generation, it was easy, at least in a cultural vacuum, to pretend that modern sexuality was, *mutatis mutandis*, the same sort of animal as ancient sexuality, only differently (if perhaps immoderately) expressed. In his groundbreaking *History of Sexuality*, however, Michael Foucault famously argued that until the late nineteenth century "homosexuality appeared as one of the forms of sexuality when it was transposed from the practice of sodomy into a kind of interior androgyny, a hermaphrodism of the soul. The sodomite had been a temporary aberration; the homosexual was now a species."[8] That is to say, that before the medicalization of sexual discourse, the analysis of sexuality was largely confined to *sexual practice*: the rather humdrum and mechanical actions involving a set of culturally determined body parts (including the penis, the vagina, the anus, the mouth, and a grab-bag of other erogenous zones). Certainly, such sexual practice could, and must, be implicated within larger spheres of cultural activity (including marriage, religion, criminality, and leisure), but the actions per se were not indicative of identity, merely of expression appropriately or inappropriately executed. On Foucault's reading, as nineteenth-century Europe saw a revolution in the discourses of Truth—from religion and social theory to the medical sciences—the study of sexuality itself petrified sexual actions into sexual *conditions*, thus establishing the notion of a permanent sexual identity (or, rather more chillingly, the notion of a *cure* for otherwise permanently deviant sexual practice). Before 1870, sexuality was a matrix of actions; after 1870, an immutable aspect of identity.

One of the curious consequences of Foucault's radical approach to sexuality is that, by starting Volume One with the Greeks and Romans, the philosopher forced classicists to respond to the bleeding edge of contemporary cultural criticism. This was an unusual, and not particularly

---

piece, however startling to the modern reader. As Varro puts it, slaves are "talking tools" (*instrumenti genus vocale*, RR 1.17.1).

[8] Foucault 1980: 42.

comfortable development for a field that prided itself on avoiding the
jargon and even explicitness of scholarship in contemporary cultural
studies; suddenly, the world was waiting for professional classicists to
weigh in on the merits of Foucault's heavily theoretical analysis of ancient
sexuality. One must bear in mind that this is the same field in which a
1934 volume entitled *Sexual Life in Ancient Rome* produced the following
analysis of the *Priapea*, a set of raunchy sex poems: "This singular collection is an important document for the study of sexual life under Augustus.
However, we can give no examples of it in our present volume."[9]
Obviously, self-censorship in classics had a noble pedigree; a standard
1961 Oxford edition of the poems of Catullus by C. J. Fordyce notes coolly
(and notoriously) that "this edition is intended to meet the need for an
English commentary for general school and university use" and that "a few
poems which do not lend themselves to comment in English have been
omitted." These "few poems" include Catullus' astounding poem 16, which
begins *pedicabo ego vos et irrumabo* ("I will screw y'all up the ass and in
your mouths") and one wonders which language Fordyce would have
preferred for a commentary.[10] (Italian was the obfuscating tongue of
choice for Harvard's Loeb series of classical translations; the translation
of Greek into Latin was always an option open to squeamish Hellenists.)

To its credit, the field of classics rose to the challenge, engaging Foucault's work with candor, sophistication, and (especially among second-
wave feminists) a healthy skepticism. Classicist-turned-cultural-critic
David Halperin stirred the waters with (among other writings), a feisty
"hagiography" of Foucault ("As far as I'm concerned, the guy was a fucking
saint"[11]), while feminist critic Amy Richlin continues to sound notes of
caution about the troubling ideological bases of Foucault's own theories of
ideology ("In general, Foucault's work on Greek and Roman sexuality is
remarkable for its omission of women . . .; of prior feminist work; and of
Roman culture. That any classicists should in turn base their work on the

[9] Kiefer 1934: 247.
[10] Fordyce 1961: preface. Every poem mainly (or even partly) touching on homosexuality has been
cut (including 15, 16, 21, 28, etc.); for poems involving heterosexual sex, Fordyce allows the
Latin to appear but maintains a discreet silence in the commentary. For instance, in the famous
poem number 11, *Furi et Aureli, comites Catulli*, Catullus' mistress Lesbia is secretly taking on
three hundred lovers at a time, an action glossed with the startling phrase *omnium ilia rumpens*,
"bursting the loins of all of them." Fordyce ignores this entire image and instead composes a
paragraph on the word *ut*, meaning 'where' (125).
[11] Halperin 1995: 6. For Halperin's clarification of his Foucauldian stance—he prefers the term
"historicism" over "social constructionist"—see Halperin 2002: 1–23. (See also his response to
the unfavorable, feminist criticisms of his work, 2002: 6.)

principles Foucault evolved out of this seems bizarre to me.")[12] Even
Victorianists have noted the internecine warfare among classicists: the
brawl in classics has spilled over into a wider field of cultural studies.[13]
(Classicists often stress the utility of their discipline for other fields of
humanistic endeavor; still, it is disconcerting when it actually happens.)
A particularly fractious debate broke out in the pages of the *History of the
Journal of Sexuality* concerning the materiality—that is to say, the existence
—of *cinaedi* in the ancient world, or self-identifying "passive" homosexuals.[14] The existence of such *cinaedi* would lend support to an "essentialist" view of homosexuality, which argues for the general continuity of
sexual desire between antiquity and modernity. A "radical reappraisal" of
ancient Greek homosexuality, by James Davidson, takes this position even
further by arguing for a sexual system that valorizes desire between men of
equal age and civic status, instead of the more generally accepted system of
desire by men for adolescent boys.[15] In a scathing review, Thomas
K. Hubbard accuses Davidson of "pandering to the 'gays in the military'
and the 'gays in the church'," and worse yet, to "gay-marriage fetishists."[16]
For Hubbard, Davidson's politically correct reading of the evidence
inappropriately retrojects modern sexual concerns into the ancient
world: Davidson's antiquity is not antiquity at all, but merely modernity
disguised.

Of course, reading modern or "American" sexual behavior back onto
antiquity, while a popular pastime, is fraught with peril. In his witty,
influential article on ancient Roman sexual practices, Holt Parker conducts
a thought experiment in which the Roman historian and ethnographer
Tacitus wakes up to find himself suddenly in Toledo, Ohio. As Parker
neatly demonstrates, the sexual mores of modern Ohio (apparently chosen
as representative of Middle America) would completely baffle Tacitus;
straight men advertising their "muff-diving" skills would be anathema to
any straight-thinking Roman male, and Ohioans' squeamishness—even
ignorance—about same-sex attraction would be similarly confounding.[17]
The matrices of attraction that informed a Roman's sexual life—taking into

---

[12] Richlin 1991: 169.
[13] See for instance, the admiring stance of Behlman 2003: 459. "[Classicists] are instructive for
their more energetic, bolder critiques of Foucauldian ideas [than Victorianists], and as in the
case of David Halperin, even stronger defenses of Foucault's usefulness for conceptualizing
history."
[14] For a broad overview of the debates within classics over ancient sexuality, see Karras 2000. For
the debate concerning the materiality of 'passive homosexuals' in Rome, see Richlin 1993.
[15] Davidson 2007.   [16] Hubbard 2009.   [17] Parker 1997: 62

account the object's sex, orifices, and citizen status—become problematic when applied to modern, Western sexual *mores*. And yet, as a cultural touchstone, the classical world holds a privileged place in the inquiry concerning homosexuality; in the quest for genesis, one can search for origins either through physical science (biology and zoology) or through social science (psychology and sociology).

Plato's *Symposium* and Neo-hellenism

One of the reasons that the classical world so attracts gay and lesbian readings (and readers) is that, at least before Foucault and the recent boom in gender studies, readers on both sides on the ideological spectrum could agree that the ancient world was absolutely a hotbed of homosexual desire. Such a perception is aided by the fact that Plato's *Symposium*, a seminal philosophical document on desire, features homoerotic love as a primary theme, including the love of an older *erastes* ('lover') and younger *eromenos* ('beloved') for each other. For many later readers, the *Symposium* proves both the existence and power of same-sex desire, even through the powerful diachronic shifts in cultural patterns (from late antiquity through the Renaissance) and attendant power structures.

Historically, the *Symposium* has been a dangerous document for analysis, particularly for analysts of a socially conservative bent, and one encounters all sorts of rhetorical strategies for avoiding its central sexual concerns while emphasizing Plato's humanity or brilliance. One such tactic is omission or convenient quotation, such as found in the Pope Benedict XVI's 2005 papal bull on love, *Deus est Caritas*.[18] In a document that covers, *inter alios*, Virgil, Sallust, Aristotle, and Augustine, it would be hard for the Pope to justify the omission of Plato in a history of theories of love; on the other hand, Benedict's concluding argument concerning desire is distinctly *un*-Platonic: "From the standpoint of creation, *eros* directs man towards marriage, to a bond which is unique and definitive; thus, and only thus, does it fulfil its deepest purpose" (11). As proof, Benedict adduces Adam and Eve from *Genesis* but also—a bit surprisingly—Plato's *Symposium*: "Here one might detect hints of ideas that are also found, for example, in the myth mentioned by Plato, according to which man was originally

---

[18] Mostly conveniently found in English online at: www.vatican.va/holy_father/benedict_xvi/encyclicals/documents/hf_ben-xvi_enc_20051225_deus-caritas-est_en.html. Purists may of course consult the Latin as well.

spherical, because he was complete in himself and self-sufficient. But as a punishment for pride, he was split in two by Zeus, so that now he longs for his other half, striving with all his being to possess it and thus regain his integrity." Benedict hastens to add that this close connection between *eros* and marriage has "practically no equivalent in extra-biblical literature."

In the case of Plato, that is something of an understatement. Benedict first confuses author and character—the myth to which he alludes is narrated by the character Aristophanes, not Plato, per se—and, moreover, the speech is antiquity's most eloquent celebration of male same-sex desire (and one in which opposite-sex desire is decidedly second fiddle). Through a series of historical and interpretative accidents, however, Aristophanes' speech has nearly usurped in prominence the other five speeches of the *Symposium*. All of these speeches figure desire as homosexual; Aristophanes' speech is merely the gayest of the bunch, for reasons to which we shall soon return. Pausanias' introductory speech finds the highest form of desire in those who are attracted to the male (181C); perhaps comfortingly to the modern mind, Pausanias especially lauds those attracted to post-pubescent males, "who have begun to form minds of their own" (181D). The physician Eryximachus attacks the nature of Eros from a medical angle, along with some highfalutin rhetoric concerning the twin forms of love: one healthy, good, and chaste, the other common and prone to debauchery (187D). After Aristophanes' speech, the tragic poet (and host) Agathon spins a lovely, even schmaltzy, yarn concerning the nature of Eros the God: a young, delicate, devastatingly handsome boy without a shred of violence or injustice in him (196B). This is followed by a typically Socratic evisceration of Agathon's argument, in which the argument shifts from the nature of love-as-god, to the nature of love as a desire for beauty (a beauty figured as a lack, and therefore an object of love, 201B). Socrates next relates his own personal interrogation by the wise woman Diotima, who argues that Eros is a continual process of seeking its own lack, which, following in a step-wise progression, ultimately ends in the soul's quest for beauty; gazing upon this great sea of beauty, the soul then "gives birth to many gloriously beautiful ideas and theories" in unstinting love of wisdom.

The *Symposium* famously concludes by shifting from the esoteric musings of Diotima/Socrates to the drunken ramblings of the beautiful playboy Alcibiades, who crashes the party only to find his own object of desire, Socrates, in attendance. After the metaphysical ruminations of Diotima, Alcibiades' speech comes across as coarse and humorous – and quickly devolves into the carnal. After hitting on pretty-boy Agathon, Alcibiades confesses that his true object of desire has always been Socrates, who nevertheless seems far more interested in abstract beauty than Alcibiadic beauty. Alcibiades describes the effect of his thwarted desire in terms nearly Sapphic:[19] "the moment he starts to speak, I am beside myself: my heart start leaping in my chest, the tears come streaming down my face..." (215E). Alcibiades' frustrated attempts at sex/courtship—from an awkward moment alone (217B) to a sterile wrestling match (217C), to a couple of dinners (217D) to a drunken pass and embrace under a cloak (219B)—escalate into the desperate maneuvers of a man hopelessly in love. Moreover, even Alcibiades notes that his passion for Socrates subverts "ideal" Athenian expectations of homosexuality, in which the older partner is expected to take the lead, and the younger expected to endure such courtship for the sake of future pedagogical rewards. The final episode of the *Symposium*, then, ironically presents an affair—and a desire—that is more comprehensible in the context of American homosexuality than Athenian homosexuality, in which distinctions of age and class carry less weight than more intangible aspects of attraction.

But let us return to Aristophanes' speech. Aristophanes' speech has attracted more than its lion's share of attention because it not only describes the origins of *Eros* but the origins, it seems, of sexual preference; it is thus one of few surviving documents from antiquity to touch directly upon this matter of enduring philosophical, theological, and scientific inquiry. In Aristophanes' fable, humans began existence as rolling wheels of concatenated arms and legs, eight to a spheroid, with double genitals, double faces, and a superfluity of ears. They were of three types, composed either of two males (offspring of the sun), two females (offspring of the earth), or one of each, and thus androgynous (offspring of the moon). Unfortunately, these spheroids were also ambitious; they attempted a *coup d'état* against the gods of Olympus but were defeated. Zeus was in a quandary: wiping out the humans meant wiping out the gods' sole opportunity for worship, but obviously the humans merited *some* sort of punishment. Zeus opted to split the humans in half (to diminish their strength) and arranged for Apollo to tie up the literally loose ends (creating, in the process, wrinkles, navels, and breasts).[20] The result, alas, was tragedy: "each half longed for its other half" and when he or she would find it, the two

---

[19] See the so-called "pathology of love" in Sappho's fragment 31.

[20] There are of course many different ways of reading this particular fable; Bakhtin's analysis of the grotesque, most clearly adumbrated in *Rabelais and His World* would seem to fit well here. At 1968: 319, Bakhtin argues that comic visions of the body in the west tend to be implicated in the processes of rejuvenation and even expulsion (urination, defecation, childbirth, etc.) and by extension to transmogrified or hyperbolic body parts (big breasts, large rumps, protruding

halves would only embrace until one died from hunger. The survivor would then seek out another, similar, survivor, until one succumbed to hunger, and so it continued: a virtual Virginia Reel of death (191B).

Obviously, this condition could not continue; further alterations were in order. Zeus thus rotated the genitals to the front—before this switch, humans would plant seeds in the grounds, like cicadas (191C). Frontal coupling satisfied the urge to "become one" while allowing procreation. Heterosexual coupling might in fact result in procreation, but "when male embraced male, they would at least have the satisfaction of intercourse, after which they could stop embracing [and] return to their jobs..." (The absence of a separate description for female–female coupling is perhaps indicative of ancient Greek attitudes concerning female sexuality.) This particular section concludes with arguably the most plangent lines of the entire *Symposium*: "This then, is the source of our desire to love each other. Love is born into every human being; it calls back the halves of our original nature together; it tries to make one out of two and heal the wound of human nature" (191D). These unassuming, poetic lines are radical in their implications; one, that humans are ontologically flawed and two, that desire is biologically determined, that is to say, "orientation" (as a modern concept) is produced by nature, not nurture.

Though immutable, not all orientations, according to Aristophanes, are of equal value. Those who lust after the opposite sex may well become lechers (both male and female, 191D); women who run after women become simply lesbians (another instance in which Aristophanes seems to have comparatively little to say about this crucial prong of sexual orientation). The superior orientation is, of course, male homosexuality; these are "the best of boys, because they are most manly in their nature" (192A). Aristophanes even goes out of his way to defend such boys against charges of shamelessness; on the contrary, such lads are "bold and brave and masculine" and only marry out of custom, rather than inclination. They would be happy, in fact, to live life unmarried, that the mere action of

bellies, etc.). This is in contradistinction to "classical" constructions of the body as clean and Apollonian: chiseled abs, symmetrical profiles, "closed" bodies. View through this lens, the first half of Aristophanes' speech is definitely folk-humor: we humans are entirely circular, with strangely placed genitals, and a penchant for rolling along in bumbling, comic ways. The second half of the speech is, by contrast, *un*-grotesque: the idea of a slicing is completely contrary to the spirit of grotesquerie, which emphasizes the fluid rather than the discrete. So the second half of the speech is "tragic" in that it no longer concerns the comic body as outlined by Bakhtin but, rather, bodies that are struggling to achieve the comic body once more, a process that is itself an imperfect reflection of Eros.

belonging to another is enough to provide happiness (a fine *mot* for contemporary advocates of same-sex marriage). Reiterating his themes previously expressed, Aristophanes avers that such a couple "never wants to be separated from each other, not even for a moment." (192C).

Even in a post-Foucauldian era of healthy skepticism concerning the social construction of homosexuality (Greek or otherwise) there is something seductive about this particular speech; in a review of the relevant secondary literature on the *Symposium*, John Thorp argues that the speech both confirms the possibility of a "psychically deep" desire for men, by men, as well as the possibility for a "life-long predilection" for same-sex unions. Thorp thus draws the conclusion: "Greek homosexuality seems very close to our own category in fundamental ways. Of course, it may still be the case that homosexuality is a social construct, but if so, it is striking that the Greeks and we have constructed it so similarly."[21] For many readers, Aristophanes' speech—which is likely to be a gloss as well on the theatrical flair of Aristophanes, the comic playwright—achieves its power by combining a fairy-like tale with Platonic wit. For Richard Hunter, "We may well smile as we recognize something of ourselves and our own sexual pursuits in the comedy of Aristophanes' half-people … The logic is that of the etiological 'just-so' story."[22] Composed as a *jeu d'esprit*, the speech is "inventive, witty, appealing, naggingly suggestive, but at heart utterly empty." That is to say, it fails as a philosophical argument, if rather a triumph on the level of entertainment. Stanley Rosen, fascinated by the speech's gloomier implications, draws quite different conclusions: "[This speech] has proved to be a tragedy rather than a comedy. The situation is as dark for Zeus as it is for mankind. The second operation was as much a failure as a success."[23] On Rosen's reading, the half-men can only live lives of extraordinary desperation, as they continually attempt to repair themselves through *eros*; any further splitting of humans into quarter-men, would make us like "profiles on tombstones," and so we're stuck in a existence in which the only cure for attraction (*any* attraction) is death. A bleak assessment, indeed.[24]

To my mind, the most striking modern reception of Plato's *Symposium* is found not in a philosophical text but in a hard-rocking Broadway

---

[21] Thorp 1992: 61.   [22] Hunter 2004: 64–65; 70.   [23] Rosen 1968: 157.

[24] Lescher 2006: 338 notes that the kaleidoscopic nature of Plato's text makes it especially amenable to warring interpretations: *The Symposium* features "the absence of a single and clear dominant message" and so later readers, artists, and thinkers are offered a smorgasbord of conflicting narratives and ideals to puzzle out.

musical, *Hedwig and the Angry Inch*. John Cameron Mitchell first conceived the idea of a musical after seeing a stage adaptation of the entire *Symposium* in Los Angeles in the early 1990s; he later handed a copy of the *Symposium* to composer Stephen Trask and asked him to make a song based on it. Trask's brilliant reformulation of Aristophanes' speech [189c–193e] made its debut in 1994 in Mitchell's/Hedwig's act at the Squeezebox, a dance party in downtown Manhattan. As Mitchell states in a later interview, Aristophanes' speech has always been the nucleus of *Hedwig*: "[The song 'The Origin of Love'] has always been the centre – we had that before we had a story. There was a myth, a 2,500 year old myth, that was always the centre of it."[25] As a full-fledged musical, *Hedwig* premiered off-Broadway in 1998, to critical acclaim; it was subsequently filmed with James Cameron Mitchell again as the titular Hedwig. *Hedwig* made its Broadway bow on April 22, 2014, in a production starring Neil Patrick Harris, who nabbed a Tony award for his performance.

In form, *Hedwig* is something of a two-hander, with Hedwig and his inamorato (the cunningly named Tommy Gnosis) played by the same actor, with support from a dubiously gendered friend named Itzhak. The musical begins with Hedwig—a boy—falling head-over-high-heels for an American G.I. stationed in West Germany; immigration to the United States, however, requires the ruse of a heterosexual marriage, and so Hedwig consents to a sex-change operation. The surgery, alas, is botched, leaving Hedwig with just an "angry inch" and a dubious gender. Hedwig eventually falls in love with Tommy, a young and feckless American rocker; in another nod to the *Symposium*, Tommy's last name, in Greek, translates as "knowledge," and so symbolizes not only Hedwig's erotic inclinations but his epistemological journey as well. Throughout *Hedwig*, the title character *lives* Aristophanes' speech through a continual cycle of men, of "other halves," though always concentrating on his own true love, Tommy. (*Thomas* is Hebrew for 'twin': another piece of etymological wordplay on Aristophanes' original tale of gemination.)

It is something of a surprise, however, when Hedwig, in "The Origin of Love," not only alludes to Aristophanes' speech but renarrates it in an American idiom. First, there is the medium of song: light to hard rock (scored for electric guitar, rhythm, and vocals). Next, the visuals: an animated sequence (by Emily Hubley) displaying Zeus' severing of the spheroid humans and the subsequent erotic complications (see Figure 2.1).

---

[25] See Sypniewski 2008.

Figure 2.1. An original human is split in half, in Emily Hubley's animated version of "The Origin of Love."

Lastly, the language: a lightly updated, slangy version of the tale that ties the universalizing fable to a *specific* love affair, thus placing the Greek myth within its American social context. Some verses of the song are startlingly close to the Aristophanic original; for instance: "Folks roamed the earth/ Like big rolling kegs./ They had two sets of arms./ They had two sets of legs." Other sections—such as the introduction of the Norse god Thor and an unnamed Indian god of surgery—seem content to blend world mythology with Greek. But the song's concluding stanzas again tie Hedwig's ill-fated affairs to a specific reading of Aristophanes' original speech:

> So we wrapped our arms around each other,
> Trying to shove ourselves back together.
> We were making love,
> Making love.
> It was a cold dark evening,
> Such a long time ago,
> When by the mighty hand of Jove,
> It was the sad story
> How we became
> Lonely two-legged creatures,
> It's the story of
> The origin of love.

Hedwig's ode-to-Aristophanes emphasizes, ironically, the tragic elements of the comedian's speech: the desperate attempt by two halves to "shove [themselves] back together." Humanity thus finds its origins not just in bipedalism, but in sheer loneliness. Jove's lightning, which strikes the original humans "like shining blades/Of a knife" finds its mortal reflection in Hedwig's botched surgery, thereby constructing Hedwig as the original human: our sexually scrambled Adam.[26] Thus Trask and Mitchell's *Hedwig* uses Plato's *Symposium* to locate same-sex desire as a *primary* human impulse: a nod in the direction of "essentialism," in which gay desire may be traced back directly to the start of it all: the Greeks.

Hedwig's initial Off-Broadway run was the culmination of four years of musical experimentation in the punk scene in Manhattan; though Mitchell's adaptation of the *Symposium* might indeed have been perceived as

---

[26] See Peraino 2005: 249 on the conflation of biological and socially constructed gender in *Hedwig*: "When Hedwig, the male-to-female transsexual character (played by a man), kisses Yitzhak, the former 'drag queen' who is Hedwig's husband (played by a woman), the parallel and cross relations between the composite bio- and neo-genders, the 'real' and 'fictional' genders, create a union that is simultaneously homo and hetero—a perfect, undivided sphere like the original earth, original humans, and original love."

Figure 2.2. The whimsical CD cover art for *All About Love.*

revolutionary by Middle America, as a *musical,* it was fostered and developed in the welcoming artistic climate of New York City itself. But what happens if a production of the *Symposium* is produced *specifically* as an act of social resistance? In fact, a musicalization of the *Symposium,* produced in Colorado Springs, Colorado in 1997, was figured as just that. *All About Love,* with music and lyrics by Mark and Lauren Arnest, and a book and direction by Murray Ross, updated Plato's dialogue to a swinging, literally gay, 1930s cocktail party (the musical and literary overtones of the closeted Cole Porter are surely not coincidental: see Figure 2.2). Since Colorado had recently weathered the uproar over its Proposition 2 constitutional amendment prohibiting munici-palities from enacting gay-friendly legislation (1992), this production of *All about Love,* then, had a political sting, one noticed and remarked upon by critics: "So why is this show courageous? Because these men are on stage in the center of family-values land—Colorado Springs—dancing and kissing and talking about loving other men. At one point, it's mentioned that there are 'all these damn religious groups promoting abstinence.' Call me a fool, but this seems gutsy—considering the surrounding landscape."[27] In fact, one author of the show seemed disappointed that they only had one walk-out during the run of the production (offended by an anatomically exuberant satyr, as it happens); otherwise, Mark Arnest is "sad to report that we got not a single protester."[28] It might be that the audience for an evening of Plato *à la* Noël Coward is (to put it coyly) self-selecting, and therefore unlikely to elicit

---

[27] Thom Wise, *Rocky Mountain News.* Sept. 5, 1997.
[28] http://home.earthlink.net/~marnest/reviews.html. Accessed March 20, 2007.

protest; it is certainly worth noting that the (professionally obligated) critic, whose sympathies appear neutral, situates the production within the wider space of contested "family values."

For the director Ross, staging *All About Love* brings into focus the dialogue's gay underpinnings: "Once you put Plato's words into the mouths of actual people you are struck by something often ignored: all these people are either gay or bisexual, and the love under consideration has a clear basis in homoeroticism. For most of the last two millennia, commentators have failed to point out that the largest, most wide-ranging discussion of love in western history is carried on by a group of homosexuals..."[29] This statement is a bit hyperbolic: commentators have been nothing short of obsessed with the homosexual underpinnings of the *Symposium* since well before 1997. And yet, there's something to Ross' point that the *performance* of the *Symposium* radicalizes the *Symposium* in ways that written editions cannot do (and have not done). The Colorado *Symposium* situates Plato's *Symposium* within one of the hoariest of American art forms—an old-fashioned musical comedy—and thus, as a performance piece, it's un-skimmable: the audience is compelled to watch all of the performance in real-time, however uncomfortable the performance and however explicit the motifs. Parts of *All about Love* are more explicitly gay-affirming than others; surprisingly, Aristophanes' speech, for decades a gay call-to-arms, receives a gender-neutral treatment. As adapted by Arnest, the speech is now a plaintive love anthem entitled "Love and Found," and therefore less an *aition*, a 'foundational myth,' concerning homosexuality than a rather more straightforward recognition of mutual attraction between *any* genders:

> For there's not one Soul destined to be hale and whole
> All are split in two and always wonder how and with whom
> They were first linked in that silent space
> before each was cast
> with no past
> On the farther shore

The rest of the verses constitute variations on this theme (while eliding the intervention of Zeus and thus providing a more specific focus on the poetics of loss). The big gay anthem, it turns out, is Alcibiades' bawdy tango "Nothing at All," in which the young playboy describes his disappointing attempted seduction of Socrates: "I saw a fine romance coming

---

[29] http://home.earthlink.net/~marnest/director.html

my way/ If only he got the chance, I knew he would love me…" The reference to a "fine romance" cleverly alludes to the Dorothy Fields/Jerome Kern standard, popularized by Fred Astaire and Ginger Rogers in *Swing Time* (1936), and here appropriated (in a campy fashion) by Alcibiades. The song becomes, however, bluer in its subsequent verses:

> So I asked him to come to the gym
> And we got in a bit of a tussle
> He'd certainly give in to his whim for me
> (*Others, shouting variously:* And then what happened?)
> Nothing at all.
>
> When we got into a clench
> Though hard as a rock, he wouldn't give an inch
> That's when I feared
> There would be no lay today.

Here, Socrates rebuffs Alcibiades' advances at the gym—even when clasped by a rock-hard suitor, Socrates hews to his philosophical precepts concerning *eros*—and a night spent by Alcibiades' side results in "nothing at all." The final song of *All about Love*, then, though "gay" in content, ultimately performs the same function as in the original dialogue: it destabilizes contemporary notions of same-sex desire by radical separation of the physical from the cerebral, and the private from the public. In spite of— or perhaps because of—its form as a dizzy musical comedy, *All about Love* re-appropriates the Socratic dialogue as a peculiarly American commentary on contemporary gay life, in the heart of "family-values" Colorado.

Both *Hedwig* and *All about Love* reinscribe modern homosexuality into antiquity in a way that valorizes such an orientation: these are left-leaning, progressive takes on a modern, controversial social issue. The odd thing about the *Symposium* is that even those of a diametrically opposed ideological bent—socially conservative—can create a largely *identical* construction of ancient same-sex desire. They just interpret its moral repercussions *very* differently. For instance, in his 1931 manifesto on Greek morality, the American literary critic and essayist John Jay Chapman fulminated:

> But to the historical student, to the man who not only knows something of books, but something of the world, the 'Symposium' of Plato is seen to have been in every age since Plato the most effective plea for evil that one can point to or recall. The moral disease which it inculcates is apt to break out in any age and to poison the young. The 'Symposium' has already been the *vade mecum* of those who accept and continue the

practice which it celebrates. To them it is a sort of lurid devotional book
—the sulphurous breviary of the pederast.[30]

Obviously, Chapman does not mince words. He further decries the fact
that most contemporary books on Plato are extremely accommodating to
"a modern Miss Nancyism"[31] (a lovely phrase, that) and thus take little
notice of the *Symposium*'s obvious moral failings. In expressing his
general exhortation to read Platonic Greek, Chapman finds himself,
therefore, in a moral quandary. One possible recourse is to emphasize
the *Symposium*'s historical virtues, as opposed to its philosophical or
humanistic qualities: "[The Symposium] shows the depth to which [the
Athenians'] favorite vice had penetrated their moral instincts. Yet we
have to remember that they themselves were not conscious of evil. The
degeneration in question is not personal but racial, a thing indigenous
and ingrown as part of the most coördinated and articulate civilization of
which we have any record."[32] Like many critics of the Greco-Roman past,
Chapman is enthralled by the general *idea* of antiquity, but appalled by
specifics. He attempts a certain damage control by emphasizing that the
Athenians' vice was *racial*, rather than individual; that is to say, Plato
couldn't help it, with a conception of "evil" so naïve he couldn't possibly
recognize his own.

Chapman's conclusion, however, is an important document in the
history of classical reception, and worth quoting in full:

> There is a special reason why young Hellenists should understand the
> 'Symposium,' namely, that they may be fortified against another class of
> 'Platonic' literature which they will meet in the world on leaving the
> university. This consists of modern books and essays, written in language
> more veiled than that of Aristophanes and Diotima. Such writings
> continue the teachings of Plato as to Love. They are the direct descen-
> dents of the 'Symposium,' with this difference, that they lack the gaiety of
> the original, which is now replaced by caution and innuendo—made
> necessary by the penal laws of civilized countries. They are written by
> intellectuals who fancy themselves as Hellenists and as recoverers of the
> lost mysteries of Attic sensibility. Such books are unmistakable. A certain
> preciosity of style, an artificiality in the arrangement of words, the pose of
> an exquisite balance in the sentences, betray the influence of Neo-
> Hellenism. This vehicle veils indoctrination into Greek vices. The books
> are propaganda.[33]

[30] Chapman 1931: 133.   [31] Chapman 1931: 120.   [32] Chapman 1931: 132.
[33] Chapman 1931: 134–6.

What is amazing about this passage is that Chapman here recognizes contemporary receptions of the ancient world and attempts *to fight back* by appeal to the original text, which he has already lambasted as the world's "most effective plea for evil." At least Plato has the virtue of being open in his vices; these *modern* books, however, are Plato "veiled," and constitute "propaganda" barely skirting the "penal laws of civilized countries." Such propaganda may be spotted, Chapman avers, by its obvious neo-Hellenism, including balanced clauses and a preciosity of style. (Weirdly, this warning itself comes in a sentence featuring balanced clauses and a preciosity of style; psychoanalysts and ironists, take note.) And while one might be eager to dismiss Chapman's warnings as the work of a crackpot social theorist, Chapman is in fact correct in his perception, if not in his evaluation: neo-Hellenist work in the 1920s and 1930s often *did* employ the rhetoric and literature of the ancient world as a "cover" for discourse concerning homosexuality.

In his 1924 work *Corydon* (written variously over the previously decade and published surreptitiously), André Gide posits an argument between a skeptic of homosexuality and a gay academic significantly named after the homosexual shepherd of Virgil's second *Eclogue*, who burns for the beautiful youth Alexis (*formosum pastor Corydon ardebat Alexin*, 2.1). As the argument progresses, Gide's title character notes the physiological oddity that "the male has much more to expend than is required in order to answer to the reproductive function of the opposite sex and to ensure the reproduction of the species" (104); Corydon's solution "is the same one ancient Greece advocated" (105), to wit, homosexuality.[34] After all, Corydon confesses to his interlocutor, "From your earliest childhood you have been brought up as I have; you have been taught to venerate Greece, of which we are the heirs"; the Greeks, he continues, are especially to be prized for their perfection in artistic achievement and their "aptitude for harmony" (106). And yet, Corydon laments, "as soon as Greek morals are mentioned, they are deplored, and since they cannot be ignored, they are turned from in horror" (107)—in precisely the ways that Chapman's horrified rant about the *Symposium* applauds the Greeks in general but not their moral code. Moreover, as if to annoy Chapman, Gide has framed his worked as *explicitly* neo-Hellenic: a series of Platonic dialogues, featuring a scholar with a Greek name taken from a homoerotic poem of Virgil. The form of the work thus allows Gide, as author, to broach a controversial topic under cover—and approbation—of antiquity.

---

[34] All quotations and references from Gide 1925/1983.

Figure 2.3. Charles Cullen's flamboyant illustration for Lucian's "The Little Flute Girl."

Similar trends occurred on the other side of the Atlantic as well. A 1928 illustrated edition of Lucian's *Dialogues of the Courtesans*, produced by (apparently) two gay Manhattanites, allowed marginalized sexual activities—including homosexual liaisons—to be broached under cover (and protection) of "classical literature." Lucian's dialogues—a witty send-up of stock character types from Attic literature, including avaricious prostitutes, lecherous tricks, and pushy madams—allow the adapters to dilate on some decidedly outré sexual behaviors, including S&M, fellatio, and homosexuality (strikingly, both male *and* female). A. L. Hillman's translation often riffs on Lucian's original Greek—including such formulations as "Then they obliged me to take . . . between my lips, saying 'Try a new melody, genial little flute player!'"—while Charles Cullen's illustrations feature curiously androgynous and hyper-sexualized male figures, replete with tongue-in-cheek phallic symbols and a general air of sexual ambiguity (see Figure 2.3).[35] But it's in Hillman's introduction that we find the appeal to antiquity—and a precious neo-Hellenism—that Chapman so abhors:

> The translator has endeavored to keep constantly in mind the kindly
> humanism with which Lucian wrote these tales so descriptive of one

[35] Hillman and Cullen 1928: 94–5.

phase of Greek life. Lucian discusses intimate sex details with the frankness of one not immoral, but influenced by a system of morals that finds
everything that is natural both beautiful and good.

These dialogues can hardly be offensive to the intelligent modern; for,
somehow, our own civilization is changing, and as it becomes richer and
fuller, it seems to have more in common with the civilizations of
antiquity.[36]

These paragraphs are rich in the language of gay and lesbian ideological
appropriation, all the more so because they preface a neo-Hellenic translation and edition. On Hillman's reading, Lucian, and by extension, all
ancient Greeks, do not engage in immoral sexual behaviors but act on
purely "natural" impulses; because these impulses are natural they are thus
"beautiful and good" (a phrase lifted out of innumerable dialogues of
Plato). From this point, we discern the inevitable bridge to modernity: an
"intelligent" modern can hardly be offended by the dialogues because our
own (American) civilization is changing, and as it improves (as it becomes
"richer and fuller") it paradoxically forges stronger links with the civilizations of the past. The best thing that could happen to America (and
American sexual morality) is thus a return to antiquity's frankness concerning homosexuality. Lucian can cure us of our shameful turn from
civilization's treasury of erotic expression.

Homosexuality, Psychology, and the Ancient World

Something of the state of confusion concerning pre-1970s analyses of
ancient Greek sexuality can be deduced from the writings of the ethno-
psychologist George Devereux, who analyzed Greek sexual practices
through a Freudian lens, with decidedly mixed results; this trend in the
reception of ancient sexuality, as originally published in specialized classics
scholarship, will reappear in some startlingly high-profile mass media
(including a standard college textbook). Like Chapman, Devereux stressed
the *familiarity*, the *humanness*, of the Greeks—but a familiarity unfortunately marred by perverted sexual practices. (Even that conclusion reifies
the idea that, after all, we moderns have our perverts too—and so, we're
like the Greeks!) Devereux's analysis of Sappho's fragment 31 is a case in
point. Though we've only the first few stanzas from the poem still extant,

[36] Hillman and Cullen 1928: Preface. See Jenkins 2005 for an extended analysis of this
fascinating work.

it's probable that Sappho has a crush on a woman who is (unfortunately) already betrothed to a man. The poem begins with an eroticized glance of smoldering jealousy—"He seems to me like a god – the one sitting and facing you – hearing your sweet voice and laughter..."—and ends with Sappho's erotic meltdown, as all her senses fail one by one: ears, eyes, skin, soul. Devereux's analysis skips the pathos and goes straight to the pathology: "[E]ven if there existed no explicit tradition concerning Sappho's lesbianism, her reaction to her male rival would represent for the psychiatrist prima facie evidence of her perversion. This finding does not imply that she was not *also* a schoolmistress or the leader of some feminine cult group, particularly since, even in our day and age, 'tweedy' games-mistresses and the like are far from rare."[37] The phrase 'games-mistress' might better be translated into American English as 'gym teacher,' a pervasive modern stereotype delightfully skewered by *The Onion's* satirical 1999 news story, "Community Bands Together to Get through Lesbian-Gym-Teacher Crisis."[38] By comparing the Sappho of ode 31 to modern gym teachers, Devereux continues a centuries-long project of equating ancient sexual impulse with modern desires—and even modern stereotypes.

Moreover, Devereux arrives at this *truth* concerning ancient sexuality not through philology or history but through the discourses of science: "[T]he [ancient] speculation that [Sappho] was a prostitute (Sen. *Ep.* 88, etc.) is hardly credible. It does, however, reinforce the view that she was a lesbian: female homosexuality is notoriously common among prostitutes (cf. any serious monograph on prostitution).... It would seem desirable, in classical studies, to spend less time on proving that some gossipy tradition is manifestly untenable on *logical* grounds, and to start examining what latent *psychological* truths such objectively untrustworthy canards contain."[39] It is a shame that Foucault never laid eyes on this lovely specimen of cultural criticism: it features *exactly* the sort of shift in discourse that Foucault claims created modern homosexuality (and with it, the modern homosexual). Firstly, Devereux disparages historical methods of inquiry (the "logical" grounds of historical fact); next, he privileges the discourse of psychology, through which we discover truths "objectively"; and in addition he promulgates the (frankly, crackpot) notion that prostitutes are commonly lesbian by appeal to anonymous, "serious monographs" by

[37] Devereux 1970: 21.   [38] www.theonion.com/content/node/39094
[39] Devereux 1970: 31n2.

social scientists. (Counterevidence is presumably to be found in frivolous monographs on the same subject.)

In his 1967 piece "Greek Pseudo-Homosexuality and The 'Greek Miracle'," Devereux attempts to exculpate the entire Greek race from the "perversion" of homosexuality by arguing, in essence, that it was just a phase, one that "while behaviorally real, was psychologically spurious."[40] Devereux's "relentless application of psychoanalytic and ethnological insights will prove that the *average* Greek … was not *psychiatrically* a pervert, despite his homosexual behavior. In some respects, he was perhaps even more heterosexually oriented than modern man." I will spare the reader the tortured reasoning that goes into that line of thinking, but Devereux's division of the question goes something like this: (1) Greek homosexuality was a phase of most men's existence as adolescents (2) Greek men seem to have adjusted to opposite-sex desire later in life, with non-neurotic consequences (3) true homosexuals are always neurotic thus (4) Greeks were not homosexuals even though they acted like them. The explanation for the "social prolongation of adolescence,"[41] on account of which Greek men acted in sexually confused ways well into their twenties, is chalked up to a pandemic of "inadequate fathering,"[42] which compelled young men to seek father-substitutes for generations. The most curious part of Devereux's article is his strangely uplifting conclusion that this pseudo-homosexuality created, in part, "the Greek miracle"; "the prolongation of a charmingly adolescent intellectual presumptuousness"[43] fostered the native Greek penchant for scientific and mathematical inquiry, and so, these pseudo-homosexuals, in their charmingly naïve way, advanced the human race while fumbling through their sexual misadventures.

Until, of course, the root of all evil, Plato, appeared; Devereux thus advances a line of argument of which Chapman would surely approve: "The 'Greek Miracle' came to an end when one of its most brilliant and also emotionally least mature representatives—reacting *against* his own adolescent emotionality—froze the graceful spiraling of adolescent fantasy into a dereistically orderly crystal."[44] What had been a cultural *jeu d'esprit* was now ordered by Plato—in the *Symposium*, among other works—into a pathological homosexuality (69); behavior was now, on Devereux's reading, codified. When Greek homosexuality mimicked the form of modern adolescent experimentation, it produced the "Greek Miracle"—but as behaviors for cultural and physical *adults*, well, this is beyond the pale.

---

[40] Devereux 1967: 69.   [41] Devereux 1967: 76.   [42] Devereux 1967: 70.
[43] Devereux 1967: 91.   [44] Devereux 1967: 91.

By creating, and valorizing, ancient homosexuality, Plato made permanent an inclination that was at best "abnormal" (91). Greece was now gay.

Devereux's later analysis of Euripides' tragedy *Hippolytus* is even more damning in its construction of "modern" homosexuality within ancient myth.[45] At first glance, however, *Hippolytus* might seem an unpromising text for an investigation of homosexuality of any sort: the plot concerns the Queen Phaedra's lust for her proud and apparently asexual stepson, Hippolytus. At first Phaedra keeps her secret to herself, and soon induces a near deathlike state of lovesickness. Indeed, Phaedra would likely have taken her secret to the grave were it not for the importunate badgering of her nurse. The nurse's subsequent interview with Hippolytus goes terribly awry; Hippolytus is horrified by his mother's desires, and flees the scene. In shame, Phaedra hangs herself, but not before indicting Hippolytus, in a suicide note, for attempted rape. Theseus, her husband, therefore curses his son to a miserable death; Poseidon fulfills the terms of the curse by summoning a sea-monster to spook Hippolytus' horses as he drives his chariot by the sea. The *dénouement* is terrible: Hippolytus is torn to shreds among the rocks; Theseus discovers, through the goddess Artemis, his wife's deception; and a brief sentimental scene of reunion between father and son concludes with Hippolytus' forgiveness and his apotheosis into a hero of religious cult.

Because of the erotic underpinnings of this family romance, Devereux claims the ability to analyze the *Hippolytus* through modern psychological and sexual categories, thereby receiving the *Hippolytus* as a gay/lesbian text. After outlining his qualifications for passing judgment on the sexual orientation of Euripides (!)—including fieldwork among the Mohave Indians as well as patients in his clinical practice—Devereux concludes: "My inability to detect any indication of homosexual tendencies in the surviving writings of Euripides should therefore carry some weight" (68). This is a perfect example of classical reception: as filtered through a psychologist's lens, Euripides is "straight." In the same vein, Devereux introduces his "last and clinically most certain interpretation" of Hippolytus' relationship with his father, Theseus. "Boy children, hag-ridden by their panicky dread of the erotic-hostile impulses mobilized by their

---

[45] All quotations from Devereux 1985. It is odd that Devereux misses the chance to mine some supporting ancient testimony concerning Euripides' sexual proclivities: Athenaeus, for instance, records that "Sophocles was as much a lover of young lads as Euripides was a lover of women" (*Deipnosophistae,* 13.603). Perhaps Devereux doesn't wish to broadcast that Sophocles would have gotten on famously with Hippolytus.

oedipal conflicts, sometimes shy away from their normal ('developmental neurosis') oedipal conflict by restructuring it into a so-called 'reverse Oedipus.' In such cases the boy identifies himself with his father and develops latent (passive) homosexual impulses toward the father" (73). Hippolytus' curious statements at ll. 997–998—that he knows how to make friends who avoid wrongdoing, who avoid evil pronouncements and the rendering of base services—"imply a denial of homosexual practices and homosexual prostitution rendered in payment for services rendered" (74–75). Thus Hippolytus situates himself as a self-recognizing, but tormented homosexual, who recognizes his impulses, but who cannot carry through on their vulgar physical consequences. ("Euripides' dislike of fashionable, homosexual athletes is obvious," Devereux observes (75).)

Hippolytus' latent homosexuality "is perfectly congruent with Hippolytus' hatred for his father" (75), and, according to Devereux, such hatred ricochets back on himself; his murderous impulses become self-directed. Thus Hippolytus' conspicuous "anal eroticism"—the root and fundament, so to speak, of homosexual longing and aggression—manifests itself in Hippolytus' death-wish: he desires to turn back the clock to a time before his mother's fall from grace to "sluttishness." This can only happen when Hippolytus again "ceases to exist"; or, as Devereux tastelessly puts it: "chariot (and automobile) 'accidents' are made to order for such purposes" (76). Thus Devereux constructs Hippolytus' death as an ancient version of a modern suicide-by-automobile, fueled by gay self-loathing. Though Devereux deflects criticism in his introduction about producing a character assassination of Hippolytus—he is criticizing, he says, only the *encomiasts* of Hippolytus—this is purely rhetoric (xi); he has little good to say about this "self-destructive narcissist" (86). Only bleeding heart "Occidental eulogists" might imagine that Euripides *should* have admired the prototype of "a lakonizing, priggish, conceited, horse-crazy, athletic, sex-phobic, virginal, 'orphic' dandy..." (92).

Now, it might be easy to dismiss Devereux's derogative "queering" of antiquity as the product of a 1960s and 1970s hysteria concerning the American Psychological Association's *de*-pathologization of homosexuality in 1973; in that sense, Devereux's work reflects the turmoil of that controversial decision, as his readings of Sappho and Euripides ferociously resist at least one rising trend in American social discourse. One of the strengths of reception studies is its insistence that even scholarship—for all of its vaunted predilection for "objective" truth—can never be quite objective: scholars of the ancient world are just as socially conditioned (and ideologically biased) as the artists who seek inspiration. Gay and lesbian appropriations of antiquity are not, of course, confined to gay and lesbian readers, nor are such appropriations necessarily valorizing; psychosexual analyses of the ancient world can find dissemination in a whole host of media—including pedagogical texts. Stephen L. Harris's and Gloria Platzner's *Classical Mythology: Images and Insights*, a widely adopted American college textbook, is designed to be a sort of "one-stop" shopping solution for introductory mythology courses. Instead of having to order an expensive swath of individual primary and secondary texts, instructors of mythology can, instead, assign selections from a pre-chosen mix of Greek and Roman literature, critical analyses, and archaeological data. Though the cost is cheaper than buying the texts separately, the resulting tome is hefty in price and just sheer heft (in 2009, over three pounds). It also means that students tend to regard the authors as authoritative, since conflicting viewpoints are often subsumed under an overarching narrative of mythological progression, from early cult to the disintegration of "paganism" under the late Roman Empire.

When Harris and Platzner present, then, an idiosyncratic take on the god Apollo, it's worth investigating how gay and lesbian subtexts are presented in a manner that seems superficially friendly, but ultimately laden with a number of less-than-positive stereotypes, stereotypes largely indebted to mid-century Freudian/psychoanalytical takes on the ancient world. On the one hand, the book seems admirably forthright in its presentation of the god Apollo's bisexual affairs: "Like his father, Zeus, he formed liaisons with members of both sexes, but unlike Zeus, he was typically unlucky in love" (241). Next follows a brief catalogue of Apollo's affairs, including Daphne (turned into a laurel tree); the boy Cyparissus (who dissolves into a cypress); the boy Hyacinthus (whom Apollo accidentally kills with a discus); and the woman Coronis, by whom he has his child Asklepius (and whom he later kills in a fit of jealous rage). But it's the student-directed "Questions for Discussion and Review" that frame the matter most curiously: "Discuss Apollo's generally unsatisfying love affairs. Why does myth present the most physically and intellectually gifted young male Olympian as almost invariably suffering erotic rejection or loss? Is it because he is an ephebe, lacking the mature authority that ensures Zeus' success in love?" (257).

That last question is nothing if not leading. At the least, it features an unexamined and ultimately dubious assumption that Zeus was successful in love. If by "successful," one means "prodigiously reproductive," yes, then Zeus was certainly successful: Zeus can boast of many children, usually through rape, though that rather stretches the definition of success.

Timothy Gantz, in *Early Greek Myth*, argues that Zeus' liaisons are "primarily unions with mortal women" (61), including Dia, Danae, Europa, Semele, Alkmene, Io, Aigina, Kallisto, Leda, and "in the same category" the boy Ganymede; Gantz also argues that Zeus' role as father "is generally restricted to the act of procreation" (61). Leda, for instance, is abandoned after giving birth to an egg after her congress with Zeus in the form of a swan (320); Zeus kidnaps Europa while disguised in the form of a bull (210) and thereafter gives birth (in various traditions) to Minos, Rhadamanthys, and Sarpedon; Io is turned into a cow and later impregnated by Zeus through the touch of his hand (Aeschylus, *Prometheus Bound* 790–815); Semele is accidentally incinerated by Zeus after conceiving Dionysus. While these various acts may be seen as successful in terms of progeny, it's curious that Harris and Platzner consider them successful in terms of "love" (Zeus' only long-term relationship, with his wife and sister Hera, is obviously rocky by any sort of modern standards of connubial bliss). Moreover, the chapter on Apollo emphasizes the god's homosexual liaisons by omitting many of his (reproductive) heterosexual liaisons, including an apparently happy romance with Cyrene (mother of Aristaeus, Pindar, *Pythian* 9); Evadne, who bears Iamos (Pindar, *Olympian* 6.35); and Thero, who bears Chairon (*Hesiod*, fr. 252 MW), among others.

   All of which is to say that the chapter—and the study question based on it—presents Apollo as a frustrated homosexual (in the face of much evidence) and Zeus as a successful lover, with his "mature authority" (again, in the face of much evidence). Put another way, Apollo, while undoubtedly "physically and intellectually gifted," is ontologically doomed to unsuccessful affairs, particularly of the homosexual bent. This is a strange reading of Apollo and one searches for its genesis. The answer is not far a field: the bibliography in the "Recommended Reading" lists Robert Eisner's *The Road to Daulis: Psychoanalysis, Psychology, and Classical Mythology* (1987), and points out for particular approbation the book's insightful analysis of Apollo and his various love affairs.[46]

   The title of Eisner's chapter—"Apollo and His Boys"—does not inspire confidence, for reasons already enumerated; it may be cute, but it is not particularly accurate given Apollo's propensity also for women. The

---

[46] And variously reviewed. A rave from Lois J. Parker: "A brilliantly crafted work" (*CW* 1988–1989 **82**: 215); a pan from Simon Goldhill: *CR* 1988 **38**: 75–6. Goldhill: "[The thesis is] pursued by E. with shaky scholarship, insufficient rigour of argumentation, and a general unawareness both of the questions such a thesis involves and of the scholars who have already discussed the topic."

introductory subsection states one major aim of the chapter: "Apollo is not a *senex* figure, like Zeus or Jehovah, but the archetype of ever-youthful sterility ... He is a narcissist" (141); and from narcissism, Eisner segues inevitably to homosexuality ("Freud recognized the narcissistic component of homosexuality" (147)). Apollo's many children, of course, present a problem for both the god's purported sterility and his homosexuality, and so rhetoric comes to the rescue: "With few of his loves does Apollo succeed in procreating, in establishing his line, in finding a productive expression for his eros... Gods cannot die, but they may lead very lonely isolated lives" (143). For Eisner, *eros* is only successful if *productive of children*; Apollo's five children—at least—are considered "few" and so Apollo must forever lead his lonely homosexual life. Worse yet, the women he so admires are not really women at all: "Apollo, then, loves boys and boyish women, prefers narrow and unvoracious hips" (147).[47] That is to say, women are merely boy-substitutes, and their hips, like a boy's buttocks, geared towards non-productivity (i.e. not "birthing hips"). The nymph Daphne is specifically singled out as a "tomboy," another neutering. In Eisner's framing of the question, then, Apollo "plays the role of the patron god of homosexuality" (147).

Many of Eisner's observations have little support in any sort of text; indeed, they often read as a fantasia on Apollonian themes. For instance, after an excursus on the boy Narcissus, who, from self-love, wastes away into a flower, Eisner continues: "Narcissus' self-absorption strikes us as god-like—'Olympian,' we call it. Indeed, Narcissus resembles Apollo in his disdain for normal connections. Although Apollo embodies the Hellenic ideal, he was still a god and the gods are all bored. Like immortal children on a perennially rainy day, they need us adults to amuse them" (153). So far, Eisner has carefully tiptoed around the pathological aspects of Apollo's sexuality; but the inclusion of "normal" gives away the game. On Eisner's reading, Apollo, read *exclusively* through his sexuality, is abnormal, deviant; he is narcissistic, and implicitly puerile, trapped in arrested development. We are the "adults" who must amuse *him*, a trope that thus constitute a reversal of the usual metaphorical world in which the gods are *our* parents. Eisner's disquieting portrayal of Apollo's sexuality finds a reflex, too, in its depiction of (older) Athenian homosexuals: "And in the gymnasium, a youth's narcissistic preoccupation with the appearance of his body and the development of its musculature and mechanisms was

---

[47] "Unvoracious hips" is also an unfortunate refraction of the concept of Freudian concept of the *vagina dentata*, the 'toothed vagina,' a manifestation of castration anxiety.

Figure 2.4. Copy of Praxiteles' "Lizard Slayer." Louvre, Ma 441.

promoted, prolonged, and admired. The ancient gym's lack of floor-length mirrors was more than made up for by the glittering eyes of its older patrons" (147). That is to say, a young man could see the results of his gym work-out in the (leering) expressions of the older men: the (modern, American) floor-length mirror finds its ancient counterpart in eager, aged eyes.

Lastly—and as a sort of *summa* of his argument—Eisner analyzes a famous statue of Apollo by Praxiteles (see Figure 2.4).

> The most youthful Apollo of those to come down to us—A Roman copy of Praxiteles' state of the god as *sauroktonos* or 'lizard slayer'—shows just such a boy as must have broken the hearts of the elderly pederasts of Athens. . . . Instead of a powerful athlete manfully drawing his recurve bow, P. gives us a slender, sinuous, and sinew-less youth about to impale the little reptile with a hand-held arrow. . . P. shows us the god as he once, for a brief moment, was—luscious and cruel—before he became the tormented, frustrated lover we know from the myths. As he tormented

the lizards who adored him, so, when he becomes the adorant, will he be
tormented in his turn. Apollo, it seems, would have it no other way. (147)

Here, Eisner's "queering" of the *sauroktonos* statue elides the most common interpretation of the statue—that it's a whimsical joke based on the
adult Apollo's later slaying of the Python[48]—and reads it instead as a
metaphor for Apollo's psychosexual persona. Instead of drawing a recurve
bow "manfully" (notice the implicit antithesis between manliness and
homosexuality), Apollo instead toys with a lizard in much the same
way that boys (and women with unvoracious hips) will toy with *him*.
The decadent tone of Eisner's description—the phrase "luscious and cruel"
could be lifted from a Thomas Mann short story—indelibly links homosexuality to social pathology.

So, through a roundabout way, Eisner's "queer"—but hardly sympathetic—reading of Apollo has found its way into a modern textbook; and
through that textbook to American undergraduates. This is a powerfully
skewed ideological reception of antiquity, and shows the often serpentine
path that such receptions can take: from Freud, through a scholarly
Freudian reading of myth (Eisner), to a mass-market paperback that
disseminates the results without challenging the method or the statistics.
Harris and Platzner's "ephebic" and "unsuccessful" Apollo thus reinforces
(to my mind) outdated notions of male homosexuality, and propagates
mid-century stereotypes that have much to do with Mart Crowley's "The
Boys in the Band" but nothing to do with Apollo.

Homosexuality and the Limits of Metaphor *Dionysus in 69* and *An Arrow's Flight*

One of the aims of this chapter—even this book—is to locate and analyze
the *metaphors* employed when adapting classical myths to modern American contexts: what aspects change, and why? A particularly spectacular
example of "Americanizing antiquity" occurs in the central scene of Richard Schechner's *Dionysus in 69*, a countercultural take on Euripides'
Bacchae. Performed by The Performance Group as a free-form meditation
on the ancient text, *Dionysus in 69* takes classicist William Arrowsmith's
popular dramatic translation and transmogrifies it into a performance

---

[48] See for instance Pollitt 1972: 154 on Praxiteles' "genial, low-key humor": the statue is "clearly a
burlesque" on Apollo's heroic slaying of the Python.

piece with elements of ritual, peep-show, exorcism, political tract, and coming-out story. The evening famously opens with a chorus of scantily clad women re-enacting the birth of the god Dionysus, largely by lining up in a row and then forming a replica of a birth canal with their legs. They then push through this canal the infant Dionysus—played by William Finley—and the psychosexual subtext to the play is off to a roaring start. As the *mise en scène* switches to Thebes, the elder statesman Cadmus and his advisor Teiresias express their disappointment in the reception given to Dionysus in the *polis*—not a good omen—while the young Pentheus, King of Thebes, makes his entrance, disturbed at reports that a priest of Dionysus is on his way. Pentheus is here played by William (Bill) Shephard, bare-chested and clad only in shorts; like many members of the cast, his costume is designed to emphasize the character's—and the actor's—access to sexuality.

The orgiastic aspect of the evening blurs the line between actor and character, and between character and audience. Contemporary accounts of the event emphasize that *every* aspect of the evening was a performance—including the act of simply watching. Reactions to this hypersexualized and viscerally physical *Bacchae* differ. Admits one disappointed spectator: "This time I joined in the dancing, but the fondling pile was so far away I could not easily join it."[49] Given the improvisational nature of the performance, misapprehensions were bound to occur: "[W]hen I saw *Dionysus in 69*, one young woman began slugging a performer to stop him from continuing what she had allowed to begin."[50] Furthermore, amidst all of the groping and nudity, a certain amount of interpretative nuance seems to have been lost: "I still cannot follow the Euripides lines or understand their contribution to the evening."[51] This was, in a sense, all part of Schechner's plan: in his theoretical writings, which emphasize the anthropological bases of performance, Schechner aims for an experience that blends elements of ritual, play, and music. Text is merely one part of the equation.[52]

But in the case of the *Bacchae*, that text is hardly inconsequential; for all its liberties, *Dionysus in 69* is still a version of Euripides' play. Though to some extent *all* of *Dionysus in 69* engages in transgressive re-enactments of Euripidean moments, it is fascinating that the most "homosexually charged" moment arrives precisely at the point of (traditionally) greatest interpretative difficulty by scholars and readers. (We will see similar

[49] Kostelanetz 1989: 149.   [50] Isaac 1970: 434.   [51] Kostelanetz 1989: 150.
[52] For an anthology of Schechner's cross-cultural theories of performance, see Schechner 1988.

developments in feminist re-envisionings of the *Odyssey* and the *Aeneid* in Chapter 5.) Having imprisoned Dionysus—whom he thinks is merely an effeminate devotee of the god—Pentheus soon finds Thebes in catastrophe: an earthquake hits the palace, the Eastern "stranger" escapes from his prison, and the women of the city continue their revelries in the wilderness as marauding Bacchants, crazed followers of Bacchus. A second interview between Pentheus and Dionysus reveals that Pentheus would happily spy on the Bacchants—presumably for military reconnaissance—but the king is at a loss how to proceed. In one of the most magical, yet curious, scenes in ancient drama, Dionysus convinces Pentheus to cross-dress as a woman.

This famous scene has received famously conflicting interpretations. For Dodds, it represents "a psychic invasion" of Pentheus by Dionysus (172); Pentheus' reactions are thus "if not [those] of a maniac, at least of a man whose reactions are ceasing to be normal" (175). His subsequent transformation, by way of a wig, miter, and linen *chiton*, marks him as a "giggling, leering creature, more helpless than a child, nastier than an idiot" (192).[53] In other words, Pentheus has gone wonderfully, theatrically insane. Or perhaps the scene symbolizes, on a more expansively psychosexual level, "the defeat of male phallic power by the female," a defeat which, metatheatrically, "symbolically effac[es]the distance between spectator and actor" and thus constitutes "a sinister mirror-image of the play's effect upon its audience, its *theatai*."[54] Put another way: the embarrassing transvestitism of Pentheus creates a play-within-a play that makes problematic the real-life experiences of Athenian males dressing as Bacchants in the "real," outer play; the *Bacchae*'s (dis)robing scene thus deconstructs the entire notion of theater (and is hence appropriate for a play concerning the god of drama). A more ritually oriented analysis of the scene stresses the possible "transvestitism of 'mystic initiation', though a transvestitism that could, if made public, expose the initiand to mockery" (216).[55] Here, Richard Seaford stresses the *ritual* dimension of the crossdressing scene: that Pentheus' humiliation lies not in the cross-dressing, per se, but doing so in a public forum. (A decidedly conservative and heterodox reading of the play decries the modern emphases on ritual and sexuality, "two inherently dull subjects which nevertheless hold endless fascination for the late-twentieth-century mind" (6).)[56]

If we take a closer look at the language of the scene, we find clues to why Schechner adopted a radical substitution for his adaptation:

---

[53] Dodds 1960: 172; Dodds 1960: 175; Dodds 1960: 192.   [54] Segal 1997: 205, 225.
[55] Seaford 1996: 216.   [56] Leinieks 1996: 6.

{Δι.} στεῖλαί νυν ἀμφὶ χρωτὶ βυσσίνους πέπλους.	D. Now throw linen robes around your skin.
{Πε.} τί δὴ τόδ᾽; ἐς γυναῖκας ἐξ ἀνδρὸς τελῶ;	P. What is this? Shall I turn into a woman, from a man?
{Δι.} μή σε κτάνωσιν, ἢν ἀνὴρ ὀφθῆις ἐκεῖ.	D. So the Bacchants do not kill you there – if you seem a man.
{Πε.} εὖ γ᾽ εἶπας αὖ τόδ᾽· ὥς τις εἶ πάλαι σοφός.	P. Again, you have spoken well. How clever you are, and have been!
{Δι.} Διόνυσος ἡμᾶς ἐξεμούσωσεν τάδε.	D. Dionysus trained me in all these things.
{Πε.} πῶς οὖν γένοιτ᾽ ἂν ἃ σύ με νουθετεῖς καλῶς;	P. How best to go about the things that you advise me?
{Δι.} ἐγὼ στελῶ σε δωμάτων ἔσω μολών.	D. I shall take you into the house and dress you.
{Πε.} τίνα στολήν; ἢ θῆλυν; ἀλλ᾽ αἰδώς μ᾽ ἔχει. ll. 821–828	P. In a dress? A female dress? But shame possesses me.

Whether the scene is analyzed in terms of performance theory (metatheater); psychology (madness); or ritual (initiatory garb), the Greek text neatly leads up to Pentheus' horrified gasp at the thought of donning female (*thelun*) garb: though it would be desirable to glimpse the women (812) and pathetic to see them drunk (814), the key emotion here is *aidos*, 'shame.' The entire dialogue builds to this crucial psychological moment: though Pentheus recognizes the potential for shame, he further inquires about the robe, his hair, and the thyrsus, the sacred (and gender-marked) implement of Bacchants. At this moment, his fate his sealed: as he exits the stage, Dionysus notes sardonically that this hunter of women has fallen into his net, where he will pay the penalty with his life (847–848). Dionysus also predicts that Pentheus will endure the necessary concomitant to shame: ridicule ("I desire for him to be an object of mockery as he is led through the streets in the guise of a woman...", 854–855).

As Schechner relates in his diary/script of *Dionysus in 69*, The Performance Group struggled to find an American "equivalent" for this particular scene of cross-dressing; it's also telling that this scene, as performed by the Group, has the most variations, both "written" (for the four combinations of actors and actresses playing Pentheus and Dionysus) and improvised (because energetic members of the audience occasionally try to help out Pentheus, "offering comfort or routes of escape"). It's striking too that Bill Shephard (Pentheus) and Bill Finley (Dionysus) feel compelled to seek an equivalent for Euripides' original text; sensing that mere cross-dressing (particularly in the late 1960s) lacks the necessary humiliating force, they search for an American cultural equivalent to the Greek one. Their solution? Same-sex desire.

As Schechner describes, a scene concentrating on homosexuality seems a proper way to mortify this oh-so-American Pentheus:

> In Euripides, Pentheus is possessed and humiliated, rewarded and destroyed. [The actor Bill] Shephard suggested homosexuality as the counterpart. It was the most difficult thing he could think of doing in public. The homosexual kiss is supreme revealment and concealment at the same time. Dionyus's purpose works through Pentheus's submission. And both performers taste something that attracts and repels them. Neither is homosexual. To many homosexuals in the audience the scene is titillating. Sometimes, as much from anxiety as from amusement, spectators shout encouragement to Pentheus. Unwittingly, they mortify him as Euripides intended: 'I want him made the laughingstock of Thebes.' (unpaginated)

There is much to note, here. First, that in the rehearsal period, the idea for the kiss came from the *actor*, not the director (or fellow actors): it is not only that a homosexual kiss is mortifying to Pentheus, but to the actor *playing* Pentheus: Shephard is relying on his cultural experiences as an American to posit the single most mortifying thing that could happen to him in Manhattan in 1968. Secondly, the audience for this kiss is explicitly bifurcated; (male) homosexuals experience one emotion (titillation) while the rest of the (heterosexual?) audience experiences anxiety or amusement. If the original, Euripidean scene treats the audience as a corporate body of fearful or pitying spectators, the Schechner adaption is calculated instead to *divide* his audience into gay and non-gay readers. (Sexual identity thus informs the work's reception.) Lastly, Dionysus's intention to make of Pentheus a public laughingstock is brought to fruition by the "unwitting" audience of jeering New Yorkers, who, in shouting out to Pentheus, thus play their parts just as Dionysus/Schechner intended.

But more: though Schechner is obviously proud of the theatrical effect of the kiss, the real shock of the scene isn't in the kiss per se, but in that kiss's promise to fulfill the terms of Pentheus' contract with Dionysus. In the Euripidean original, the arrangement was to don women's clothing, an exchange rendered in *Dionysus in 69* like so: "Dionysus: First I want you to relax. To be open. To be open to me. I want you to be vulnerable. To be very loving and very relaxed. Bill, I want you to be a woman for me." The last line could very well be a translation for γυναικόμορφος, 'in a woman's shape,' Euripides' term for Pentheus' transformation after the scene (855). But then the kicker:

PENTHEUS: What specifically do you want me to do?

DIONYSUS: Specifically, I want you to take off my shirt and my pants and my underwear. Then I want you to caress my body all over. I want you to caress it very slowly and carefully. And then I want you to caress my cock until it gets hard. And then I want you to take my cock in your mouth and caress it with your lips and your tongue and your teeth. I want you to suck my cock. Bill, I want you to suck my cock.

The alternate text, with Patrick McDermott as Dionysus, is even more explicit (perhaps even a bit purple):

And then I want you to lick my legs. And eat my hair. And then I want you to bite my ass. And then I you to put your tongue in my crotch and lick my crotch and hold my balls up in your hands and make me feel good and send me up, man, send me up! And put my cock in your mouth! Bill, put my cock in your mouth!

In each case, in order to make the mortification sharper, Pentheus is addressed by the name of the actor ("Bill"), and not as Pentheus; this strips away any comforting pretense of fictionality, and instead confronts the audience with a cruising scene straight out of the seediest of gay dives. Though Schechner constructs the kiss as the moment of revealment/concealment, it is actually the off-stage fellatio that consummates—so to speak—the humiliation of the actor: the on-stage kiss might be shocking, but notionally, it's the fellatio—under a trapdoor—that makes the scene so wildly, crudely "gay."

As Pentheus disappears into the trap (both literally and figuratively), Finley-as-Dionysus crows: "Friends, skeptics, fellow Bacchae. That man is ours. To be more precise, he's mine. To quote Euripides: 'For sane of mind, that man would never wear a woman's dress, but obsess his soul and he cannot refuse.'" Here Finley make explicit the cultural equivalency between Euripides' cross-dressing-madness and the previous scene's focus on homosexuality; it is also problematic in that it draws potentially unwelcome parallels between insanity and same-sex desire. Finley attempts a sort of interpretative damage control, then, by focusing less on the *object* of desire, and more on the *process* of desire: "Now what this means is this: Bill Shephard has to know me. He has to submit to me." Finley here stresses that the mortification of the previous scene didn't necessarily concern homosexuality, but of sexual repression more generally. Perhaps this is so; there are other versions of the scene in which Dionysus, played by a woman, orders Pentheus to "put your mouth inside my cunt and bite it gently with your tongue" (etc.), and the scene proceeds along generally

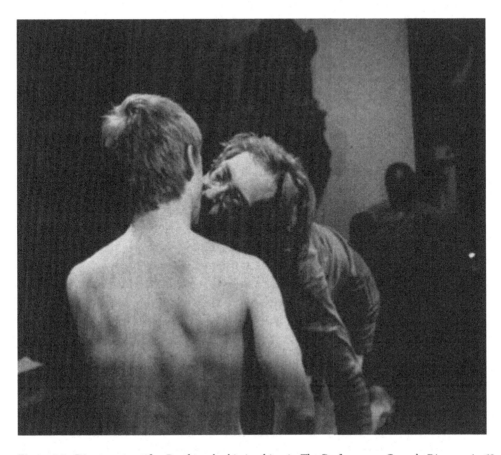

Figure 2.5. Dionysus mortifies Pentheus by kissing him, in The Performance Group's *Dionysus in 69.*

heterosexual lines. But the heterosexual scene also has less bite, so to speak: Shephard's original impulse was for a homosexual scene, and the compulsion to make love to a woman does not quite capture the cultural taboo of a same-sex kiss (see Figure 2.5).

Subsequent to the off-stage fellatio scene, the chorus begins a group "caress," intended to "liberate the energies Euripides describes in this play." When Pentheus re-emerges, he is the *opposite* of Euripides' female-garbed Pentheus: he is naked, vulnerably so. Dionysus next goes through the Euripidean motions—teaching Pentheus first how to dance: "Then you raise up the other foot and the other arm . . . And you go like this. And like this, Bill." As indicated in the stage directions, Dionysus' last tender moment with Pentheus is again figured as a homosexual one, but with ominous implications: *Dionysus caresses, perhaps kisses, Pentheus, marking him with blood.* It's an unlovely image, this homosexual kiss of death, one that nevertheless signposts the logical progression from social death/ mortification to *actual* death and mortification. Indeed, Pentheus' mother, Agave, calls for Pentheus' head with the cheery exhortation: "We must kill this animal. Remember, violence is as American as apple pie." The "Americanization" of the *Bacchae* has not only updated Pentheus' mortification, but made a cliché of his death.

The conclusion of *Dionysus in 69*—including Agave's shock at her own murderous impulses and the famous curse of Dionysus—pursues other themes, but always with a metatheatrical twist. In fact, Dionysus' curse is explicitly linked to contemporary political contexts, including the 1968 presidential campaign. But Dionysus also comments on Bill Shephard's/Pentheus' metatheatrical predicament: "He put me in the pit and he did what he should least of all have done. He told the truth. He had nothing for me. He didn't satisfy me. Now he has only a false death, some stage blood, and the promise that he has to do the same damned thing tomorrow night." Dionysus then runs for American president ("Yes, I am running for President. Who else have you got? ... A vote for Finley in 68 brings Dionysus in 69.") As Schechner notes, the Dionysus of the play's end is a combination of "tyrant" and "fascist," who's only too happy to mortify—in every sense—Bill Shephard every evening, on the way to satisfying his political ambitions. His seduction of Pentheus, then, isn't rooted in desire at all, but is instead an act of supreme cruelty and calculated sadism: homosexuality-as-weapon, enabled by American revulsion of the same. By substituting homosexual sex for (ritual) cross-dressing, Schechner and his company politicize the *Bacchae* through the discourses of (homo)sexuality. Unlike valorizing metanarratives of homosexual experience (as above), Pentheus' conversion/coming-out is not intended as a Pollyanna celebration of the ubiquity of homosexual experiences through time: rather, it channels contemporary fears and even loathing through the prism of a specific sexual behavior.

In *Dionysus in 69*, the central scene of cross-dressing is metaphorically replaced with an American equivalent, one with highly charged homosexual overtones. I turn now to another text which makes a similarly crucial *metaphorical* substitution in its examination of modern (homo)sexual mores. In some respects, Sophocles' *Philoctetes* is an unlikely candidate for a gay or lesbian reception of antiquity. Compared to the strongly pacific spins given to wartime productions of *Trojan Women*, *Hecuba*, or even *Children of Herakles*, Sophocles' tightly structured play of betrayal and disillusion appears a difficult play to locate along any ideological spectrum.

Though war is certainly a *theme* of *Philoctetes*, and in some senses also its conceptual genesis, the play is at base a meditation on the Athenian notion of *philia*, 'social cohesion,' and the related processes of communal inclusion and expulsion. Like many Greek myths, the narrative of Philoctetes features a number of important variations, spread across multiple sources, and including even a brief mention in Homer's *Iliad* (2.716–728). In this primary epic of the ancient world, Philoctetes is AWOL from the catalogue of ships and heroes because he is waylaid in Lemnos, "where the songs of the Achaeans had left him in agony from the sore bite of the wicked water snake." The Sophoclean plot is considerably more involved. Philoctetes, a Greek from Thessaly, is an ally in the attack on Troy. En route to Asia Minor, the Greeks stop off at the island of Chryse, where Philoctetes unwittingly stumbles across a shrine sacred to the island's eponymous nymph-goddess and is bitten on the foot by a snake. The wound festers, and despite the best efforts of the Greeks to cure it, the flesh putrifies. Torn between pity and revulsion, the Greeks (led by Odysseus), abandon Philoctetes on a deserted island, allowing him only his bow with which to hunt.

This is the backdrop, so to speak, of Sophocles' play. While Philoctetes suffers the consequences of (effectively) ostracism, the Greeks continue their unsuccessful siege at Troy. Unable to breach the walls, they discover through the prophetic powers of the captured Trojan Helenus that Philoctetes, ironically, is the key to success: "[Helenus] prophesied all these things—and more—to them, and that they should never sack the towers of Troy until, by powers of persuasion (εἰ μὴ τόνδε πείσαντες λόγῳ/ ἄγοιντο), they should bring Philoctetes from the island where he now lives (*Ph.* 610–613)." To the Greeks, this oracle is, at the least, distressing, and more so because violence—the easy currency of a warrior—is explicitly ruled out. Philoctetes must be persuaded by *logos*, 'speech,' and not by sword.[57] Worse yet, Odysseus, the foremost orator among the Greeks, led the charge to abandon Philoctetes and so obviously cannot approach Philoctetes without fear of reprisal. Instead, Odysseus dragoons into service Neoptolemus, Achilles' adolescent son, and the sort of fresh-faced lad whom Philoctetes might trust, even in suspicious circumstances. Neoptolemus' mission, then, is to befriend and betray Philoctetes, and thereby sacrifice the niceties of interpersonal bonding and redemption to the

---

[57] Roisman 2005: 60 argues that the division between *biê*, 'physical might,' and *mêtis*, 'mental cunning,' already schematized in both Homeric epics, is further polarized in the characterization of Odysseus here: a man composed entirely of words.

greater demands of war. As Odysseus bluntly argues: "I know well, my boy, that you are not, by nature, apt to utter or enact wicked deeds (*kaka*)... However, let us be called 'just' at another time. Cast away shame for me for just one day: for the rest of time, may you be called the most righteous of men" (*Ph.* 79–85).

Sophocles thus constructs a lovely antithesis between *philia* and popular concepts of morality, between the emotional bonds of individuals and Duty to the Greater Good. In some ways, however, the antithesis is *too* beautiful, *too* exact: after befriending and betraying Philoctetes and tricking him out of his bow, the young Neoptolemus changes his mind and confesses the entire conspiracy, thereby turning the tables on his master and endangering Odysseus. At this crucial moment, the play is perfectly balanced: Philoctetes remains implacable; Odysseus, irrepressible; Neoptolemus impotent. From these three characters, there can be no more forward impulse—each has staked out an extreme ethical position and so the play, for a moment, is as still as stone. Only an extreme measure can shatter the impasse, and so Sophocles introduces his (in)famous *deus ex machina*: the god Herakles, who, descending from the heavens on a huge stage crane, solves the problem with the ethical equivalent of a mallet. "You (=Philoctetes) will come with this man (= Neoptolemus) to the city of Troy; you will first be healed of your painful sickness (*nosos*); then, having been chosen as the greatest in virtue among the army, you will slay Paris—the start of all this evil—with my bow; then you shall sack Troy..." (1423–1427).

And so Odysseus wins; not because of a *logos* that is persuasive per se, but a *logos* that is divine and therefore irresistible. Herakles' prophecy ties up all loose ends: Philoctetes will go to Troy; he will be healed of his sickness (*nosos*); his bow will kill Paris; and Troy will fall. The detail about the bow is a particularly nice touch: even internally to the play, there is debate about whether Philoctetes' physical presence is required or just his bow. As Herakles makes clear, both are integral to the final destruction of Troy, and so the *deus ex machina* proves himself a conclusive interpreter of oracles as well as effective motivational speaker.[58]

Mark Merlis' terrific 1998 novel, *An Arrow's Flight*, reconceives Sophocles' *Philoctetes* in ways consonant with a late 1990s *milieu*, but with some surprising twists. To judge from a talk Merlis delivered to the Foundation for Hellenic Culture shortly after the novel's publication, the choice of

---

[58] See Roisman 2001 for an argument in which Herakles is in fact Odysseus in disguise.

Philoctetes as a foundational text was something of a happy accident: "People who read *An Arrow's Flight* assume that I hunted around for the right Greek myth to frame a story of modern gay life. But I didn't: I just set out to do a rendering of the play. In fact, it started as a play, it only became a novel later on. And I initially intended to tell the story 'straight,' in both senses." [59] In the project's original form, then, Merlis was attracted to the central ethical paradox at the heart of Sophocles' play: the collision of public necessity and private conscience, all narrated "straight." Merlis' choice of adjectives here is telling: by "straight," Merlis means both that he intended the project to be identifiably Sophoclean (ancient in setting, dramatic in form) as well as "straight" in argument, a political meditation on the role of the individual in the state.

But Merlis eventually abandoned the project, deeming the story "kind of silly," dealing as it did with "a smelly wound and magic bow." He subsequently returned to the project as a novel, and, arrestingly, a *gay* novel. Though Merlis had originally envisioned his *Philoctetes* as a "straight" project, it's conspicuous that Merlis managed to latch onto the only Greek play in the entire canon to lack female characters. On the one hand, the original play invites the "straightest" of readings: three (heterosexual) men quarreling over matters of state. On the other hand, it also invites a homosocial reading: a play without women in which personal bonds—bonds of *philia*—are equal, and arguably even superior, to state-mandated bonds of unit cohesion and military service. The generational gap already present in the original play becomes, in Merlis' hands, the cultural gulf between gay men who prospered—and succumbed—in the late 1970s, and the younger, brasher breed of gay men feeling their way through the 1990s. Through a deft interweaving of Greek myth and American *mores*, Merlis explores both the possibilities of Greek metaphors for American life, but, also—most crucially—the limits of metaphor in the age of AIDS.[60]

The lengthy first third of the novel presents a character study of Neoptolemus as a dissolute and self-absorbed young gay man, thereby setting up the study of (ethical) contrasts in the latter parts of the novel. Though his grandmother was only "a B-list goddess," he was still a "hemidemigod" and stunningly, effortlessly beautiful (5). Frustrated by his traditional upbringing on Scyros, Neoptolemus disappears into the Big City and a neighborhood that seems to be—though unnamed—a duplicate of Downtown

---

[59] www.markmerlis.com/Hellenic2.htm
[60] For a scholarly application of the Philoctetes myth to the problem of the *pathologization* of American urban populations (principally, the homeless) see Feldman 2001.

Manhattan. His beauty wins him easy money: he even dreams fleetingly of his grandmother Thetis and enjoys his "sense of unrecognized entitlement" (28), an entitlement enabled by his peculiar genealogy. Though first employed as a waiter, Neoptolemus discovers a more lucrative career as a go-go dancer and hustler. His advertisement for tricks boasts of his "archer's body" (55)—a clever phrase that appeals to prurient interest through its martial language and imagery. His ad, which also includes details concerning reliability, versatility, discretion, and location, omits one crucial aspect, however: "you might see the very same thing today, except it would also say *safe*. That omission by itself tells you how very long ago this all was, back in the age of heroes" (55–56).

This is one of the first times in the novel that the narrator retreats from his story in order to comment on the distance, in time, between the present day and this fabled age of heroes. The narrative implies that desire must now recognize its potential for peril and thus locates the novel's "present" time, jarringly perhaps, as the age of AIDS; the Age of Heroes, the age before AIDS, is thus located as sometime in the late 1970s. A later chapter begins by reminiscing about life "long before the plague" (85), in which the opening gambit of innumerable tragedies and epics—the plagues on Thebes, on Athens, on Troy—descends upon New York City. We are in plague time, the narrator suggests; and this particular version of *Philoctetes* explores love in the time of pestilence.

After setting up the character of Neoptolemus and planting indications of impending doom, the narrator kicks the Sophoclean plot into high gear. Odysseus, having discovered that Philoctetes holds the key to destroying Troy, discovers as well that Neoptolemus—also referred to by his nickname, Pyrrhus, 'red-head'—is necessary as well. He recites the relevant oracle to his assistant, Phoenix: "'When Philoctetes' bow is brought to Troy, then shall the hero son of Achilles take up the sword of his father, and Priam's children raise loud their lamentations.'" When Phoenix expresses surprise that he'd never heard the full oracle, Odysseus deadpans: "It was classified" (200). This is a typically Merlisian trope, in which a classical text (here, an oracle) is reconfigured into its modern reference: here, classified military information. Merlis is more subtle, however, in his first full description of Philoctetes, whom the soldiers discovered still living—if not exactly thriving—on Lemnos:

> There was none of him to spare. He was at that eerie point in the
> downward glide when every redundant ounce has been pared away, as
> by a carver, but just before the carver has done that one stroke too many,
> here and then here, leaving at last bright eyes peering from a cranium all

stripped of flesh. One of death's passing jokes, this moment: to Pyrrhus, Philoctetes looked perfect, taut as a panther. To Admetus, who recalled him strutting with the other overfed officers ten years earlier, he looked like an admonition. (224)

This introduction of Philoctetes is a masterpiece of compression, in which Philoctetes' physical condition is focalized through two different interpreters. Philoctetes' body, to the naïve Neoptolemus, looks "perfect": lean and sinewy, a remarkable gay body. Admetus, who accidentally traded away his mortality and who will never die, takes, however, the long view: comparing Philoctetes to his earlier days, Admetus senses an admonition (an admonition, implicitly, of death).

In Sophocles' play, Philoctetes' proud self-introduction, a trope of Greek tragedy, links disease and identity indissolubly: "I am Philoctetes, son of Poeas, whom two generals and the Cephallenian king cast out wickedly upon this solitude: I, who am wasting away with a savage disease (*nosos*), caused by the savage bite of the man-destroying serpent" (*Ph*.263–267). Genealogy and pathology here intertwine: Philoctetes' short outburst segues from parentage, to crime, to the disease that continuously rots him. Likewise Philoctetes links physical disease to social death: "The men who wickedly cast me out jeer, and yet tell no one else–while my disease (*nosos*) always blooms and grows ever greater" (257–259). Philoctetes' enemies have only two modes of social interaction—mockery and silence. Meanwhile, as Philoctetes indicates, his disease grows ever more powerful.

Merlis' Philoctetes similarly meditates over the cause—and the meaning —of his *nosos*, 'disease.' At first, Philoctetes was baffled by his snake bite: "A pair of tiny sores, like a dieresis: No bigger than pinpricks, each oozing the merest droplet of something yellow. So tiny, yet something baleful about them. Like the eyes of the snake itself, but sightless" (241–242). Here, Merlis neatly links the physical manifestation of the wound—snake's eyes —to the fangs that caused the injury. Next, in Merlis' hands, the "noxious smell" inherent to so many versions of the Philoctetes tale becomes, quite literally, its metaphorical referent, the social aversion to a "mysterious wound that will not heal" and that might "be catching":

You could see it on their faces, this kind of weird mix of terror and disgust, pity and contempt. People didn't visibly retreat from me, they just happened, so casually, to stroll over to the other end of the ward room ... But the way everybody treated me now—as if my wound literally gave off a bad smell, that's what some people said, can you believe it?—it all got to me ... I didn't believe at first that I had gotten the wound because I had—what was the word?—transgressed. (243)

Philoctetes' mythical "bad smell" is reinterpreted as the social manifestation of hysteria, as rumor of Philoctetes' mysterious wound makes its rounds. As Philoctetes himself notes, there's nothing about the wound itself that's particularly distressing; rather, its mysterious origins provoke conflicting, yet entirely negative, emotional responses. Each observer's reaction concludes, however, in the same *physical* activity: a casual "stroll" to anywhere else. At the same time, this audience of interpreters first postulates the reason, the *aition*, for the wound: Philoctetes had transgressed. Philoctetes didn't believe in his transgression at first—but certainly did believe it later. The effect thus generates its own cause.

The novel also generates, in modern-day terms, the "natural cause" theory of Philoctetes' transgression. In archaic myth, such as in Homer, no reason is ever given for *why* the snake bites Philoctetes, and it's part of the power of Sophocles' play that Philoctetes' accident seems so innocent, even freakish: it could have happened to *anyone*.[61] In Merlis' novel, the onlookers have their own ideas of what constitutes a natural cause. Philoctetes' own doctor figures that Philoctetes *deserved* the bite: "I heard about his life, in the city, before [Philoctetes] was called up. You can't imagine the way he lived, the things these guys did with one another. I know my anatomy, and let me tell you, the things I heard about: they just weren't meant to be" (195). Or, as Pyrrhus paraphrases it, "You're saying they crossed some boundary," Pyrrhus said. "Broke some natural law" (195). Sophocles' literally natural transgression—a misstep in a rural grove—is reinterpreted as a social transgression rooted in natural law (and as such, Merlis here taps into the language of the American "culture wars," and "traditional family values"). By having a doctor first formulate the law of transgression, Merlis also emphasizes the complicity of the medical profession in whipping up prejudice: relying on his expertise in anatomy, the doctor applies teleology to body parts.

In one of the most extraordinary passages of the novel, the narrator ruminates in an extended fashion on the distance in time between the present age of men and the previous age of heroes. It's a trope with fine classical precedents; Homer does the same at critical points throughout the *Iliad*, reminding the audience that heroes are different than "such as we mortals now are."[62] In *An*

---

[61] See Shein 2013: 1–7 esp. 3 for an overview of archaic and Attic variations on the myth of Philoctetes. For a catalogue of mythographers' later rationalizing and moralizing accounts, see Shein 2013: 1n1.

[62] *Iliad* 1.272; 5.304; 12.449; 20.287. Kirk 1990 notes on 5.304 that the narrator here "contrast[s] heroic strength with that of the singer's contemporaries," thereby emphasizing the gap between the generations of myth and the present day.

Arrow's Flight, the narrator provides a metaphorical equivalent to the gay American counterculture of the 1970s:

> They were the heroes, the very Eronauts, of love. And first among them was Philoctetes. . . . They had crossed every frontier, circumvented every inhibition, acted out their deepest wishes and their shallowest fantasies. . . . They were lawless in the manner of heroes. They sailed west without a chart, beneath night skies with unnamed constellations . No one will ever go that lane again, not even if the cure is found. Partly because we will never own our bodies again, as they did. We are vectors now, or vessels, sources of transmission; our bodies belong to the unseen. Well, it has always been so, we have always belonged to the fates. We just never thought the Fates were so tiny. (231–232)

As so often in the novel, Merlis plays with metaphor: gay men of the 1970s were sexual Argonauts, which Merlis transforms, punningly, into *Eronauts*. In antiquity, the *Argo* is the first ship, the Argonauts the first explorers; but this discovery is not without its darker side. The creation of the *Argo* is also figured as the first step in the decline of mankind, as humanity lurches from an ideal state into one pocked by commerce and pillaging.[63] Merlis transforms the metaphor from one of exteriority—gay men as Argonauts— to one of interiority—gay men as Argos: from sailors to ships, from masters to vessels. The *real* Argonauts turn out to be the viruses of HIV, swimming in our blood as agents of Fate. Homer's narrator takes it as a point of fact that a monumental distance in time separates us from our heroes; Merlis stresses an identical gulf between the present and previous generation of gay men.

For the greater part of the novel, Merlis retains a singular fidelity to the basic outline of Philoctetes' story, both the Sophoclean version and those culled from other sources. The narrator even ponders the eternal fascination of ancient poets who depict—whether in words or in paint— Philoctetes' suffering: "The reader will have seen the image on a hundred vases. Heaven knows why this motif was so popular for a while. [The phenomenon thus draws] from the anonymous poet in the *Anthology* his famous reproach: . . . "—and here Merlis includes a short conflation of two poems. The first is by Julian the Egyptian, found in the *Anthologia Graeca*, 16.113. This original ends like so: "His skin is parched and shrunken to look at, and perchance feels dry even to the finger's touch. Beneath his dry

---

[63] Catullus 63.1–7 explicitly links the creation of ship faring—the *Argo*—with its ultimate purpose: the pillaging of the golden fleece.

eyes the tears stand frozen, the sign of sleepless agony."[64] The other (16.3) is by Glaukos of Athens, and includes the line: "Admirable painter, would you have not done better to free the suffering man of his misery?" Merlis' conflated version is more punchy, but recognizably drawn from both classical sources:

> Even to paint Philoctetes is to make his misery perpetual.
> His skin is dry, and from his dry eye hangs a tear,
> Frozen, that the painter could have wiped away. (337)

On the one hand, this ancient poem describes Philoctetes much as the novel's narrator has, in fact, described Philoctetes. As the narrator continues in his defense: "if we didn't make [Philoctetes'] misery perpetual, no one would remember him at all" (337). To the extent that the modern and ancient narrator share a common goal, and a common technique, it's to stress the misery of Philoctetes' existence and thereby create a compelling narrative: one in which the physical characteristics of the disease (the dry skin, the suppuration of the wound) provide a source of eternal tears, "frozen" timelessly in art. Wiping away the tear would wipe away the lynchpin of the story. Julianos of Egypt, Glaukos of Athens, Sophocles, and Merlis all require for Philoctetes to suffer and to suffer and to suffer.

But then, a narrative swerve: a surprise. "Anyway, he is wrong, the poet, about this: the tear does not hang forever but drops at last on the sheet. Philoctetes was through crying . . ." (337). Up to this point Merlis has been scrupulous in preserving the structure of his metaphorically "American" *Philoctetes*; this departure not only shocks, but disorients, since Merlis *explicitly* disavows the ancient sources. From this point on we, as readers, stumble blindly into the climactic scene of the novel and encounter the same impasse as in the Sophoclean play: Philoctetes is angry and will not go to Troy—but Troy must fall by Philoctetes' bow. As we have seen, Sophocles finessed the problem with the introduction of Herakles, and Merlis toys with that same solution: "This is the point in the drama when Heracles is lowered from the rafts on pulleys . . . [There's] no other way out of that hospital room: Heracles must order them to go. And must promise the cure" (358).

This is the first time in the novel that Philoctetes' condition is described as something non-static, non-eternal. It had seemed up to this point that Philoctetes would be eternally disabled, but never mortally so, just as in the Sophoclean play. But Merlis' equation of the sickness *explicitly* with AIDS

---

[64] Translated by Bowersock 1994: 76.

paradoxically breaks the metaphor. General sickness, *literary* sickness, is easily curable with the stroke of a pen. Merlis' equation of Philoctetes' sickness with a *specific* modern illness shatters the illusion of the disease's fictionality, and indeed shatters the metaphorical basis of the novel altogether:

> Here is what is missing: no one has mentioned the cure. Philoctetes is supposed to obey, unthinkingly, the command from the recently deified hulk who used to boff him, so long ago. Now Philoctetes will leap out of bed and go with Neoptolemus to the ship. When they get to Arisbe, at the foot of Troy, Machaon, son of Asclepius, will dress Philoctetes' twin wounds with divine salves. He will bathe Philoctetes and anoint him with oil. Until his whole body shines, that body that was a gift to the city, shines as though it had returned from the dead. Then he and Neoptolemus will crawl inside a giant mock-up of a horse and –
>
> But I didn't promise to get us to Troy; I said I would get us to where we were. (358–359)

First, Merlis races through the "expected" ending of the novel, the ending one might anticipate if Merlis were to adhere to a Sophoclean outline. Herakles would appear; Philoctetes would be whisked off to Troy and cured; then both he and his young friend would take Troy, thereby fulfilling the terms of the oracle (and of mythological history). But as the narrator wryly indicates, it was nowhere mentioned in the novel that the oracle would come to fulfillment. In fact, it *can't* come to fulfillment. Philoctetes can't be cured because, sadly and self-evidently, there is no cure for AIDS. "Maybe some son of Asclepius is, right now, concocting that miraculous salve," the narrator observes, but until that time, Herakles cannot appear. The real moral nexus of the novel is not in the relationship between Neoptolemus and Philoctetes, but between Merlis and generation wiped out by AIDS: "If I owe nothing else to the dead, I can at least refrain from wheeling out Herakles."

And so, just as angrily as in the Sophoclean play, but free now from the commands of a *deus ex machina*, Philoctetes does what an enraged American man might do when confronted with a room full of wheedling, so-called "friends": "As with a sudden resurgence of strength, Philoctetes sat up. And broke the bow over his knee" (364). Thus ends the novel proper. And so Philoctetes—and his bow—never go to Troy; the Greeks go home; and Troy never falls. In a brief epilogue, it is clear that Philoctetes is dying, and that dozens have preceded him, having contracted HIV/AIDS through (apparently) Neoptolemus' one fling with Philoctetes and from then to a host of Greek sailors. In a hospital antechamber, a friend asks

Neoptolemus about his HIV status. Neoptolemus implies that he's negative but then adds "So far. I haven't, you know ... checked" (370). At this, "the future grew a little murky."

In other words, Neoptolemus refuses to get tested: that is one oracle he doesn't wish to know.

Queering the Canon

I began this chapter by noting how contemporary gay and lesbian cultures often reinscribe themselves into the past through a series of metanarratives: narratives that displace or revise previous constructions of the past. There is, however, nothing sneaky or underhanded about this displacement: indeed, meta-narrators can be their own best advertisers. For instance, Andrew Calimach's provocatively entitled *Lovers' Legends: The Gay Greek Myths* explicitly takes Achilles and Patroclos as the first mortal homosexual pair. As the cover for Calimach's book indicates, the stories are "restored and retold" by the author, and it is worthwhile to examine that particular metaphor more closely. The idea of restoration is a loaded one, as if the original stories were damaged by barbarians, like classical artifacts or statues. Only an expert, it is implied, can restore them to their original shape, and original "gay" function. Such a formulation also constructs the stories themselves as the direct objects of willful destruction, which need to be restored and then (as a result of their previously battered and neglected state) reintroduced to a modern audience. After a fairly perfunctory retelling of some of the events of the *Iliad*, Calimach launches into the meat of his retelling of the relationship between Achilles and Patroclos: "Alone again, Achilles prayed to Zeus, soaking the earth with wine, and begged him to grant his friend success and safe return. His prayer came straight from the heart, for Patroclos was his one true love. At gatherings they always sat apart from the crowd, their arms around each other, laying their plans, and when all turned in, they two shared a single blanket" (p. 105). After the death of Patroclos, Achilles laments "Why so ungrateful, after all our kisses? Why so uncaring for the holy union of our thighs?" (p. 106). The prose is a bit stiff, but not so far off from the fragment preserved from Aeschylus' *Myrmidons*: "Why did you not feel reverence for the holiness (*sebas*) of our limbs,/ you who are so ungrateful for my many kisses?"[65] By "restoring" the fragment to its rightful place in a more extended narrative

---

[65] Mette fr. 228a.

of the *Iliad*, Calimach rescues the gay reading of the relationship from the forces of oblivion (and anti-homosexual ideology).

That Calimach has some ideological axes to grind is made clear from his biography on the dust jacket: "Having spent his early years under dictatorship, Andrew Calimach has a particular appreciation for human rights, and considers the right to love and be loved as the most basic right of all." Calimach's *Gay Greek Myths*, then, figures itself as an anti-authoritarian act of resistance, an advocacy for human rights. An afterword by Heather Elizabeth Peterson lauds the book as presenting love stories that "will reach the ears of a wider audience than has hitherto been privileged to hear the true myths and legends of the world" (117). It's the epithet "true" that leaps out at the reader: in Calimach's world-view, the myths we have received have been generally "false": "myth and folklore have been co-opted by mass market commercial interests beholden to the imperative to appeal to all and to offend none" (118). Thus the ancient world must be repackaged in niche presses, continuing a process begun in the late nineteenth century and continuing through the twenty-first.[66]

In a similar vein, Robert Drake's *The Gay Canon: Great Books Every Gay Man Should Read* is an explicit call-to-arms for gay men, as a *community*, to reclaim literature: "The gay community has no clear-cut sense of functional literary history" (xx). To this end, Drake advocates for gay men to sign a *contract* (xxvi) to meet as a book club and plough through some twenty-five centuries of gay canonical works. It's hardly a surprise that *The Gay Canon* likewise begins with Achilles and Patroclus: "For gay readers, *The Iliad's* queer heart beats within the breast of its ultimate hero, Achilles ... [Achilles' decision to sacrifice his own life] lends credence to the argument that Patroclus was more than just his friend, that Patroclus was his companion, his lover" (21). Drake is quick to note, however, some problems in the Homeric construction of homosexuality: "They share an affinity for slave women, but this only suggests a portrait of men wildly in love with their own maleness: fucking and fighting together,

---

[66] Weirdly, Calimach "regrets" that there is nothing here about the love of women for one another (120); a footnote to the same page argues that all copies of Sappho had been systemically pillaged by Pope Gregory VII in the eleventh century. True enough, but the fragments themselves have provided voice for lesbians since at least the nineteenth century, and in a project concerning 'restoration', one might think that Calimarch could have included a reworking of at least two Sapphic poems (Frr. 1 and 31: "Invocation to Aphrodite" and "He Seems to Me Like a God"). Calimach's own omission of Sappho thus skews his readership towards gay men, thus fracturing even more its potential audience. See this book's coda on fracturing (pp. 221–8).

fighting for each other and fucking each other" (22). The logic here is dubious and Drake seems to acknowledge that fact; he quickly shifts his pro-gay argument from a pseudo-logical analysis to a more direct emotional appeal based on the reader's presumed proclivities: "That Achilles and Patroclus were lovers cannot be doubted, but as for how their love manifested itself within their hearts and bodies, we have only our intuition, and our erotic leanings, to guide us" (22). That is to say, our *own* erotic experiences can be easily mapped onto ancient texts, providing a method both of illumination and interpretation.

This canonization of classical authors continues as a general trend in gay and lesbian anthologies of poetry. In his recent *Gay Love Poetry*, editor Neil Powell includes Theocritus' *Idyll* 23 and Virgil's *Eclogues* 2 and 7 under "Nature Boys"; shorter lyrics from Solon, Alcaeus, Catullus, Martial, and the obscure Strato of Sardis under "Lads' Loves"; and selections from Virgil and Homer are filed "In Memoriam."[67] (No classical authors seem to have made the cut for "Street Life" and "As It Is," perhaps reinforcing the notion that ancient homosexuality was the stuff of bucolic, or perhaps martial, fantasy.) In each subsection, a gap of several hundred years separates the classical authors from e.g. Sir Philip Sidney (1554–86) or Michael Drayton (1563–1631), a chronological leap that really does blur the distinction between antiquity and modernity: the classical authors wrote "gay" love poetry just like our more familiar poetic brethren. The Everyman's Library Pocket Poets series likewise features Sappho and Virgil alongside Whitman and Gertrude Stein in its collection *Love Speaks Its Name: Gay and Lesbian Love Poems* (2001); the ancient poems are variously strewn throughout the work—including sections on "Longing," "Anxiety," and "Aftermath"—in yet another attempt to efface the very real differences between ancient and modern homosexuality. In his introduction, J. D. McClatchy notes that "between classical times and the Renaissance, the poetry of homosexuality was largely underground" (15) and further argues that a defining feature of gay and lesbian poems is its interrogation—even occasionally celebration—of forbidden desire. Read against such a background, Sappho's poem fragment 94V, here entitled "I have had not one word from her" might be seen as a poem of persecution. Though a fragment, this is obviously a poem of dissolution, in which the beloved complains, "This parting must be/endured, Sappho. I go

---

[67] Powell 1997: 1. See the introduction to Chapter 1: "The pastoral provides one of the oldest strands of gay love poetry. The classical tradition of rustic love which is often unreciprocated or obstructed or at least delayed is represented here by Theocritus and Virgil."

unwillingly." (213, tr. Mary Barnard). Where "she" goes is unclear, but off to a (heterosexual) marriage seems a good guess. In the context of other "furtive" poems—such as A. E. Housman's poetry—Sappho's poems too seem like furtive glances at forbidden desire.

As we have seen, metanarratives of gay desire tend to start with Achilles and Patroclus, the Adam-and-Adam of Western gay mythology. In 2001, the San Francisco-based illustrator Eric Shanower launched an incredibly ambitious retelling of the Epic Cycle in graphic novel form, including the canonical *Iliad* and *Odyssey*. By the end of the novel's projected seven volumes, it will have encompassed all major events of the Trojan War, including the rape of Helen, the sacrifice of Iphigenia, the death of Patroclos, the death of Achilles, the Trojan horse, and the return of the Greek soldiers, including Odysseus. *Age of Bronze* has been extensively researched: this is no mere fantasia on Greek themes, but a sustained inquiry into the archaeology of the ancient world, one then fitted into the general narrative arc of the Epic Cycle. Shanower's enormous bibliography runs for multiple pages and contains over a 150 bibliographical items, including journals such as *Archaeology, the American Journal of Archaeology*, and *Natural History*, scholarship by such figures as Mabel Lang, Emily Vermeule, Timothy Gantz, and ancient sources such as Statius, Homer, and Dictys of Crete. In his slim issue *Age of Bronze: Behind the Scenes*, Shanower talks more specifically about the historical underpinnings of the novel: "From the beginning I knew I wanted my version of the Trojan War set in the world where it would have taken place ... [For Nestor's palace] Carl Blegen's excavations there provided a wealth of information—painted floors, fragments of painted walls, even pieces of the roof structures" (7).[68] For Priam's palace, in the East at Troy, Shanower must confront an archaeological record damaged by the zealousness of its original excavator, Heinrich Schliemann: "No one knows what a Late Bronze Age Trojan palace looked like. In *Age of Bronze* I have based the Trojan culture on the Hittite culture ..."(10). In constructing his narrative of the ancient world, then, Shanower works with the best of available scholarly evidence.

Shanower reinforces the verisimilitude of the narrative by cleverly weaving well-known archaeological artifacts and images into the fabric of the story itself. For instance, the famous Lion Gate at Mycenae is here figured as the welcoming gate for Odysseus and Agamemnon. A red-vase painting of Achilles tending to Patroclus' wounds (Berlin F 2278) is neatly

---

[68] Shanower 2002.

Figure 2.7. Achilles patches up Patroclus in the comic *Age of Bronze*.

Figure 2.6. Achilles patches up Patroclus, on Sosias' vase from approximately 500 BCE.

transferred back to the Bronze Age where it belongs (see Figures 2.6 and 2.7). Minoan hairstyles—as featured, say, on the frieze at Akrotiri on Thera, Crete—here adorn the hair of Helen, and of the women at the Mycenaean royal court. Even the enigmatic female figurines of an ancient religion—the so-called "touch-down" goddesses—find both representation and a purpose, as Helen raises her arms in an identical gesture during a moment of religious contemplation. Throughout *Age of Bronze* Shanower is scrupulous in preserving, to the extent that he is able, a link between his narrative and the tangible remnants of Europe's archaic past.

In his plot, too, Shanower remains remarkably faithful to his ancient sources. The ending thirty pages of *Sacrifice*, Shanower's retelling of the Iphigenia tale, are obviously indebted to Euripides' version of the myth, including such odd details as Agamemnon's "double letter" scene (in which the king recants an earlier deception intended to trick Iphigenia into coming to Aulis—and by so doing, attempts to avert the tragedy to come). One story arc, however, holds a bit of a surprise: that of Achilles, his wife Deidamia, and his comrade Patroclus. A hint of possible complications occurs just after Achilles tends to Patroclus' wounds; the close physical proximity draws from Patroclus an awkward "Achilles...," followed a frame of pure silence: two men staring at each other. Patroclus breaks the silence by turning away, muttering "Nothing..." Two months pass; Achilles, spending the night beside his wife, dreams instead of young, lithesome, Patroclus; he rebuffs his wife's advances for sex and the two argue. As Achilles gazes out on the

Figure 2.8. Achilles surprises Patroclus with a kiss in *Age of Bronze*.

shore from his balcony he spots Patroclus, precisely as in his dream. Hastily throwing on a cloak, Achilles runs to the shore. Patroclus next confesses his desire to leave—he feels unwelcome in the house of Achilles: "Look, you know as well as I do that no one wants me to stay." Surprised, Achilles exclaims "I do!" and then falters in his speech: "I. . ."

The modern American reader may or may not know what to expect after this fumbling on the seashore; in retrospect, however, nothing is so clear or ineluctable as Achilles' swooping kiss on Patroclus (see Figure 2.8). Even Patroclus is surprised, eyes wide with amazement. He quickly recovers, however, returning the kiss with passion and a bit of tongue, before inviting Achilles to elope with him from Skyros (after a night of passion "in a place where we can be alone together"). As the two frolic gaily on the seashore, Deidamia gazes mournfully on, sad spectator of a surprising little play. (Contemporary fans can even order T-shirts of this climactic moment from the Age of Bronze website. I have.) In many ways, Shanower's gay-themed episode is a more sophisticated, and certainly more moving, example of gay appropriation than those tales retold in Calimach's *The Gay Greek Myths*. In Calimach's collection, the collection is *explicitly* appropriated, and marketed, as gay-friendly. Shanower's graphic novel, however, presents a gay-friendly spin on Achilles and Patroclus as part of a larger, "veristic," account of the ancient world; there are no overt indications of a post-Foucauldian critique of the social construction of homosexuality, and no broadsides or polemics about social justice. The homosexuality of Achilles and Patroclus is presented matter-of-factly, if a bit soap-operatically; the embarrassment that Achilles and Patroclus feel at their emotions also seems a nod to a specifically American (or at least Western) discomfort with a socially problematic phenomenon. Shanower's Achilles and Patroclus couldn't be gay-er, but it's a 1990s sort of gay-ness, far distant from the unabashed *erastes* and *eromenos* of Plato's *Symposium*.

X-rated Sophocles: Alice Tuan's Ajax

I end this chapter by examining not just a GLB appropriation of antiquity but a queer one; by queer, I mean theoretical and artistic practices that "powerfully problematize a wide range of socially constructed and arbitrary regimes of the 'normal' and the 'natural.'"[69] As we shall see, queerness is not a substitute for amorality—one can have both a queer and highly moralistic reading of a text—but it shunts aside the duality of hetero/homosexuality in search of other, competing discourses of sexuality (including discourses informed by ethnicity, power, race, and class). As it happens, a "queered" classical text can comment perceptively and breathtaking on modern sexual mores and hypocrisy: one particularly radical transformation of a canonical Greek tragedy does just that (see Figure 2.9).

In Austin, Texas, in late 2005, I read a review of a play entitled *Ajax* (*Por Nobody*) by Alice Tuan; the review read, in part: "[*Ajax* is] a sick & twisted work of brilliance ... In a perverse and utterly bleak sort of way ... it's as funny as hell. Listen: Somewhere out there, in the vast world of art, there lurks a vile plague known to mortals as Thomas Kinkade. This is its antidote."[70] I was intrigued that a play apparently adapted from Sophocles could be constructed as an antidote—in Greek, a *pharmakon*—to another artist, in this case a devoutly Christian artist specializing in scenes of natural and family harmony. Somewhat to my surprise, this *Ajax*, as presented by Austin's Salvage Vanguard Company, was a staged reading and the reasons for this decision soon became clear. *Ajax* features so many acts of sodomy involving so many implements and so much bloodshed, that it is in fact legally, ethically, and I would suspect, physically impossible to perform as written. And in that inheres a radical queerness, as an evening of "fun" starring four porn stars and swingers devolves into a

---

[69] Bravmann 1997: ix. Portions of this analysis appear also in Jenkins 2010, in a special edition of the journal *Helios* dedicated to ideologically inflected receptions of antiquity in drama.

[70] Wayne Alan Brenner, *Austin Chronicle*, Oct. 29, 2004.

Figure 2.9. Advertisement for Salvage Vanguard's production of *Ajax (Por Nobody)*.

Sophoclean-inflected reflection on the nature of sexuality, taboo, and fame in American Los Angeles.

In a sense, Tuan's *Ajax* is tragedy turned inside out: it takes the sexual subtext of many Greek tragedies—the taboo marital liaison of Oedipus, the rape of Creousa in the *Ion*, the marriage to death in *Antigone*—and makes that subtext text: *Ajax* chronicles a terrible drug-fueled evening in the life of four porn stars, one that ends, appropriately, in tragedy. Like Edward Albee's *The Goat* (2003), Tuan's *Ajax* is less a direct adaptation of a Greek tragedy than an exploration of what a goat-song—or *trag-oidos*—means in the context of American theater. Tuan's clever use of classical allusions and stage techniques, however, roots the play in the most ancient of performance traditions even as it pushes the boundaries of contemporary sensibilities concerning sexuality and orientation.

Tuan earned an MFA in 1997 from Brown University, under the mentorship of Paula Vogel, author of *How I Learned to Drive* and *The Baltimore Waltz*;[71] Tuan has already seen performances of her plays in

---

[71] Vogel's *Hot'n'Throbbing* (1994) also employs pornographic themes in its serious exploration of women's domestic and sexual abuse.

New York City, Seattle, Sydney, and Los Angeles, including the prestigious Mark Taper Forum. Though much of her work concerns Asian-American experiences, *Ajax* is rather its own animal, as Tuan set out to write a play "that no one will ever dare to stage."[72] Indeed, *Ajax* is so transgressive—in all senses—that it can really only be played as a piece for voices, with an actor reading the stage directions as a type of narration.[73] (In this respect, it furthers the line of shocking classical reception begun by Sarah Kane, whose version of Seneca's *Phaedra* opens with Prince Hippolytus watching porn and masturbating with a sock; it concludes with his on-stage disembowelment.[74]) For instance, here is a sample stage direction from early in Tuan's *Ajax*: "[Jesse] opens [Alma's] towel, licking a line down her spine. His tongue follows her buttock crack down to the inside. He eats (58)." Or, in a similar vein, "Offstage, ALMA sodomizes JESSE with the gun (82)." In Salvage Vanguard's production, the actress playing the narrator, Lee Eddy, stole nearly every scene: the stage directions were so over-the-top and so uncomfortably graphic, that the response was (usually) laughter from the audience. The presence of the narrator also helped, on a broader narrative level, to complete the inversion of tragic conventions: the one thing that usually separates theater from all other forms of narrative is the absence of a controlling, external voice, and is the one thing that Tuan's piece, because otherwise unperformable, compels to be placed back into performance.

The plot of the show is a bit exiguous, being mostly a catalogue of the various sexual permutations of the quartet of characters. In brief: porn stars Alma and Annette throw a sex party for two unknown tricks, Jesse and Alexander, neither of whom is emotionally stable (as becomes rapidly apparent). Jesse has certain violent tendencies that manifest themselves in gunplay while his friend Alexander insists on being called *The Great*, a nod to the Macedonian general. After the gun accidentally goes off in the first third of the play, the second and third movements increasingly involve the interplay of sex and violence, including a gruesome Euripides-like mutilation and a concluding nod to Sophocles' play. By investing this Los Angeles play with tragic Greek imagery, Tuan attempts, like many modern

---

[72] www.huffingtonpost.ca/alice-tuan/ajax_b_1755773.html. Accessed April 21, 2014.

[73] *Ajax (Por Nobody)* has recently been anthologized in the collection *New Downtown Now: An Anthology of New Theater from Downtown New York* (edited by Mac Wellman, Young Jean Lee. Minneapolis: University of Minnesota Press, 2006). A review by Heather Mays (in *Theater Topics* 2008 18: 92) notes laconically that the collection is "not for the faint of heart." Page numbers in this chapter refer to the original publication in *Play: A Journal of Plays*.

[74] Kane: 2001.

American playwrights, to define American tragedy (and American morality) against its ancient antecedents.

It is obvious from the first moments of the play that Tuan enjoys playing
with the curious juxtaposition of American porn and symbolically-charged
myth. Our introduction to Alma, for instance, presents her as "sit[ting] on
the long, tiled block with an apple corer in hand, preparing to eat a
pomegranate" (35). This pomegranate eventually ends up smeared on the
tiles of the floor, an event which, when the men arrive, provokes the
following exchange:

ALEXANDER: Someone just been murdered here?
ANNETTE: Oh that. It's pomegranate.
JESSE: Maybe it's month juice.
ANNETTE: (*flirty*). Maybe. (46)

Tuan's sense of playfulness—even if off-color—is abundant here: to a
classicist, particularly of an anthropological bent, a pomegranate can sym-
bolize *both* death (in its blood-red color) as well as fertility (because of its
multiple seeds). As Helene Foley points out, the pomegranate is thus a
perfect food for the girl Persephone in *The Homeric Hymn to Demeter*
because, having been kidnapped to the underworld by the god Hades, her
ingestion of the pomegranate seeds thus symbolizes both her maturation
into womanhood (symbolic sexual intercourse) as well as death (a ritual
binding to the god of the underworld).[75] In Tuan's *Ajax*, Alexander interprets the pomegranate in one "ancient" sense (death) while Jesse latches
onto the other (sex), thereby outlining the twin thematic poles of the play.
Moreover, Annette uses the entire classical subtext as a chance to be "flirty."
In a later scene as well, Annette proves herself a surprisingly perceptive
reader of classical texts. After discovering that Alma occasionally works
under the stage name "Penelope" and that Alma's partner took the name of
"Dick Odyssey," Annette dryly notes during a seduction scene that "I'm glad
you're helping ... Penelope ... enjoy herself. She'd become quite the
waiting, weaving wife there" (59). This is an obvious allusion to the Homeric
Penelope's deceptions while waiting for Odysseus' return (see *Odyssey*
19.158); it also reinforces the striking disparity between the chastity of the
Homeric Penelope and the randiness of her Californian counterpart.

While all of these classical allusions help construct the architecture of
the play as a text that slides constantly between categories—modern satire

---

[75] Foley 1994: 56–7.

and ancient tragedy—the real crux of the tragedy is in the odd relationship between Jesse and Alexander. Towards the beginning of the play, they establish what seems to be an arbitrary rule, that if engaged in a *ménage à trois* with one of the women, they would never look at *each other*: "JESSE to ALEXANDER: OK! I won't look at you when we're doing the ass-mouth thing, OK?" (45). (By ass-mouth thing, Jesse means dividing up sexual positions between anal and oral penetration.) Crucially, this is the *only* transgression alluded to in the entire play; any other combination of psychosexual behaviors is apparently fair game, including sodomy with guns, sex with sheep, the insertion of edible wienettes into one's vagina, a comparable insertion of dollar bills into the vagina, and, as hard as it is to compress similar actions into a single Latin abbreviation: *et cetera*.[76] The only "rule" is no homoeroticism—and from that prohibition, weirdly enough, springs tragedy.

The subtextual layer to all this is, of course, Sophocles' *Ajax*, and a quick review of its themes helps situate the climax of Tuan's *Ajax* as an ironic, even impassioned riff on the cultural bankruptcy of Southern California. As in his *Philoctetes* (with which the *Ajax* shares many similarities, including the character of the dubiously sympathetic Odysseus), Sophocles uses figures of the heroic Greek past to comment on contemporary ethical concerns. As we learn from a brief mention in the *Odyssey* (11.543ff) and from the so-called Epic Cycle, the death of Greek hero Achilles (after the events of the *Iliad*) caused a power vacuum among the Greeks;[77] Ajax, by all accounts the second-best fighter among the Greeks, and a hero of legendary size and power (*Il.* 17.279–280; *Od.* 11.469–470; *Od.* 24.17–18), should have inherited the title—and the weapons—of "The Best of the Achaeans." Instead, Thetis, Achilles' mother, presented the arms of Achilles as the prize in a contest; versions differ, but in any event Ajax (unfairly) loses the contest to Odysseus through the collusion of Athena. In some accounts—including the one that Sophocles adopts—Ajax becomes enraged and intends to assassinate Odysseus and the two leaders of the

---

[76] Strictly speaking, it is wieners (i.e. small hotdogs) that are destined for a vagina, but Annette twice hypercorrects their name to wienettes (43–44), without further explanation. Three possible reasons present themselves. One: this is actually the proper name of a (fictional) consumer product, like *Raisinettes*. Two: Annette is employing a diminutive to stress the cuteness of the appetizers. Three: Annette is provocatively re-gendering the "masculine" *wien-er* into the "feminine" *wien-ette*. I prefer this last explanation as it dovetails with the queering of gender roles throughout the piece: in Tuan's play, not even thumpingly obvious phallic symbols like wieners are free from a scrambling of their customary gender.

[77] Stanford 1963: xix–xxiv.

Greek army, Menelaus and Agamemnon. Athena dazzles his eyes and Ajax instead slaughters a pack of sheep (Sophocles adds the alarming detail that Ajax continues to torture the sheep he believes to be Odysseus, *ll.* 105–110). When Ajax returns to his senses, he dispatches himself out of abject shame: the most famous male suicide in Greek myth. His act of suicide is preceded by twin monologues of almost unbearable beauty: the first a "deception" speech that convinces his family and friends that he goes merely to bury his sword as expiation and purification; the second precedes the "burial" of the sword within his own chest.[78]

The two speeches reinforce the notion of a hero trapped in an inappropriate epoch: as an exemplar of the heroic world, Ajax is, in many sense, imprisoned in the wrong play, adversary to the fast-talking, even lawyer-ly Odysseus, whose rhetorical chops and demagogic appeal mirror those of the historical Themistocles and Alciabides.[79] Indeed, Ajax's speeches hinge on the notion of Time, writ large, a force that "innumerable and lengthy, reveals all things and hides them in turn" (646–650), just as Ajax's eyes were eclipsed, but his crimes soon exposed. Tapping into deeper metaphors of seasonality, Ajax avers that he will learn—in time—to revere the two sons of Atreus (667), just as winter must yield to spring, and the cycle of the night must give way to the chariots of the day (673–674). He recognizes his disastrous confusion of friend and enemy—*philos and ekthros* in the Greek—and seeks to make amends; he guarantees to his wife and friends his eventual salvation (692). When alone, however, Ajax plants his "slayer" (*sphageus*) in the ground so that its point is most keen; this unlucky sword from a former enemy, Hector, may be hateful (*ekthros*) in appearance, but kindly (*eunoustaton*) in its literal execution (815–822). A catalogue of invocations marks Ajax as, paradoxically, a pious man: Zeus, Hermes, the Furies, the Sun, and Death are all invoked as Ajax makes his final preparations for his posthumous reputation and possible revenge. With a final flourish—as if already dead and reporting his own demise— Ajax announces that "Ajax utters this, his final word: the rest I will tell those below in Hades" (864–865). The larger themes invoked in the two speeches—of a society, even a time, no longer tolerable to an Ajax[80]—find amplification in the play's argumentative conclusion, in which the sons of Atreus, attempting to block the burial of Ajax, square off against Odysseus and Teucer, Ajax's half-brother, in a showy display of forensic skill. The

---

[78] For a discussion of the speeches as a thematically linked pair, Hubbard 2003: 158–171, esp. 161–3.

[79] Stanford 1963: xxi.   [80] Knox 1961: 27.

brawn and valor of Ajax thereby segues, on the level of *theme*, to the showy logocentric world of contemporary Athens, where battles are won by wits, not weapons, amid a blizzard of words. The play ends with the eventual conciliation of the two Greek generals to the burial of Ajax.

We return now to Tuan's *Ajax*, which hasn't on the level of plot seemed to be following Sophocles' play much at all; it's only when the single "rule" of the plot is transgressed (as in Ajax's tragic transgression) that the Sophoclean resonances become clear. This moment of homoerotic transgression is preceded—in appropriately tragic fashion—by dramatic foreshadowing. During a scene of deeply unfortunate gunplay, Tuan slips *echt* Sophocles into the play; the hostess Alma, frightened by the gun, yells out in fear:

ANNETTE: You fucking fucks, get out of here. . . . IO! IO MOI MOI!
JESSE: Let's get back to the social
ANNETTE: Well
ALMA: IO MOI MOI! IO MOI MOI! AIAIAIAIAS (p. 72)

At first—and perhaps second and third sight—this seems highly postmodern and peculiar; "IO MOI MOI" is a Greek tragic lament corresponding roughly to "woe is me"; there is, however, no intimation that Alma actually knows Greek. It is just that her cry of dismay, instead of coming out in Valley Girl-inflected English, mirrors a cry from three different characters in Sophocles's *Ajax* (Ajax, l. 333, Tekmessa, l. 891, Teucer, l. 974). The cry of AIAIAIAIAS puns—as in Sophocles' play—on Ajax's name, which is spelled AIAS in Greek, and which has then an onomatopoeic relationship to his fate: as the Sophoclean Ajax sadly notes, he has become his own cry of woe, *aiai* (ll. 430–433).[81] But there is no Ajax in Tuan's *Ajax* – or is there?

This question brings us back to *Ajax*'s central tragic moment and central tragic symbol. We learn earlier in the play that Alexander, having lost a music contest (an allusion to the Sophoclean judgment of arms), steals a neighbor's prize and brings it to the sex party. The on-stage revelation of the theft is stunningly theatrical: "ALEXANDER slowly appears. He walks in a trance towards ALMA. He holds a mounted prism, a foot tall, slim with a sharp point. It is an American Music Award" (60). In Salvage Vanguard's production, the narrator exaggerated the preposterousness of

---

[81] See Stanford 1963: 115 for a brief discussion of the Greco-Roman belief in the link between personal names and destiny, best exemplified by the Latin phrase *nomen omen*: 'your name is your fate.'

the award by invoking it in the same awed tone of voice one might use for the Shroud of Turin. In case the audience might not catch the allusion to Sophocles' play, Tuan—through an impromptu song of Alexander—makes the parallel explicit: "A prism of light/ Sharp as a warrior sword/ Thick at its base/ Designates America's/ Best, glory hallelujah/To you yeah, o precious, Double Penelope" (62). Tuan is mischievous here: Alexander's allusion to the warrior sword not only provides an apt metaphor for the American Music Award, but also for himself: unwittingly, Alexander inscribes himself as the play's titular Ajax. (Even Alma accidentally inscribes Alexander as Ajax, as she warns: "You hold on tight to that, Alexander the Great. Don't let it get inside anywhere it shouldn't" (69).)

Sophocles' Ajax is defined by his transgression; so too Tuan's. Thus during the play's climax, Alexander and Jesse have sex simultaneously with Alma, remembering always not to break their one rule. Alexander, however, appears to be having problems with self-control:

JESSE: I'm not crossing the line with you any more. Stop fucking looking at me. . .
ALEXANDER: I never hurt you
JESSE: You would if I crossed the line again. . .
ALEXANDER: C'mere
JESSE: No
ALMA: Uhn
ALEXANDER: C'mere
JESSE: No (88–89)

The moment of greatest transgression is at the same time the moment of greatest dramatic complexity, as Tuan runs Greek tragedy and Hollywood tragedy *simultaneously*:

> Stage direction: A high pitched 'meh, meh, meh, meh,' (mix of sheep and cat) as the three seem a porn flick. Alma begins to bleat like a sheep while Annette calls out for her cat, Aja,

ALMA: (high-pitched) meh meh meh meh meh meh meh meh meh
ANNETTE: A-JA . . . (90)

Here, Tuan blends the slaughter of the sheep—from Sophocles' *Ajax*—with a series of bizarre puns from the original play: Annette's cat, Aja, is Ajax's cry of angst, his name a soul-scream. The timing could not be more apt, since this is the moment—at last—of fateful transgression:

> In slo-mo, ALEXANDER grabs for JESSE, kisses him square on the mouth. JESSE breaks it up, smacks ALEXANDER with his fist. ALEX- ANDER starts to beat off, as JESSE grabs ALEXANDER's hand to stop. . .

> JESSE grabs ALEXANDER's balls: an excruciating and silent scream.
> A beam of light hails down as JESSE twists off one of ALEXANDER's
> balls. JESSE stares at what seems to be a bloodied pomegranate in his
> hand ... (90)

Where to begin an analysis of this charming moment? First, the physical manifestation of the "transgression," the homosexual kiss, is, within the context of the drama hilariously tame—which is what makes the consequences so very shocking. In a play in which characters have been inserting half the kitchen into their orifices, a mere kiss seems almost mawkishly sentimental. But that kiss is also one indicator of a true, piercing same-sex attraction—a taboo attraction that Jesse apparently can't tolerate. Jesse's revenge is therefore a good, old-fashioned, Greek tragic mutilation. Instead of gouging out Alexander's eyes—as does Hecuba to Polymester in Euripides' *Hecuba*, or Oedipus to himself in *Oedipus Tyrannus*—Jesse leapfrogs over any possible Freudian implication of blindness-as-castration, and skips straight to the castration. (Los Angeles, it seems, abhors a subtext.)

Tuan then segues to the evening's most hilariously macabre moment by describing Annette's frantic attempts at a clean-up, grabbing a convenient bottle of cleanser: "ANNETTE sprinkles Ajax on ALEXANDER's trail of blood" (90); as if a good American *hausfrau*, she even reads the canister's directions to make sure she is properly attendant to Madison Avenue's instructions: "Wet surface/ Sprinkle AJAX freely/ Rub lightly to make a paste with sponge or pad./ Clean and rinse" (91). But the cleanser Ajax's instructions—even when intoned like a quasi-magical charm—cannot, at this point, prevent the Greek Ajax from re-emerging, as the castrated Alexander makes a sudden reappearance:

> ALEXANDER paints with blood on the tiles, screaming. All run from
> him like sheep, and huddle together in the corner. ALEXANDER places
> the American Music Award on the long block. It shimmers red. He
> staggers, holding his crotch blood in.

> ALEXANDER: meh meh meh weep
>   meh meh meh leap
>   meh meh meh sleep

> He falls and impales himself on the American Music Award. (92)

Alexander's final soliloquy is obviously a minimalist parody (weep–leap–sleep) of Ajax's famous speech before falling on his sword; Alexander barely manages to bark out a rhyming, ovine stanza before impaling himself on the very symbol of American artistic bankruptcy. The play ends quickly thereafter, with Jesse beating a hasty retreat, and Annette and Alma expressing their keen disappointment in how their party turned out.

Happily, critics seemed to understand the play: that far from being a glorification of obscenity, *Ajax* is an outraged attack on American licentiousness, superficiality, and especially sexual hypocrisy. D. J. R. Bruckner's notice in the *New York Times* describes the play as a broadside on modern hedonism, emptiness, and self-abuse while Ken Urban's review for *New York Theater* notes that "beneath the pornographic attention to detail lies the work of a moralist."[82] Indeed, Tuan targets the hollowness of Los Angeles' pleasure-and-entertainment culture, an emptiness exposed by the sharp contrast with the deeper structures of Greek tragedy. Though on a surface level, the play seems to celebrate—or at least exploit—a West Coast atmosphere of sexual experimentation, the narrative demonstrates that American taboos are at least as deeply ingrained as Greek ones: that homosexual desire still languishes under the stigma of degeneracy, and that for all of America's purported tolerance of "lifestyle choices," Hollywood largely banishes from its own narratives any hint of homosexual desire. Of course, Tuan herself seems to indicate that her radical approach—porno Tragedy with a gruesomely queer twist—isn't likely to be everyone's cup of tea. In a wonderfully metatheatrical moment, Annette, desperate to clean up Alexander's blood with cleanser, reads the bottom of the can: "You must be completely satisfied with the performance of AJAX or you'll receive your money back" (91). The evening thus concludes with the depressing—and hilarious—conflation of Greek tragic performance with the literally reassuring bromides of American commercial advertising.

To conclude: it is a commonplace of cultural criticism that gay and lesbian versions of antiquity are constructed from a generally leftist or progressive point of view: volumes such as Calimach's *The Gay Greek Myths* explicitly emphasize the restoration of a GLB antiquity as a human rights project. But the retrojection of modern homosexuality into the past can be, equally, a conservative reaction to contemporary degeneracy, one that traces homosexual impulses to a primal, ineradicable Western flaw, even neurosis. Both Tuan and Schechner see in homosexuality the final vestiges of a Greek-like sense of taboo, one that can be exploited in the adaptation—and transmogrification—of Greek tragedy, while Merlis explores not only the metaphors of homosexuality, but of homosexuality's

---

[82] *New York Times*, Nov. 5, 2001; www.nytheater.com/nytheatre/archweb/arch_024.htm

grim attendant: the plague of AIDS. In a sense, such receptions, however elaborate, take us further and further from the *actual* circumstances of ancient same-sex activity, but closer and closer to their *meaning* in the modern imagination, as antiquity remains a site for the contestation and construction not of ancient sexuality, but our own.

3 | Classics and ideology

It's one of the ironies of ideology that it's often easier to identify the ideological biases inherent in the art of other cultures than in the art of one's own. Let us start, then, by examining a particularly obvious ideological reception of the classical world—from a culture that's not only non-Western, but (in a sense) non-Terrestrial. In the comic book version of the American television series *Star Trek* (1978), writer George Kashdan and illustrator Alden McWilliams recount the continuing travails of *Star Trek's* U.S.S. Enterprise, boldly going where no ideologically motivated passengers have gone before. Continuing their (apparently self-justifying) mission of "discovery and exploration" (15), Captain Kirk, Mr. Spock, and the rest of the crew accomplish a routine rescue of another Federation starship when, alas, they are captured by the gravitational pull of a hitherto unidentified planetoid (3). Though Kirk and Spock express understandable alarm, the rest of the crew respond lazily and listlessly; indeed, Ensign Chekhov even asks—in the comic book version of a Russian accent—"Can't ve enjoy the scenery avhile?" As the cover of the volume darkly intimates, Kirk and Spock are about to journey through "an odyssey of peril!"—and this specific episode, adapted from the *Odyssey's* "Lotus Eaters" (9.63–104), is but the first of several Homerically inspired adventures on this new and frightening planet.

The promised perils come fast and furious. The teleported "Away Team"—of Kirk, Spock, and Dr. "Bones" McCoy—is first attacked by cannibals (depicted, somewhat unfortunately, as semi-clad aborigines, pp. 7–8) and further molested by a sandal-shod giant with one enormous eye. (In a troubling development, McCoy breaks his Hippocratic oath and turns his cauterizing laser on the giant's pupil. This is surely a haunting moment in intergalactic medicine (9).) The half-human Spock—whose knowledge of Earth's classical literature dwarfs that of the Earthlings around him—finally explains that this pattern of adventures mirrors that of "an ancient Earth legend, about a general returning from battle," and briefly narrates the Homeric underpinnings of their own story. As Kirk and Bones dimly recall their literature courses, Spock continues: "The gods were testing Ulysses... toying with him ... by filling his journey with deadly terrors!" (12). The appearance of the gods themselves confirms Spock's interpretation: as they once terrorized the ancient Ulysses on the old planet Earth, so too do these mysterious, power-mad entities now terrorize the inhabitants of their current planetoid—and any interlopers thereupon.

And so Zeus (and Hera, and Hermes, *et alii*) force the Away Team to navigate many of the *Odyssey*'s most famous adventures, including the billowing winds of Aeolus and the seductive song of the Sirens. (As a precaution, Kirk's ears are plugged by Bones' surprisingly versatile medical gauze.) The Federation officers even survive a harrowing gunfight with the monsters Scylla and Charybdis. At journey's end, the Away Team is surprised to discover a "copy" of ancient Greece, filled with "childlike" and "almost primitive" inhabitants (that is to say, Greeks, 21). Zeus joyfully declares that these new Greeks "worship only pleasure" (22), just like the gods themselves on Olympus. The Away Team is *appalled* by this information, not out of some intrinsic empathy for these Greeks (who seem, in fact, as happy as clams), but at the *ideological implications* of the gods' actions. As Kirk explains, "Now hold it, Zeus ... you Olympians are entitled to your fool customs, but you have no right to impose them on others!" Spock chimes in: "Indeed, it is a violation of the prime directive of the United Federation of Planets, which forbids interference in a people's evolution!" Zeus, to his peril, scoffs at the Prime Directive ("Bah! What do I care for the laws of puny mortals!"), and is rewarded with a debilitating blast from the Enterprise's tractor beam. Humiliated in front of his subjects, Zeus—and the rest of the Olympians—departs "Greece" for good (see Figures 3.1 and 3.2).

It turns out, then, that the entire plot, though powered by the inherent excitement and dramatic interest of Homer's *Odyssey*, actually serves to reinforce the justice, wisdom, and importance of an ideological consideration: the Federation's insistence on any planet's right to its own political self-determination and (r)evolution. The primacy of this Prime Directive is additionally reinforced by the attributes accorded to its defenders and detractors: the valiance, skill, and (at least in Spock's case) deep learning of the Away Team, as opposed to the cruelty, megalomania, and petulance of Zeus and his "Olympian playmates" (24). The text's deeper structure—the substratum of Homeric epic—lends further gravity to this narrative of ethnography (indeed, the Away Team inadvertently replicates line 3 of the *Odyssey* when it discovers "the cities and mind" of a new people: the Greeks). The "moral" of this Odysseanic adventure, moreover, is converted into law, as Kirk recommends to the Federation that the "planetoid be

Figures 3.1 and 3.2. Two pages from an *Odyssey*-themed *Star Trek* comic (1978).

issued a nomenclature and declared a non-self governing region under Chapter XI of the Articles of Federation" (24). (The meaning of that last phrase is a bit opaque, but presumably indicates that the planetoid must be henceforth regarded as politically independent.) The comic's title—"What Fools These Mortals Be"—thus proves to be ironic: even a *god* would be foolish to cast aspersions on the Prime Directive!

There are, of course, different levels of appropriation at play here: Star Trek's Federation is commonly read as a metaphor for the liberal, Western democracy of the United States of America, and the Federation's Prime Directive—that insists that all nations have an inalienable right to self-determination—has clear linkages to America's Cold War foreign policy throughout the 1960s and 1970s.[1] Indeed, it is not too much of a stretch to see in *Star Trek's* power-mad Zeus some traces of the USSR's Leonid Brezhnev, whose invasion of Czechoslovakia (1968) clearly violates the Prime Directive: Captain Kirk would be *aghast*. And while the *interior* narrative of Star Trek Issue #53 transparently pits two political ideologies

---

[1] The bibliography concerning the political metaphors of *Star Trek* is truly daunting. For a good recent overview, see John Shelton Lawrence 2010: 93–111, "Star Trek as American Monomyth," especially the subsection "Star Trek's *American Mission* in the original series."

against each other—utilizing the framework of the *Odyssey*—the comic book's *external* referents are both contemporary and metaphorical: this is both a version of the *Odyssey* and a vision of modernity at once.

The next two chapters of this book thus look at strongly ideological appropriations of antiquity that—like the *Star Trek* comic book—function not only as versions or adaptations of classical texts, but as commentaries on current events, most often with a political point. Sometimes the metaphor is implicit—as in *Star Trek*—and sometimes explicit: for instance, the very title of Conall Morrison's play *The Bacchae of Baghdad* erases all doubt. And while America has *always* had an ideological debt to antiquity—its Senate and statuary are the least of its borrowings[2]—the events of 9/11 have brought into focus the urgent appeals to classical precedent, from both Left and Right, from both artists and politicians. It's hardly an overstatement to observe that America's invasion of the Middle East was an invasion of antiquity as well, and that the massive (over)production of classically themed films and pop culture owes something to this pivotal event.

But the post-9/11 Second Gulf War—and the ensuing post-9/11 classical receptions—did not appear *ex nihilo*; there was, of course, the First Gulf War, which engendered less flamboyant (but still fascinating) pre-9/11 classical receptions. For instance, the Library of Congress catalogue heading for the book *Dateline: Troy* (1996/2006) combines two seldom-employed rubrics: *Trojan War–Juvenile literature* and *World-politics—20th Century—Juvenile literature*. It's a generally felicitous pairing, though also—as we will see—a tendentious one, as author Paul Fleischman and artists Gwen Frankfeldt and Glenn Marrow demonstrate not only "the relevance of the past and the resonance of the present" (so the dustcover) but engage in some surprisingly pointed criticism of mid-1990s American politics. The form of the book stays consistent from beginning to end: sparely narrated episodes of the Trojan War populate the left-hand pages (with prose composed with middle-school children in mind), while the right-hand pages offer sophisticated and surprising collages of modern, "related" newspaper clippings. (With its striking reuse of print media and fonts, the book's debt to pop art is clear.) The goal is thus to initiate a dialogue between classical "myth" and the all-too-real episodes of war and invasion in the twentieth century, particularly as filtered through the lens of modern political reporting.

---

[2] For the intellectual indebtedness of the Founding Fathers to the authors and ideals of classical antiquity, particularly as refracted through *The Bill of Rights*, see Wiltshire 1992, esp. 103–83.

Some of authors' juxtapositions are unlikely to raise hackles. The Trojan War's inordinate length—ten years—is illuminated by a *New York Times* article of 1987 entitled "Afghan War: In Year Seven, a Deadly Stalemate" (38–39), which analyzes the war of attrition between Soviets and Afghan insurgents and recalls, therefore, the protracted siege of Troy by the Greeks. Achilles' threat to abandon the Greeks—a threat on which Achilles makes good after his mighty quarrel with the general Agamemnon—hilariously invites comparison to baseball player Darryl Strawberry's temper tantrum during training camp ("He says he'll walk out if the Mets don't satisfy his contract demands," 48–49). Achilles' new armor—with a helmet of "unsurpassed strength" and a breastplate that "shone brighter than fire"—is winningly compared to the Pentagon's development of impervious tank plating ("It's really a major advance," marvels Pentagon spokesman Fred S. Hoffman, 58–59). And the Greek leaders' oath to defend Helen's honor—a sort of loose military compact—finds its modern counterpart in the activation of Army reservists on the eve of the Korean war (August 1950, pp. 24–25).

Some of the juxtapositions, however, are apt to ruffle feathers, and the authors' generally pacifist and left-leaning views inform their use of parallels: not all juxtapositions are created equal. For instance, the pregnant Trojan Queen Hecuba has nightmare visions of a burning city, and sends for Calchas, "interpreter of omens, readers of dreams and the future." This is compared to the screaming headline "Reagans use astrology, aides confirm"—one of the more embarrassing stories to run in the Santa Cruz Sentinel (1988, pp. 10–11). ("President Reagan and his wife Nancy are both deeply interested in astrology, and Mrs. Reagan is particularly worried about the impact of astrological portents on her husband's safety, the White House spokesman Marlin Fitzwater said Tuesday.") When reviewing the unpleasantness at Aulis, on the eve of the Greek invasion of Troy, the authors become even more cynical: the sacrifice of a hecatomb—100 oxen—is juxtaposed with the *Denver Post's* 1991 headline "[George H. W.] Bush declares this Sunday to be a day of prayer," and notes Bush's insistence that there will be no cease-fire in Kuwait (29). (As if to comment on America's misguided priorities, this newspaper article is buttressed by a weekend circular ad for a holiday "SUPER SALE" for brand name fashions—all of which is cradled by an American flag (see Figure 3.3).)

Most extreme, however, is the authors' illumination of Euripides' *Iphigenia*, which relates how Agamemnon's daughter Iphigenia, though tricked into coming to Aulis under false pretenses, nobly gives up her life, with "no protest": "'My life's but a little thing,' she spoke. 'Willingly will I give it up

A thousand ships, from every corner of Greece, gathered at Aulis for the invasion. Though Agamemnon promised his soldiers success, he knew that Troy would not be easily taken. Solemnly, he sacrificed one hundred fine bulls to almighty Zeus, beseeching him to favor the Greeks. From one hundred fires the scent of roasting meat, beloved by the gods, rose toward the heavens. The following morning the fleet set sail.

28

Figure 3.3. Juxtaposed classical text and modern image in *Dateline: Troy.*

for the sake of so noble a cause.'" This is juxtaposed with a *Los Angeles Times* piece from October 1967: *War Protester Burns Herself to Death Here,* a column which begins "A woman who left her purse and a pickup truck filled with literature and other references to the anti-Vietnam war movement burned herself to death with gasoline Sunday on the steps of the Federal Building here" (33). The parallel, however, is inexact: the original Euripidean text offers a woman who sacrifices herself to *enable* a war while the *Los Angeles Times* story details an act of sacrifice to *end* a war. While *Iphigenia in Aulis* may (as a totality) be read as an anti-war statement, the ultimate goals of these self-immolating women are completely antithetical: the authors have allowed their loathing of war to color their interpretation of Iphigenia's original sacrifice.

Above all, the authors' *sadness* permeates the world of *Dateline: Troy*, from the ransom of Hector's body—illuminated by the May 1990 article "Pyungyang Returns Remains of 5 U.S. Soldiers on Memorial Day" (63)— to the grisly 1969 montage of *Time Magazine's* "The My Lai Massacre," which describes "the most serious atrocity yet attributed to American troops in a war that is already well known for its particular savagery" (73). Photos of the moldering corpses of the Vietnamese—including women and children—are used to illustrate the fate of the similarly hapless Trojans after the fall of their city: "Awake and asleep, young and old, the Trojans were butchered by the pitiless Greeks. It was not a battle, but a massacre" (72). This is hardly a triumphalist narrative—of the type that, say, Helen recounts at *Odyssey* 4.274–289—but, rather, a description of war from a *civilian* point of view, laced with what might seem a Virgilian melancholy. *Dateline: Troy's* last explicit comparison, describing the troubled *nostoi,* 'homecomings,' of the Greeks, lists the disasters of each "victor" in turn, from Menelaus' shipwreck, to the banishments of Diomedes and Idomeneus, to the death of Agamemnon at the hand (and knife) of wife Clytemnestra (a tale best known from Aeschylus' *Agamemnon*). For added measure, the authors even sneak in a heterodox version of Odysseus' homecoming, from the epic cycle:[3] instead of a successful (eventual) reunion with his wife, father, and son (as in *Odyssey* books 22–24), Odysseus meets a particularly grisly end: "His own son didn't recognize him—and taking Odysseus for a pirate, drove a sting-ray spear through his heart" (74). At this point, the explicit parallels end, and the calamities of these "winning" Greeks are finally juxtaposed with a montage

---

[3] On Telegonus, Odysseus' son by Circe, see Gantz 1993: 710–11.

that spans the years from November 1984 to January 1992, encompassing editorials on the "futility of war," particularly in Baghdad and former Yugoslavia, and interrogating, above all, "the human price of war."

Dateline: Troy—with its wonderful, bipartite title—thus inscribes the world of modern news within ancient narrative, but does so in a way that is hardly "fair and balanced"; indeed, the tales of Troy are used a springboard (and occasionally a soapbox) for some surprisingly tendentious readings of myth. The authors' ideologically-driven juxtapositions "spin" Troy as a cautionary tale about America's devastating intervention in foreign affairs (even through the mid 1990s) and the series' target audience—young adults—is given a lesson as well in the virtues of pacifism and conscientious objection. "Troy" thus stands (and falls) as an educational primer for Greeks and Americans alike.[4]

Orientalism and 9/11

The events of 9/11 again catapulted the Persian Gulf into the American imagination; it's little wonder that it also catapulted *The Persians*. This first extant play of the Greek canon, by Aeschylus, is also among its most curious, as it largely retells the downfall of the Persian King Xerxes from the "wrong"—that is to say, Persian—point of view. Scholars have been increasingly split on the play's slippery ideological biases.[5] What might seem at first glance an extraordinary act of postwar magnanimity (the victor's profound sympathy for the defeated after the Persian War) can also be interpreted as an extraordinary variation on Greek jingoism, as the play's complicated constellation of laments, omens, and news redound to the identical theme: the divinely sanctioned victory of the Greeks over the overreaching Persians.[6] Structurally, too, the play is a puzzle: the central

---

[4] *Dateline: Troy* saw a second edition in 2006, including new and occasionally provocative post-9/11 metaphors. The Trojan priest Laocoön's warnings concerning the Trojan Horse (p. 70) are implicitly compared to failures in intelligence-analysis in the years preceding the attack on 9/11. (A sample headline: "As suspected terrorists traversed the U.S. over a decade, signs pointing to their plans went unheeded until after their plans were carried out." The Greeks are thereby implicitly compared to terrorists.) Likewise, the troubled reception of the Greeks from Troy—including the death of Agamemnon at the hands of his wife Clytemnestra—is compared to the traumas experienced by American soldiers after their return from Iraq (74—75).

[5] See especially the overview at Harrison 2000: 103.

[6] Edith Hall 1989, especially Chapter 2. See also Said 1978: 56. "[In *Persians*] Asia speaks through and by virtue of the European imagination, which is depicted as victorious over Asia, that hostile 'other' world beyond the seas. To Asia are given the feelings of emptiness, loss, and disaster that

dramatic action—the defeat of Xerxes at the naval battle of Salamis—has
already happened, and so the play begins less *in medias res* than *post res*.
Still, it's a tribute to Aeschylus' dramatic impulses and exquisite sense of
lyricism that the play can still move the audience, even as it refracts this
momentous event through multiple prisms, including Queen Atossa,
Xerxes' grieving mother; the ghost of Darius, Xerxes' eternally frustrated
father; the somber chorus of lamenting Elders; and the prolix Messenger,
who delivers one of the most celebrated "messenger speeches" from
antiquity.

In a dazzling chapter on "Orientalism" in Greek tragedy, Edith Hall
looks less at the *structure* of the play than at its complex layers of
symbolism and imagery; for a play in which little happens in terms of
plot, very much happens on the level of postwar political ideology. On
Hall's reading, Aeschylus' *Persians* is among the West's most studied and
intricate creations of the Eastern "Other": Greek self-definition through
other-construction. So the Persians of the *Persians*—however sympathetic,
however tragic—principally serve to reinforce a whole host of stereotypes
concerning the East: these include the Persian penchant for hierarchy; the
East's unseemly attraction to luxury; and the Persians' "unrestrained emo-
tionalism." These attributes are then implicitly contrasted to the virtues of
the victorious West, which is (putatively) egalitarian; austere, and self-
disciplined.[7] So while there's no *explicit* correlation between the virtues of
the West and the defeat of the tyrannical, effeminate East, such an *implicit*
causality informs every line of the play. In the original Greek, such
stereotypes are reinforced by outlandish vocalizations and rituals; by an
extensive vocabulary of material goods (such as *ploutos*, 'wealth,' and
chrusos, 'gold'); and by widespread reference to the Persians' court hierarchy and byzantine political protocols (99). Hall attempts to rescue the
play from charges of "mere xenophobic self-congratulation" by emphasizing the concurrent strain of tragic *pathos*, but it's difficult to disentangle the
two threads. What to do, then, with the play that "represents the first
unmistakable file in the archive of Orientalism"?[8]

Or, more to the point, what to do with this play in 2005, after 9/11 and
America's subsequent invasion of Iraq? The Bush administration's official
stance—that the terrorist organization Al-Qaida, supported by Iraq, had

seem therefore after to reward Oriental challenges to the West ..." For a recent, forceful
rejection of Hall's views, see Gruen 2011 who proposes a far more sympathetic view of the
"other" on the part of both Greeks and Romans.
[7] Hall 1989: 80.   [8] Hall 1989: 99

invaded the United States—seemed to divide the world along Aeschylean lines; in attacking the nation of Iraq, then, the West was thus repelling and rebuffing Persian invaders *again* while employing rhetoric and stereotypes often eerily similar to those of Aeschylus, including an emphasis on ferocity, mysticism, and tyranny.[9] As then-President Bush remarked in one of his more frighteningly candid moments, "See in my line of work you got to keep repeating things over and over and over again for the truth to sink in, to kind of catapult the propaganda."[10]

One possible way to produce Aeschylus' *Persians*, then, would be as absolutely straight, thereby allowing the stereotypes to speak for themselves, within a framework of *implicit* irony. Wartime America is not, however, ideally suited for such an interpretative gamble; subtlety is lost on the hysterical. Instead, the American performance troupe Waterwell hit upon another solution, with a thorough reworking of *The Persians* into a postmodern vaudeville, now delightfully entitled *The Persians: A Comedy about War in Five Songs* (2005). As their mission statement indicates, Waterwell is an activist theater troupe, dedicated to effecting social change: "Waterwell strives to empower its audience to change their lives and the world in which they live."[11] One would not expect, then, a bland adaptation; and indeed, Waterwell's *Persians* impresses with its verve, especially as produced in a hostile wartime climate. Since the company was co-founded by Arian Moayed,[12] an American born in Tehran and raised in Illinois, one senses in Waterwell's *Persians* that the deeply personal is mixed with the deeply political: the Persian empire strikes back. For this production, directed by Tom Ridgeley, Lauren Cregor composed the original, pastiche songs; the Greek portions were adapted from Robert Potter's translation of *The Persians* available on the Internet classics archive (a publication method far beyond the ken of Aeschylus), as well as from versions by Raphael/McLeish, Slavitt, and Vellacott.

Waterwell only adapts about half the play directly from the Greek; the rest constitutes a fantasia on Persian themes, beginning with the funky,

---

[9] For an overview of Orientalism and the "fabricated enemy" after 9/11, see Steuter and Wills 2008: 24–33. Subsequent chapters elucidate recent metaphors of Iraq and Iraqis, including "beasts" and "monsters" (75), as well as the stereotypes of religious fanatics. There are, of course, metaphors that would never have occurred to Aeschylus: cancer and microbes, for instance (82).

[10] http://georgewbush-whitehouse.archives.gov/news/releases/05/20050524-3.html. Spoken by Bush, May 24, 2005 in (ironically) Greece, N.Y.

[11] Denton 2006: 563. The quotations from Waterwell's *Persians* all come from the text printed in this volume.

[12] In spring of 2011, Moayed was nominated for a Tony award for his performance in Rajiv Joseph's *Bengal Tiger at the Baghdad Zoo*.

contrapuntal introduction of the main characters. (For instance, the actress Hanna helpfully sings: "Listen close so the names don't confuse ya/ I play the Queen, play the Queen, Queen Atossa. . . .", 576). The ensemble next apologies for its liberties with the original text ("Watch the Persian fleets get clobbered, clobbered by the Greeks/ Aeschylus, we beg your pardon; we made a couple tweaks," p. 576). The Iran-born Arian Moayed significantly plays King Xerxes ("Xerxes is dumb . . . so we knew he had to be played by an actor who, to every role he played . . . brought such a keen sense of stupidity. . .," 577); typically, however, all four actors double or triple the various roles.[13]

This Americanization of Aeschylus begins quickly and raucously, with a flash of "MTV-style lights" and skit that introduces "MTV Persia"—a pointed satire on such reality TV fare as MTV's cult hit "The Real World." While Aeschylus' original *Persians* introduces us to the "real world" of Persian life, Waterwell's *Persians* presents us with, rather, the Real World version of Persian life, complete with rolling cameras ("we followed a typical Persian family for one week," a producer chirpily announces) and reality TV clichés ("our cameras found out what happens / when people stop being polite / and start being Persian," 578). If Aeschylus' *Persians* jump-started Western concepts of "orientalism," this reality-TV frame-work ironizes such Orientalizing by calling into question the whole idea of putting a culture "on-stage" (or on camera). The opening scene thus focuses on the nuclear Ghazi family: Mother, with both a son and a husband off to war against Greece; Grandfather, in charge of the council of Elders; Daughter-in-Law, pregnant and awaiting for her husband to return from war; and the Conscientiously Objecting Son, sporting a stylish "Greeks are people too" T-shirt.

As the cameras roll, we're confronted with—at best—an unlovely portrait of the Ghazis, who are stylized in as gauche a fashion as anything on American TV: there's Grandpa's bigotry ("[We should be] killing those feta cheese monkeys," he grouses, 549), some titillating homosexual hijinks ("MOTHER tickles WIFE to the ground and into a sexual position," 579), and a concluding (and oh-so-Greek) revelation of incest (with consequent stage direction: *Gasp*, 580). This surreal scene—one that presents the grossest stereotypes of the East as filtered through American mass

---

[13] Curiously, Waterwell's vaudeville structure emphasizes the paratactic—that is to say, highly episodic—nature of the original Aeschylean play: it's a smart choice for a play that is, as Michelini argues, "the weakest [of Aeschylus] in dramatic illusion and the most static in form" (Michelini 1982: 72).

media—then tumbles into more-or-less authentic Aeschylus, with a few alterations that cement Waterwell's metaphors of America-as-the-new-Greece. In the original play, the chorus briefly recounts Xerxes' crossing of the Hellespont via pontoon bridge (ll. 109–111), and the king's subsequent temptation of fate ("What mortal man can escape the deceiving wiles of a god?" the chorus muses, ll. 93–94). Waterwell "Americanizes" this crossing: "Imagine a thousand ships lined up across a huge body of water—picture the Hudson—a thousand ships line up across it and hundreds of thousands of soldiers marching ... into Hoboken" (580). (It's no coincidence that the Twin Towers overlooked the Hudson river: Waterwell chooses its metaphors for maximum impact.) Next comes a robing scene of Queen Atossa that emphasizes the Persian stereotype of luxury —"[Arian and Tom] peel away [Hanna's] clothes and using pearls, gloves, etc. transform her into ATOSSA" (580)—which is then followed by Queen Atossa's dream of the horse and the bird, first acted out by three actors, and then relayed, in suitably stately fashion, by the Queen herself.

In the original Greek, this twofold vision of the queen quite nearly interprets itself. Two women—one garbed in Persian robes, the other in simple Greek vestments—receive some land by lottery: one receives the Greek earth, the other, a "barbarian" province (l. 187). Atossa sees her son Xerxes attempting to yoke them both together—like horses—but in the ensuing fracas Xerxes falls from his chariot; he fails. Next she spies an eagle, king of birds, fleeing to an altar of Apollo; a hawk attacks it with particularly rapidity, and the eagle cowers, frightened. The metaphor is so obvious—the failed Xerxes as trembling eagle, the upstart Greek nation as rapacious hawk—that Aeschylus doesn't even bother to provide an interpretation; indeed, the attendant chorus tactfully assures the queen that this is just a warning, and that untoward events may still be averted by proper supplication and libations (ll. 217–223). Again, Waterwell turns this scene on its ear: after providing an almost literal version of the Queen's vision, Waterwell introduces Arian's dotty (Persian) mother, who not only essays an interpretation, but gets it *wrong*: horses are a sign of "pocket money"; the fractured yoke indicates future "freedom"; and we dream about children only when "comfortable with the path our life has taken" (582). Atossa can't believe her ears: she knows that the dream is a dire one, that it is the Greeks' "fault"—and she spits on the Greeks. Arian's mother sadly points out that Iranians—Persians—always find someone else to blame.

The following song—the profoundly sociopolitical TAHKSEER (BLAME)—cleverly looks at the events of the Iranian revolution from two vantage points, even as the song oscillates between lyrics in English and Farsi. When Tom takes the microphone, the audience is gobsmacked with a brief history of Persia from an American (i.e. "Greek") point of view—"Persians were Zoroastrian ... now they're more into Islamics / never getting laid, hating U.S.A ... But nobody cared / till they were seizing embassies, taking hostages, / doing what they pleased with our oil/ except it wasn't ours, / then they hit our towers / oh no wait that was Iraq. / or was it Osama? Who cares just so long as / we bomb anybody that reads the Koran?" (583). The rage here is palpable (thus ironizing even the title of the play, a "comedy" about war), and it's a rage that carries over into Aeschylus' famous messenger speech, in which the Greeks defeat Xerxes—or Americans conquer Iraq—in bloody battle, a speech rendered without an iota of humor: "[T]he Greek ships, seizing their chance, / swept in circling and struck and overturned our hulls, and saltwater vanished before our eyes— / shipwrecks filled it, and drifting corpses. / Shores and reefs filled up with our dead ..." (585). Persians stranded on a nearby island fare no better than their maritime brethren: "It ended when the Greeks gave one great howl / And charged, chopping meat / till every living man was butchered" (586). As indicated in the stage directions, the defeat of the Persians is re-enacted by Waterwell as a modern boxing match.

As the play nears its conclusion, the metaphors come ever more swiftly, and with ever more complex associations. For instance, Queen Atossa, devastated that the motherland has now been made a "widowland," summons the ghost of Darius, her husband; together, they survey the situation with impressive dispassion ("Baby, we're fucked," Atossa diagnoses, accurately), and together lay the blame squarely on Xerxes: "Our dumbass son thinking he got to prove something." But here, Waterwell has pulled off something of a coup of metaphor; as one reviewer put it: "[W]hen a play's premise involves a superpower's leader invading another country because the leader's father failed to conquer that country previously, hints about our current involvement in Iraq are unavoidable."[14] In other words, for the briefest of scenes, Xerxes registers not as a metaphor for Saddam Hussein, but for George W. Bush, atoning for his own father's perceived botched handling of the First Gulf War. It's a reversal of associations that will also—as we shall see—confuse reviewers of the film *300*, which similarly runs riot with the metaphors of Persian invasion and Western defense.

[14] Marlon Hurt. http://offoffonline.com/archives.php?id=459. Accessed July 6, 2011.

In the original text of *The Persians*, Hall identifies its exotic rhythms and sounds as an important component of the Orientalizing (and therefore "other-ing") of the Persians; she especially emphasizes the unseemly bouts of male lament that conclude the play, particularly those of Xerxes himself. (Even for a tragic figure, Xerxes clearly goes overboard, with remarkable runs of lamentation, including *ieh! ieh! io io!* (1004); *otototototoi!* (1051), and the completely untranslatable ἒ ἒ ἒ ἒ (977).)[15] Waterwell positively embraces that aspect of the original text by complementing the text's oriental sounds with oriental accompaniment; a daf and tombak (traditional Iranian percussion instruments) beat out a dirge; three of the actors chant; and Xerxes shifts from human speech to inhuman "howls," while interspersing "moans of grief." As in the original text, these unfamiliar, discomfiting sounds are meant to convey the radical *alterity* of the Persians, their other-ness, their not-us-ness—but with a twist.

This "Oriental" lamentation, and catalogue of the dead, sets up Waterwell's final trick, a rewriting of the Persian "casualty" list at lines 303–330, including such exotic—to a Greek ear—names as Adeues, Pheresseues, Pharnuchus, Tharybdis, and Syennesis; it even includes ethnic identifications like Artebes the Bactrian and Magus the Arab. As Ebbott notes, this is one of the more conspicuous moments in the text in which Greek social phenomena—such as epigraphic casualty lists—are grafted onto an alien culture:[16] this is how *Greeks* commemorate the dead, not Persians. (See for instance the list of Athenian dead from *c.* 460 BCE, Figure 3.4.) Waterwell's Xerxes not only emphasizes the radical *form* of lament, but, even more strikingly, the radical content:

> Samyar Razan Roshan Arash Teymour Jamsheed Sousas Pharandakes Mardook Pelegon Zarvan Dotmas Souiscanes Michael Agdabatas Peer Arah Hirbod Psammis Koorosh Jerome Daixis Isaac Seulakes Samyar Roger Yashar Liliaious Luke Memphis Tharybis Kayvan Edmund Megabazes Xanthes Mehraban Metragathes Naveen Lawrence Pasha Masistras Ariomardes Pharnoukes Ekbantana Shanin Peyshang Kayvan ... [other surnames, Persian and American, improvised as needed](591)

---

[15] Hall 1989: 83–4 notes "the almost undiluted groans, accompanied by weeping, breast-beating, and beard-plucking ... and culminating in the closing epode distinguished by its unprecedentedly high proportion of metrically integrated cries, *oioi, iō, iōa,* and *ēē*, producing an effect of near-hysteria."

[16] Ebbott 2000: 83. See Dué 2006: 57–90 for a critique of Hall's interpretation of *Persians* as a primary document of Orientalism; for Dué, much of the *Persians* continues a Homeric preoccupation with *collapsing* distinctions between West and East: "Despite elaborate costuming, exotic Persian movements, and foreign-sounding music, the Persians are shown, at least at the moment of death in battle, to be as Greek as any Athenian" (90).

Figure 3.4. Epigraphic list of the Athenian dead (Louvre Ma 863).

Thus at the moment of Persia's *greatest* otherness, of its most exaggerated Orientalism, Waterwell's Xerxes collapses the distinction between Persian and American names: casualties are casualties, the dead are dead, and Aeschylean dramatic structure be damned.[17] Moreover, by interspersing American names among the Persian ones—"Edmund" falls especially strikingly on the ear—Waterwell explicitly invokes *America's* most famous epigraphic casualty list: the Vietnam Memorial in Washington, DC. As in Aeschylus' original text—which converts epigraphy to poetry—so too does the Vietnam Memorial function as a locus of stone and sound; organizers marked the occasion of its twentieth anniversary in 2002 by reciting every name on the wall, a gesture of memory and healing.[18] So Xerxes' elegy is not just for the Persian dead, but an exorcism for *all* the dead following the 2003 invasion of Iraq, an invasion that caused—as the song argues—WOE UPON WOE UPON WOE UPON WOE UPON... (There's even a moment of grim humor, as the chorus acknowledges that "These people paid for a comedy show not for / WOE UPON WOE UPON WOE ...," 591) (See Figure 3.5). As in the original play, music and wailing build to "an unbearable noise," with nowhere, seemingly, to go: an endlessly litany of WOE UPON WOE that echoes the final verse of Aeschylus: "We will escort you [Xerxes] with full-throated wails of grief" (1079). Waterwell thus bows to the theatrically inevitable—a blackout—but reinforces the central conceit of the play with a final, soft, doo-wop version of Hoagy Carmichael's iconic "Georgia on my Mind." Only, of course, Waterwell ironically "Orientalizes" this quintessentially American tune into its hall-of-mirrors equivalent: the wistful and melancholy "Persia on my mind."[19]

In *Persians*, Waterwell skewers the Orientalizing tendencies of the 1990s and 2000s, an orientalism which is far more often discovered in its pure and unadulterated forms. Perhaps the paradigm for this impulse is Frank Miller's graphic novel *300*, a retelling of Herodotus' history of the Persian wars, with a special emphasis on the Spartan disaster at Thermopylae (*Histories* 7.138–239). First published in 1999, the *300*'s striking back cover—calculated to spur purchases in a comic book shop—couldn't be

[17] Broadhead 1960: xviii–xix notes the striking one-sided-ness of the original Aeschylean text: "It is very significant that not one Greek is named . . .. This reticence was wholly fitting in a play that was to be primarily the presentation of the Persian tragedy as seen through Persian eyes."

[18] Kellman, Laurie. "Two decades old, Vietnam memorial draws thousands to hear names on its wall." http://staugustine.com/stories/110802/nat_1110688.shtml. Accessed July 12, 2011.

[19] See Foley 2012: 144–6 for an analysis of Waterwell's *Persians* that concludes: "the production suggested that only memory, laughter, and song and dance can allow us to look more carefully at the peculiar binds we are in."

Figure 3.5. "Woe upon Woe," from Waterwell's *Persians*.

more structurally composed. It constructs Greece and Persia as virtual antitheses: "The Army of Persia—a force so vast it shakes the earth with its march—is poised to crush Greece, an island of reason and freedom in a sea of mysticism and tyranny." Here, the West is limned as enlightened and free—with no mention of its entrenched institutions of, say, slavery— while Persia is Orientalized as autocratic and tyrannical. (It's often typical of the rhetoric of ideology that it occasionally deconstructs its own under- pinnings; *tyranny* is a Greek word, not Persian, as well as a widespread form of Greek governance.[20]) There are geographical oddities as well: the vastness of Persia is juxtaposed with the "island" of Greece, as if sur- rounded on all sides, an Atlantis fending off cataclysm. The Greek penchant for *logos*, 'reason,' is divorced from any unsettling religious traditions, as the Persians themselves are branded as irrational mystics. (Again, this elides a well-established tradition of Greek popular magic, including voodoo dolls, curse-tablets, and demon invocation: this system shares a certain internal consistency, but they are surely not the pillars of the "island of reason" that the authors intend.[21])

This isn't to say that the back cover is un-Herodotean; only that it exaggerates the kernels of Herodotean structure into caricature—a carica- ture aided by some modern popularizing accounts of the Persian War. In Herodotus' original text, the meeting between deposed Spartan king Demaretus and the Persian leader Xerxes famously juxtaposes the bravery and ideals of the Greeks with the servitude and benightedness of the Persians; indeed, Xerxes is startled to discover that Greeks have embraced their own poverty (7.102.1), finding that *arētê*, 'excellence,' is their highest goal, an *arētê* ultimately derived from wisdom (*sophia*) and mighty law (*nomos*). (Xerxes' uncomprehending reaction thereby reinforces three pillars of Orientalism: luxury, mysticism, and despotism, just as outlined by Hall, above.) Indeed, as Demaretus asserts, the Spartans are so horrified by the thought of slavery (*doulosyne*, 7.102.2) that they will fight to the last man, whatever the odds (a sentiment that Herotodus has cannily included to foreshadow the disaster at Thermopylae). Xerxes scoffs at the thought that "free men" (*eleutheroi*, 7.103.3) can ever fight as well as Persians: if the Spartans were (like Persians) subdued to the rule of one man, they might

---

[20] Chantraine 1968–1980: *ad hoc* argues that *tyrannos*—along with cognate ideas *anax* and *basileus*—are probably borrowed from Asia Minor, and of undetermined etymology; he rejects as doubtful a borrowing from Etruscan *turan*, 'Mistress Venus.'

[21] See Faraone 1999: 5–15, "The Ubiquity of Love Magic." See also Graf 1997: 13–18 for an overview of the evolution of scholarship concerning the "scientific" nature of ancient magic.

become superior in nature; or, cowering before the whip, they might face overwhelming odds. Demaretus' reply is a model of brevity and elegance: "Though the Greeks are free (*eleutheroi*), they are not *eleutheroi* in every respect: for them, the law (*nomos*) is their master (*despotes*), which they fear far more than your own men fear you" (7.104.4). Demaretus not only turns Xerxes' rhetoric against him, but also transforms the concrete notions of slavery and despotism into intangibles. These Western Greeks serve a master, but an abstract one: *law*.

But as so often, the tale of Thermopylae wends its way into modern adaptations—such as the *300*—through multiple sources, and not just through the original source text of Herodotus. Indeed, Frank Miller's adaptation lists four items in its bibliography: Herodotus' *Histories*, William Golding's *The Hot Gates* (1965), WWII veteran Ernle Bradford's *Thermopylae: The Battle for the West* (1980)—and most intriguingly—*The Western Way of War* (1989) by Victor Davis Hanson.[22] Having first gained recognition as a scholar of both military history and agrarianism, Hanson is now best known as a conservative firebrand and Senior Fellow at the right-leaning Hoover Institution at Stanford University; he was an outspoken advocate of "the war on terror" in the mid 2000s, and continues to write prolifically for the *National Review*. In a follow-up volume to the film version of the *300*, Hanson notes how well the comic book captures the intellectual trends that inform the fateful battle of Thermopylae:

> *300* preserves the spirit of the Thermopylae story. . . .. If critics think that *300* reduces and simplifies the meaning of Thermopylae into freedom versus tyranny, they should carefully reread ancient accounts and then blame Herodotus, Plutarch, and Diodorus—who long ago boasted that Greek freedom was on trial against Persian autocracy; free men in superior fashion dying for their liberty, their enslaved enemies being whipped to enslave others.[23]

But for some conservative thinkers—such as Hanson—the battle of Thermopylae symbolizes not just a collision of abstracts—Demaretus' "freedom" vs. Xerxes' "tyranny"—but an ongoing battle between America and a despotism that creeps in from the East. As Hanson wrote in the aftermath of 9/11:

---

[22] Golding's short, non-fictional "The Hot Gates" is a moving account of Golding's visit to modern Thermopylae. After retracing the (last) steps of Leonidas, he muses (1961: 20), "A little of Leonidas lies in the fact that I can go where I like and write what I like. He contributed to set us free." Even here, the language of Herodotus' original histories shines through.

[23] From Victor Davis Hanson's preface to *300: The Art of The Film*, in DiLullo 2007.

[I]f we fight to preserve freedom like the Greeks at Thermopylae and the GIs at Normandy Beach, then war is the right and indeed the only thing we can do. Caught in such a tragedy, where efforts at reason and humanity fall on the deaf ears of killers, we must go to war for our survival and to prove to our enemies that their defeat will serve as a harsh teacher—at least for a generation or two—that it is wrong and very dangerous to blow up three thousand civilians in the streets of our cities.... The deviant offspring of the Enlightenment—Marxists and Freudians—gave birth to even more pernicious social science that sought to 'prove' to us that war was always evil and therefore—with help from Ph.D.'s—surely preventable .... In our new moral calculus, bin Laden figures to be no Xerxes or Tojo .... Instead we insist that he is either confused (call in Freud) or has legitimate grievances (call in Marx), and so we must find the answers within us, not him ....[24]

The metaphors and equivalences fly fast and furious here: Thermopylae is explicitly compared to the storming of Normandy (and therefore Persians to Hitler-led Germans); New York City is implicitly invoked as the new, devastated Athens (sacked by the Persians in 480 BCE); the Persian Xerxes is ranked alongside the (Arab) bin Laden and the Japanese WWII general P. M. Hideki Tojo, responsible for attacking Pearl Harbor. But it's not just America that's attacked, but the abstract notions—"freedom" and "reason"—that America, like the Greeks, hold dear.[25] This sort of ideologically loaded language finds its way into *300*—first produced between the two Gulf Wars—at regular intervals. Says Leonidas, the Spartan king, to his assembled throng: "We do not sacrifice the rule of law to the whim and will of men. That is the old way, the old sad, stupid way. The way of Xerxes and every creature like him. A new age has begun, an age of great deeds. An age of reason, an age of justice, an age of law." Another panel describes Persia as "a beast made of men and horses and spears and swords ... ready to devour tiny Greece ... the world's one hope for reason and justice." (Here, we've the Orientalizing of the East as feral, ferocious, and irrational; the Romans likewise branded the "Oriental" Egypt as fearsome, and as feral, as a crocodile.)

As a visual medium, however, the *300* not only Orientalizes Herodotus' text in terms of language, but also in iconography, style, and sequence. Surely, the most spectacular example is the interview between Leonidas

---

[24] National Review Online, Oct. 9, 2001, reprinted in pp. 66–7, *An Autumn of War.*

[25] See Tomasso 2011: 157 for a catalogue of the reception of Thermopylae in American popular culture, including metaphors for both the Alamo and anti-Communist crusades.

and Xerxes, each character embodying the West and East, law and lawlessness. At this point, we have already been introduced to Leonidas, a sensibly
clad military man who is all resolve and handsome ruggedness: the type of
leader we'd *all* follow into the breach, even a breach by hot springs.
Leonidas is thus an idealized version of Western military leadership: the
perfect combination of abstract rhetoric—freedom and reason—and concrete muscle. The introduction of Xerxes, then, is something of a surprise:
he literally dwarfs Leonidas (drawn diminutively from a Xerxes'-eye-view)
and seems calculated to register, on the level of the visual, everything that
Leonidas is *not*: he's garishly clad in luxuriant (and practically porous)
regalia; he's ethnically non-Western (dark skin, shaved head, vaguely
African lips);[26] and, most strikingly, he's sexually potent, as he sports an
impressively anachronistic bikini thong. (Xerxes' sexual proclivities are
likewise coded visually as both passive and active; though his phallus
remains a considerable focal point of attention, Xerxes's body is otherwise
over-determinedly pierced and penetrable.)[27] Above all, Xerxes is
threatening: religiously, militarily, sexually. The Orient produces impressive monsters (see Figure 3.6, from the film version of *300*.)

The subsequent scene—already staged as a covert seduction in the book
—is even more explicitly homoerotic in Zack Snyder's 2005 film adaptation, as Xerxes hits on Leonidas as if at a gay bar. (Leonidas has previously
sneered at Athenians as "philosophers and boy-lovers"; Xerxes is likely to
be disappointed.) Xerxes' preamble to seduction—a sort of Oriental
buttering-up—includes ruminations about the beauty of the Greek land,
the Greek predilection for "logic," and Greek concern for women: this is
the Orient as it gazes admiringly at the West and its unique properties. But
Xerxes wants more: he wants Leonidas in every sense, and it's no surprise
that he springs his offer of power at the same time he comes up on
Leonidas from behind. (Or, as the Romans would put it, *a tergo*.) As he
places his hands on Leonidas' shoulders—the sort of gesture that would, in
a different sort of film, result in a neck-rub and much more—Xerxes
promises Leonidas a host of powers if only he would "kneel" to Xerxes
as King. (Again, the sexual innuendo of kneeling before Xerxes is pregnant
and palpable.) Like any good heterosexual Occidental, Leonidas rejects

---

[26] Miller's visual encoding of race has engendered much critical comment. Fairey 2011: 159:
"[Miller] presents the Achaemenid Persians as morally deviant and corrupt and as ethnically
Africans and Arabs."

[27] See Fairey 2011: 166 on Miller's use of piercing (here and elsewhere) as an "external symbol of
deviance from society"—that is to say, from the norms of American society.

Figure 3.6. An orientalized Xerxes, from the film version of *300*.

Xerxes' politico-sexual offer and resigns himself to self-sacrifice: he soberly explains that even if the Spartans fail, "The world will know that *free men stood against a tyrant*"—and will again once again stand against tyranny.[28]

Though some reviewers—such as the *New York Times* A. O. Scott— dismissed the film as an insignificant object of "camp derision,"[29] other reviewers understood the film of *300* to be commenting on East–West relations after 9/11—though there was considerably less agreement on what that commentary might *mean*. Sam Hatch, online at station *wwuh.org*, argued that the "multicultural hordes of the Persians can easily be applied to the massive multinational military presence in Iraq" and that "the outnumbered Spartan rebels can easily be related to the Iraqi insurgents fighting off an American presence against all odds." In other words, Xerxes is a metaphor for a "Bush-like god–ruler," and the film can be interpreted as a subtle critique of the Bush administration. Hatch's interpretation isn't particularly persuasive, however: it's hard to imagine the average movie-goer gazing at a shaved, swarthy, body-pierced, codpiece-sporting bisexual caliph and thinking "Aha! That's George W. Bush." Indeed, John Powers, writing for the online magazine *Art & Threat*, reads the film in precisely the *opposite* way, as a thinly veiled metaphor for racial politics: "[*300*] plays on the contemporary fear that we are facing a clash of civilizations, and stokes that fear with racist imagery. By calling up old Aryan dreams of a classical world peopled by blond haired blue eyed individuals, and threatening that world with an undifferentiated dark-skinned horde, the film panders to the ugliest aspect of America."[30] Certainly, the racial aspect of the film was mercilessly mocked by the Latino Comedy Project, of Austin TX, which took a famous moment of the film—Leonidas' blood-thirsty exhortation "Spartans! Tonight we dine in Hell!"—and transformed it into an equally vociferous exhortation to illegal immigrants crossing the American border: "Mexicans! Tonight we dine in San Diego!"[31] (It's

---

[28] On *300*'s right-leaning metaphors, see also Nisbet 2006: 76, who remarks on the comic's "explicitly presentist agenda which posits freedom-loving Greece as a prototype USA and hawkish Sparta as its citizen militia."

[29] A. O. Scott, "Battle of the Manly Men: Blood Bath With a Message," http://movies.nytimes. com/2007/03/09/movies/09thre.html

[30] John Powers. "300: Racist War Propaganda with Septic Timing." http://artthreat.net/2007/10/ 300-racist-war-propaganda/. See also Steuter and Wills 2008: 101, "[*300*] pits heroic, fair-skinned Spartans against dark-skinned, marauding Persians, their indiscriminate and undifferentiated nature symbolized by the identical masks worn by their advancing hordes."

[31] This famous phrase can be found in somewhat less confrontational form at e.g. Plutarch, *Apophthegmata Laconica*, 225D5: Τοῖς δὲ στρατιώταις παρήγγειλεν ἀριστοποιεῖσθαι ὡς ἐν Ἅιδου δειπνοποιησομένους. "He ordered his soldiers to have breakfast as if about to dine in Hades."

perhaps little coincidence that Xerxes is played in the film by a Latino, the Brazilian actor Rodrigo Santoro, which thereby displaces one American "other"—Latinos—onto the another American "other": Arabs.)

Author Frank Miller himself adds to the modern descriptions of the Middle East as "barbaric"—precisely the word employed by the Greeks (and by Aeschylus) in describing the nations to the East. In a January 2007 interview with National Public Radio, Frank Miller expands on the sorts of ideological notions already present in the graphic novel *300*:

> Let's finally talk about the enemy. For some reason, nobody seems to be talking about who we're up against, and the sixth century barbarism that they actually represent. These people saw people's heads off. They enslave women, they genitally mutilate their daughters, they do not behave by any cultural norms that are sensible to us.... Where I would fault President Bush the most, was that in the wake of 9/11, he motivated our military, but he didn't call the nation into a state of war. He didn't explain that this would take a communal effort against a common foe. So we've been kind of fighting a war on the side, and sitting off *like a bunch of Romans* complaining about it. [emphasis added][32]

The first items in Miller's catalogue of barbarism—his word—aren't particularly surprising: egregious acts of slaughter (decapitation), slavery, bodily mutilation, and a general "otherness" in cultural norms. "They" are not us; *they* are our foe. When Miller calls for action, it's telling that he presses into service yet another classical reference: that our current Beltway debate and dithering is characteristic of *the Romans*. I hazard that this isn't a metaphor that would occur to many classicists, the Romans being perfectly capable of invading nations on slim pretexts and with startling rapidity. (See, for instance, Julius Caesar's impressive career as an aggressor in Gaul and Britain.) Rather, Miller implicitly invokes the (putative if often dysfunctional) Roman government of a republic as an ineffective tool in wartime, and implicitly damns the current American Congress, arguing for a stronger, more Leonidas-esque executive branch. This is part of a more general trend of conservative thinkers and writers to couch the invasion of Iraq in terms of *Greek* metaphor; indeed, they need to torpedo the pesky Roman metaphors which might—in unsympathetic hands—fuel suspicions that the invasion was largely conducted in order to widen a sphere of influence, to seize and secure natural resources, and to enlarge the

---

[32] From Broken Mystic, "Frank Miller's '300' and the Persistence of Accepted Racism." www.npr.org/templates/player/mediaPlayer.html?action=1&t=1&islist=false&id=7002481&m=7002502. Transcribed at www.theatlasphere.com/metablog/612.php.

American empire in search of a new *pax Romana*.[33] The invasion thus not only played off metaphors of East vs. West but even Greece vs. Rome.

Marshall McLuhan famously declared that the medium *is* the message, but that's a bit reductive; it's just as true that a message strives to out itself by whatever medium. In the case of Herodotus, the inherent "orientalism" of the original text finds new and powerful media in both the graphic novel and in film; but the message can find its way into media even more esoteric. In 2007, NECA/Reel Games released a board game tie-in to the film, designed by Andrew Parks (with art by Ed Repka). As a war-game, *300* must have been something of a challenge to design; obviously, the Spartan player *can't* win—that's the whole point of the original sacrifice in Herodotus—so what's a designer to do? Parks' solution is fairly ingenious (and also true to the film): while the Persian player generally triumphs by slaughtering Spartans and running out the clock (marked by the traitor Ephialtes' sprint up an attractively stenciled goat path), the Spartans "win" by gaining "glory" points. (One hundred points of glory wins the game, and, one presumes, a beer.) Here, then we see the West fighting for an abstract concept (such glory would be *kleos* in Greek), while the Persians are depicted as particularly sadistic murderers. In each phase, players can play cards that affect the amount of mayhem (and dice-rolling) that turn; the cards generally reflect art and quotations from the film. If anything, however, the metamorphosis of the film into a board game strengthens the divide between the metaphor worlds of East and West. The playing cards for the Spartans generally reflect the sorts of ideals and concepts already outlined: ordinary men standing "shoulder to shoulder" in a democratic (or at least egalitarian) "stand" against tyranny. (Individual cards also allow for synergy among Spartan heroes—the Captain is bolstered by the inspiring proximity of Astinos, for example, and the sterling example of Delios rouses every Spartan warrior in his battle space.) Persian cards, contrariwise, tend to emphasize the Oriental aspects of the Persian horde,

---

[33] Indeed, adaptors of Roman material are generally suspicious of the stated goals of the Bush administration. In David Williamson's Australian adaptation of *Miles Gloriosus* ("The Swaggering Soldier") the character and playwright Plautus discovers he has little chance of obtaining Roman citizenship; in a furious Act One speech, he declares: "The Roman's [*sic*] were so up themselves it was nauseating. And their myths about themselves were nauseating. The Roman Empire brought peace and civilization to the world? The reality? It paid off the elites of its conquered satellites... then used them to help bleed off the wealth of their people [for Rome], where a large part of it went to make the Roman military machine even more formidable so it could bring 'peace' and 'civilization' to even *more* of the world. You might spot some modern parallels, but the Romans perfected the technique" (27). Williamson's adaptation is called *Flatfoot*—and the "modern parallels" are from the play's premiere in 2004.

including the "Persian Wizards" (an aspect of Persian mysticism), the ontologically feral war beasts and "monsters," and the beastly Immortals, whose teeth have been filed into (vampiric?) fangs. (The cards representing Xerxes—"God of Gods"—and his followers—"Army of Slaves"—have obvious political overtones.)

Now, *300* is not the only film to comment on contemporary international politics through classical metaphor. One would think that Oliver Stone's meditation on East–West themes—his big screen biopic of *Alexander (the Great)*—would avoid some of the Orientalism of its pop cultural brethren; this is the same director, after all, who managed to depict both sides of the Vietnam War with great sympathy and profundity in his breakthrough work *Platoon* (1986), and who surely knows how to treat "foreign" cultures with cinematic fluidity, empathy, and tact.[34] But as the Oxford historian Robin Lane Fox inadvertently discloses in his fascinating volume, *The Making of "Alexander"*, the genesis of *Alexander* (2005) was forever skewed by ideological considerations, often flowing from the film's German producer, Thomas Schühly. Lane Fox attached himself to the project largely out of academic considerations; he naturally wanted the battles to be as historically accurate as possible (indeed, he hoped that his involvement might solve some pressing historical questions concerning tactics and mechanics). What Lane Fox didn't know, of course, was that the film was destined to be a critically panned disaster, which makes the breathless prose of *The Making of "Alexander"* read like a particularly delicious exercise in irony.

Lane Fox was lucky—or unlucky—enough to be privy to *Alexander* in even its formative stages, including the correspondence between Stone and Schühly, who regularly quotes Nietzsche with admiration, and who, indeed, would have preferred a bit more Nietzsche in the final cut ("Could we not introduce ... Jews who would refuse to bow down to Alexander... we could add in a couple of Nietzsche-lines?" (35)). Indeed, Schühly even quotes Nietzsche on man's ferocious, double-edged nature: "Perhaps these 'terrible talents' are a fertile soil which give rise to all humanity in our emotions and actions. This is why the Greeks, the most human of all peoples, reflect within their characters a trait of cruelty, of a desire for

---

[34] See Nisbet 2006: 125–33 for a dissection of *Alexander's* numerous cinematic failings ("a straight-faced, heavy-handed, humorousless slog of a film," 130). Nisbet generally skirts the film's ideological biases in favor of a history of Alexander-reception—this *Alexander*, like many other *Alexanders*, goes "Roman" and ends up with a "peace-loving world conqueror" lifted straight out of Virgil's *Aeneid* (134).

destruction, as does the tiger. That trait is visible in the exaggerated, almost grotesque reflection of Greece which is Alexander the Great" (11). But there is much good in Alexander, it seems; as Schühly muses, "Was [Alexander] the first 'politician' who had the idea of integrating the different cultures into one comprehensive whole?" (11). In Schühly's admiring study, Alexander isn't then, as some historians might term him, a monomaniacal imperialist, but the first multiculturalist: he's not conquering, he's *uniting*.[35] Soldiers followed Alexander not because of the quest for "liberty" against the Persians—he is thus unlike Leonidas—but because when they gazed at Alexander, "they looked in the mirror, and saw something about themselves..." (11). Stone's response to Schühly, dated June 11, 1989, attempts to soft-pedal the project's implicit Orientalism—the inevitable clash between West and East—by transforming the screenplay of *Alexander* into a character study: "Brilliant analysis. Enemy as Greeks, not just Persians. Concept of a culture propagated by Alexander against the localization of pure Greek thinking: a brilliant theme for a character study. ..... Ah, yes Thomas: you have created in my eyes at last the true hero. I understand. Bless you ... you are truly a great producer!" (12).

Unfortunately, Nietzschean character studies of classical antiquity remain freighted with some unsettling politico-historical baggage. For instance, in his fascinatingly bizarre sketch of the Roman emperor Commodus, German historian (and Nazi Party supporter) Wilhelm Weber contributed an ideologically loaded essay to the 1936 edition of *The Cambridge Ancient History*, an account now universally derided. (A sample verdict: "Both the style and content of [Weber's] unbalanced contribution ... make one positively cringe."[36]) Whereas most historians would rank Commodus among Rome's least admirable politicians—his principal claims to fame are a fantastic drive for beast-slaughter and a thirst for daily hedonism[37]—

---

[35] Hostile reappraisals of Alexander the so-called Great have a long and glorious history; see Demetriou 2001:31–9 on the nineteenth-century historian George Grote's antipathy to Alexander's excessive orientalism and monomania, distasteful to Grote's own brand of humanistic liberalism.

[36] T. Corey Brennan. Feb. 2, 2001. # 5105. *The Times Literary Supplement*, p. 10. For a brief overview of Nazi approaches to Roman history, see Starr 1960: 150: "Modern history was often sadly corrupted to vicious ends, and the climate of opinion in Nazi Germany was far less inclined to support true research into ancient development than had been that of Imperial Germany...."; Starr further notes that Weber's chapters on Hadrian and the Antonines are tinged by "mystical fuzziness."

[37] For Commodus' considerable skills at dispatching e.g. hippopotami and giraffes, see Dio 73.10; for a thumbnail sketch of the ineffective Commodus, see Wells 1995: 255–6, especially for his unwise delegation of power to subordinates and his failed incursion on the Danube.

Weber's "youth with his fair hair and burning eyes," with a head gleaming "with divine brilliance," instead stood as a prototype of a new man, Nietzsche's *Übermensch*. The concluding page of Weber's mad, rambling biography launches into a flowery prose-poem of admiration for this ruler who could see beyond his current temporal and spatial restraints, but who remained sadly shackled by the small-spirited, inferior beings that surrounded him:

> A Spanish visionary, mystical, handsome, pliant, strong, with spirit now soaring, now sinking, a notable creature, he was in everything extreme, in obedience towards God, in power to take divinity on himself, in wild sensuality, in iron fearlessness, in animal passion . . .. His life was lived beyond the world of reason, compounded of the potencies of the body, of instinct, and of imagination. . .. [The Senate's posthumous condemnation] was not worthy of the dream, for in its waking it was so cowardly, so studious of revenge, so lacking in vision. . .. [Commodus] had grown out of an intellectualism that was breaking down; he guided life by instinct from its heights to its depths, gave to the form of the old world a content of passion and enthusiasm born of a new life and sought an Empire of happiness to be guided by men of devout obeisance to piety and the supernal. Rejected by the old, pioneer for the new, far removed from Hadrian, he was the 'rising sun' of the new world.[38]

This is, of course, pure fiction, but a fiction born of a specific time and place (Germany of 1936) and influenced by contemporary events in that nation; clearly, Commodus is being championed as a fair-haired Aryan superhero who dreams of a transformed world, a visionary "pioneer" in empire-building and leadership: in short, a proto-*Führer*, influenced by Nietzsche's ruminations in *Thus Spake Zarathrustra*.[39] Under Schühly's tutelage, the director Stone crafts a description of Alexander that is eerily similar to Weber's paean to Commodus:

[38] Weber: 1936: 392.
[39] Hindsight isn't necessary; even contemporary readers caught the political gist of Weber's scholarship. In his review of Weber's *Princeps: Studien zur Geschichte des Augustus* (Stuttgart, 1936), the British historian Ronald Syme perceptively notes that Weber's wise and mighty Augustus is nothing less than "a Periclean *Führer*"(*Classical Review* 1937 51: 29). On Nietzsche's *Superman*, see, for instance, the hieratic proclamations in the prologue to Zarathustra: "*I teach you the Superman.* Man is something to be surpassed . . .. The Superman is the meaning of the earth . . .. Verily, a polluted stream is man. One must be a sea, to receive a polluted stream without becoming impure. Lo, I teach you Superman: he is that sea . . .. I am the herald of the lightning, and a heavy drop out of the cloud: the lightning, however, is the Superman." (*Thus Spake Zarathustra*, pp. 8–10, tr. Common 1960).

> The story is beautiful – a heroic young man, a dynamic prince, then a king in his time, who struggled mightily with his two strong parents, succeeded them, and achieved of his dreams on earth. I would say he was the world's greatest idealist and as a result he took the world's greatest fall . . . .. He was clearly a man ahead of his time, or some might say, a new definition of man . . . . He made me believe in heroes.[40]

Stone's adoration dotes on many of the same characteristics as does Weber: the valorization of youth and physical beauty; the emphasis on dreaming and idealism; the implication that Alexander represented a new breed of man. Little is said of what Alexander actually *did*; much is made of what Alexander *represents*, in language largely indistinguishable from a Nietzsche-esque fantasia on antiquity.

As such, Stone's *Alexander* certainly seems right-of-center; premiering about fifteen months after President Bush's troubled invasion of Iraq, the correspondences between Alexander and Bush seemed obvious to many reviewers. (For instance, Ed Gonzalez in *Slate* magazine opines: "this half-cocked, passionately chaotic creation is ostensibly about the titular Macedonian king but doubles as an allegory for both George W. Bush's political career and Stone's own struggle with history."[41]) The film is so riddled by its unintentional campiness, however, that many viewers found it hard to fathom the *point* of the allegory ("At times, the film seems like a George W. Bush apologia, at others a condemnation, but Stone's ambivalence seems more confused than complex…"[42].) It's clear from Stone's comments in *The Making of "Alexander"* that he originally admired Alexander-as-historical-*Übermensch*; but when America's *contemporary Übermensch* unexpectedly re-enacts the events of the screenplay—the invasion of the Middle East—Stone appears to get cold feet. The resulting ill-timed allegory is a mess and Stone only gradually sorts things out in his next two films: *World Trade Center* (2006) and the Bush biopic *W.* (2008). In a sense, the imperialist *Alexander* is the first installment of a George W. Bush trilogy.

Such contemporary receptions to political events can occur with almost alarming alacrity and sophistication. Barry Unsworth's novel *The Songs of the Kings*, published in 2002, indicts American expansionist policies—including those of both Bush administrations—through the use of

[40] Stone's Foreword to Lane Fox (2004) *The Making of "Alexander."*

[41] Ed Gonzales, "Alexander," www.slantmagazine.com/film/review/alexander/1073. Orig. July 6, 2004.

[42] Scott Tobias, "Alexander," www.avclub.com/articles/alexander,4799/. Orig. Nov. 22, 2004.

surprisingly colloquial rhetoric; the novel melds the general plot of Euripides' play *Iphigenia in Aulis* with the tone and slang of modern war films and the modern academy: there is even a sly reference to the hero Palamedes' impressive curriculum vitae (91), always an asset in a global economy. Though less overtly critical of "Orientalism" than, say, the performance troupe Waterwell, *The Songs of the Kings* is even more explicitly damning of American foreign policy, which it argues is ultimately powered by considerations of lucre and capital, not human rights.

In some senses, Unsworth's choice of Euripides' *Iphigenia* as an indictment of modern warmongering is unsurprising: along with *Trojan Women* and *Hecuba*, *Iphigenia* is often interpreted and performed as a metaphor of innocence—and innocents—destroyed by war. Viewed this way, the plot easily supports such an approach. Beached at Aulis en route to Troy, the general Agamemnon discovers that only the sacrifice of his daughter Iphigenia might appease the goddess Artemis and allow the fleet to continue its course. Pressured by the army to do the unthinkable, Agamemnon elevates the demands of the army over the demands of the family, and tricks his daughter into arriving at Aulis under a false pretext: she is to be married to the Greek hero, and heart-throb, Achilles. After various reversals and tears, Iphigenia accepts her fate and yields her neck to the knife. The winds abate. The fleet sails. The war is on.

The filmmaker Michael Cacoyannis famously used the myth to criticize the military junta that ruled Greece from 1967 to 1974, and there's little question regarding Cacoyannis' sympathies or aims: on Cacoyannis' view, the seer Calchas reflects the Greek Orthodox Church's complicity with the extra-constitutional government,[43] and the priest's final capture of the frightened Iphigenia is the stuff of horror films: a ghastly specter of death grasping from the smoke and shadows. But there's a case to be made—and scholars have made it—that Euripides' *Iphigenia* does not in fact condemn war, but, contrariwise, reaffirms the value of self-sacrifice in pursuing the aims of the state, particularly when the fundamentals of Greek culture are at stake.[44] Faced with the possibility of the triumph of "barbarians"—i.e. Trojans—Iphigenia, though a wee girl of perhaps twelve, changes her mind and changes history: her death ensures the victory of civilization over the forces of lawlessness and barbarism.

---

[43] McDonald 2001: 95, "Eye of the Camera." Cacoyannis' *Iphigenia* appeared in 1977.
[44] Michelakis 2006: 75.

By the end of the novel, it is clear that Unsworth rejects any such "pro-war" interpretation of the *Iphigenia*, though merciless wordplay and multiple levels of irony obscure the point until the very last pages. In fact, for the first third of the novel, Unsworth appears to be retelling the Euripidean *Iphigenia* "straight," deviating very little from the *plot* of the original. On the level of *language*, however, Unsworth relentlessly reconfigures *Iphigenia* as a metaphor for the modern military–industrial complex, including the types of social-science discourse that surrounded the American invasion of Kuwait and George W. Bush's coming invasion of Iraq. Odysseus—the villain of the novel, and a master of modern rhetoric—explains that the sacrifice of Iphigenia is necessary because he does not wish for Agamemnon to be "marginalized" after a "demoralizing" experience for the army at Aulis (48–49); thus Iphigenia's undeniably distressing murder is justified by recourse to such modern horrors as marginalization and unit fragmentation. (Sure, murder is terrible—but so is a tepid assessment report.) Through the figure of Odysseus and his minions, Unsworth thus shellacs Euripides' plot with Orwellian Newspeak, that curious vocabulary of the authoritarian state "which had been deliberately constructed for political purposes [and] intended to impose a desirable mental attitude upon the person using them … Words which had once borne a heretical meaning were sometimes retained for the sake of convenience, but only with the undesirable meanings purged out of them. Countless other words such as *honour, justice, morality, internationalism, democracy, science,* and *religion* had simply ceased to exist."[45]

Odysseus, then, has to mask the Oldspeak of "murder" with the Newspeak of the modern American military; he is nothing if not forthcoming about his motives, as he elaborates: "On the one hand there was the desire [in the army] for power and loot, on the other the deliberate killing of an innocent. If you softened the first by mixing in notions of public service, the need for living space and wider markets to serve a growing population, and submerged the second in the heavy burden of command, the problem ceased to exist…" (155). "The killing of an innocent"—i.e. ethically charged Oldspeak—must be refashioned positively as a "public service"—i.e. your caring government in action!—and by the economic imperative to expand into international markets; negative reactions to innocents-killing are subsumed, and neutralized, by appeal to military hierarchy. As Odysseus disarmingly puts it, the solution to Iphigenia's murder is merely "a

---

[45] From "The Principles of Newspeak," in Orwell 1949: 306, 308.

question of substituting terms" (155).[46] Even more succinctly, Odysseus offers us the following *mot* for future politicians: "*Eliminate the contradictions*. They would rule the world who knew this and used it" (156). Complexity is the enemy of foreign policy.[47]

Odysseus' plans to murder Iphigenia are matched in Unsworth's novel by a deep distrust of the intelligentsia, here embodied in the seer Calchas. In Cacoyannis' film version, Calchas was a collusive, power-hungry pawn of the military; here, the philosophical Calchas plays the foil to the pragmatic, morally bankrupt, Odysseus. For Calchas, Odysseus has nothing but contempt: "As I say, he is an intellectual, unable to make himself understood, lost in useless speculation, what's the word I am looking for?" As it turns out, that word is "paralysis" (61): in the face of military rhetoric (especially after 9/11) intellectual discourse remains simply talk. Intellectuals are paralyzed by their own mouth; in fact, Calchas will not even need to be "delegitimized," because "Calchas will delegitimize himself" (60) by stupidly employing Oldspeak: the language of morality and freedom. Indeed, it is Calchas who floats the Thucydidean notion of *pretext* by arguing that the war is never "about" the stories that the bards sing: it is about "gold and copper and cinnabar and jade and slaves and timber" (167).[48] Or, just perhaps, oil.

But Calchas's message of caution never receives an audience. An important aspect of Odysseus' plan to murder Iphigenia involves the manipulation of mass media: in the Bronze Age, mass media are bards. Odysseus' plan is precise and methodical, beginning with the dissemination of small, seemingly inconsequential sound-bites and memes—*à la* the Bush administration's famous run-up to *Weapons of Mass Destruction*—and concluding with military action justified by the same organization that

---

[46] In a review on salon.com (2006), Laura Miller writes of Unsworth's take on "substituting terms": "That view of the motives of warmongers sounds a lot like the contemporary complaint that, despite the high-minded reasons it gives for invading Iraq, the United States is really after oil." www.salon.com/books/feature/2003/04/15/unsworth

[47] It's striking that mid-2000s artists are so drawn to fable and allegory in their analysis of American politics. John Patrick Shanley's 2005 play *Doubt: A Fable* putatively concerns one subject (a priest accused of child molestation) but actually demonstrates the perils of moral certainty in circumstances that admit no such certainty (transparently, the Bush administration's disastrously misguided belief in Iraq's weapons of mass destruction, part of the arsenal of "the axis of evil," 2002.) In similar vein so too does *The Song of the Kings* comment on the woeful simplification of political discourse, the "dumbing-down" of foreign policy into indubitably right or wrong, good or evil.

[48] For the three words for 'cause' in Thucydides—*prophasis*, *aitia*, and *aition*—see Kirkwood 1952: 37–61. Also Pearson 1952 on *prophasis* as an "excuse" or "pretext" rooted in rhetoric, as opposed to evidence.

disseminated the information in the first place. Thus, to a bard singing a "Song of Perseus" to the army—the tale of a hero slaying the Medusa and rescuing Andromeda from a sea-monster—Odysseus self-servingly suggests that it is "a good idea to insert a reference to the wind that detains us here" (67). In terms of narrative, such contrary winds have nothing to do with the myth of Perseus, but everything to do with contemplated military action. The bard protests that the inclusion of the winds makes no sense *artistically*; Odysseus responds: "I didn't come here to talk about art and soul and all that stuff ... I don't care whether you wrap it up in something else or tell it as a separate story, but if you know what is good for you, you'd better make sure this message about the wind goes over loud and clear, with brief repetitions in subsequent sessions to reinforce the point. It must be noised abroad, made common knowledge, disseminated on a large scale – what is the word I'm looking for?" (68). That question is never explicitly answered in the text, but some possibilities include *disinformation*, or *brainwashing*, or *media manipulation*. In fact, Odysseus' subsequent plans for media saturation include two pithy, quasi-political slogans: either WE LOVE ZEUS or ZEUS HATES WITCHES (151). Military action is thus precipitated by piety or prejudice, preferably both. It is clear that Unsworth finds both motives repugnant.

To the extent to which the West's invasion of the East is *not* about money, Odysseus proffers a multiplicity of arguments, including one that's positively Euripidean: it's about the civilizing force of Greece/America itself: "[The Trojans] are kept in ignorance and superstition, they live in the midst of squalor and bad smells, they are unhygienic, they have the wrong gods. Now we could save them from that, we could bring light into their darkness" (208). Here, any number of modern Western stereotypes of the East are foisted onto the Trojans: they are religiously, economically, and hygienically backwards. An invasion could only improve their lot, provided it is accompanied by political transformation as well. The resistant Achilles is wooed with an appeal to his "civic sense" (193) as well as the promise of frequent mentions by bards concerning his "greatness of soul," and "patriotic readiness": in essence, free advertising for Achilles' political ambitions. Another possible objector to the sacrifice of Iphigenia—to wit, Iphigenia—must be, as Odysseus puts it, "incentivized" (225): persuaded to act against her own self-interest, even to the point of self-immolation.[49] It's

---

[49] In the original text, Iphigenia's *volte face*—a surprising reversal—is motivated through appeals to nationalism (*Iph.* 1374–1401); Unsworth's Iphigenia is likewise persuaded to pursue a national good, though with an explicitly Christianized flavor.

a hideous formulation, but suitable to the plot, as Iphigenia is persuaded through rhetoric heavy with Christian symbolism to "save her people," to "take on the burden, discharge the debt, redeem the wrongs of the world" (239). Even Odysseus is impressed by her (*extremely* anachronistic) "Messianic complex." A loyal handmaiden attempts to dissuade Iphigenia, but the girl realizes the power and effect that media manipulation has had on the princess: "You are using their language. They have put their language in your mouth" (243).[50] Though the *plot* has been Greek-through-Euripides, the language is now thoroughly English-through-America.

An unexpected cessation of the winds would seem to be a savior for Iphigenia; but Odysseus worries about the consistency of his message (204) and any subsequent damage to "cost effectiveness" (205). The sacrifice thus proceeds as planned. The last sentence of the novel features Unsworth at his most sardonic; Iphigenia is indeed sacrificed, though her handmaiden slips away, an event immortalized in some versions of the song as a miraculous escape of the princess to Tauris, aided by Artemis. The narrator concludes: "But all this [story] was much later, when sensibilities and habits of thought had changed, and it was no longer considered desirable that such an ugly thing as the sacrifice of the innocent for the sake a prosecuting a war should feature in the songs of the kings" (245). The irony is keen and cutting. The whole point of the novel is that sensibilities and habits of thought *haven't* changed: that modern lingo and contemporary political jargon may be easily—too easily—shoehorned into ancient patterns of ugly human behavior. America is the new Greece, dazzled by misleading media, and eager to follow our kings, and the "songs" of our kings, wherever they may lead.

---

[50] In a sense, Unsworth's take on Euripides' play is a novelistic rumination on Nancy Sorkin Rabinowitz's thesis that every character in the play—especially the female ones—is used as a mouthpiece for a (masculine, warmongering) ideology: "As a result, although (or because) Euripides makes his sacrificial victims seems like agents, he tells us nothing about what they want, only about what men require of them. In fact, we see the fetishization of woman. . ..." (Rabinowitz 1993: 36).

4 | September 11th on the Western stage

Classical texts that directly concern politics—such as *Antigone*—or with the West's clash with the East—such as the *Bacchae*—have always provided tempting fodder for ideologically charged artists, but never more so than after the events of 9/11. For instance, the opening of Tom Kurzanki and David Hopkins' comic version of Sophocles' *Antigone* includes an impressive visual gambit. At first glance, this version seems traditional, even staid (except for, perhaps, the medium): the cover, mostly black, features a blood-soaked, if somewhat generic "Ancient Greece," with a figure—presumably Antigone—wandering among the ruins. The next two pages feature, as a prelude, a composite mash-up of Thebes/Athens, wracked by the strife of the quarreling sons of Oedipus: it's Sophocles' mythical *polis* plunged into civil mayhem. One might expect the next page to properly begin the comic with the first line of the play, Antigone's complaint: "Oh full-blooded sister Ismene, do you know of any evil that Zeus will *not* send to us as we live, evils bequeathed to us from Oedipus?" (*Ant.*, ll. 1–3). The third word of the play—αὐτάδελφον, "full-blooded sister"—neatly reminds the audience that Ismene and Antigone are sisters as well as each other's aunt: the mixed-up family mirrors the mixed-up world of the play. But no, the authors spring a surprise: the comic begins *not* with the first line (or even scene) of Sophocles, but with four selected quotations from the play— all gnomic statements about mortality and fate—superimposed upon four key events in American and world history (see Figure 4.1): the student uprisings at Tiananmen Square (1989); Jack Ruby's murder of Lee Harvey Oswald (1963); the Kent State massacres in Ohio in 1970; and, perhaps most affectingly, the attack on Manhattan's Twin Towers in 2001. Kurzanski and Hopkins thus not only translate the play into comics, but into modernity, as they search for parallels to Athenian political tragedy: they are attempting to locate moments when global political values were challenged by contemporary social forces, including civil strife and terrorism, and thereby make sense of what's at stake in *Antigone*. That's the only way *they* can make sense of the political subtext of the original play.

Though they open with a bravura gesture, Kurzanski and Hopkins shy from making explicit parallels with contemporary politicians. Nobel

Figure 4.1. Opening montage from *Antigone* by Hopkins and Kurzanski.

Prize winner Seamus Heaney explains that his otherwise fairly literal adaptation of Sophocles' *Antigone*, entitled *The Burial at Thebes*, in fact encapsulates the dictatorial bluster of George W. Bush after the invasion of Iraq: it's less an *Antigone*, then, than a *Creon*, or perhaps *The Burial at*

Baghdad.[1] As Heaney elucidates, modernity doesn't just perform the texts of Sophocles, it performs the *pretexts* of Sophocles: "Early in 2003, the situation that pertains in Sophocles' play was being reenacted in our own world. Just as Creon forced the citizens of Thebes into an either/or situation in relation to Antigone, the Bush administration in the White House was using the same tactic to forward its argument for war on Iraq ... Bush was using a similar strategy [to Creon's], asking, in effect: Are you in favour of state security or are you not? If you don't support the eradication of this tyrant in Iraq and the threat he poses to the free world, you are on the wrong side in 'the war on terror'" (76). On Heaney's reading, Creon and Bush similarly divide their citizenry into friends and enemies of the state. The tyrant Creon is a gun-slinging sheriff, a Theban by way of Texas.[2]

The metaphor falters a bit when applied to the text as a whole—is Antigone, then, a cipher for those sympathetic to the attackers of 9/11?— and even Heaney must admit that "Creon ... has a point, and a responsibility" (76); the issue is not Creon's fundamental position, but his fundamental inflexibility, his "passion and extremity," mirrored by Antigone's similar, one-sided faith in religion. In general, Heaney preserves a light touch: for instance, Antigone stresses that she would receive far more support from her fellow citizens except that they are "so afraid to sound unpatriotic" (32); this translation explicitly politicizes Antigone's statement in Sophocles that the citizens would speak "except that fear clasps their tongues" (εἰ μὴ γλῶσσαν ἐγκλῄοι φόβος, *Ant.*, l. 505). Heaney thus makes unmistakable the *specific* fear: fear of being branded unpatriotic (or, as McCarthy once dubbed it, un-American). Throughout the text, Heaney takes advantage of Sophocles' opaque language as opportunities for sharper political jabs: Antigone's opening lament that "evils from our enemies are marching towards our friends" (πρὸς τοὺς φίλους στείχοντα τῶν ἐχθρῶν κακά, *Ant.*, l. 10) becomes "the ones we love ... are enemies of the state" (5). (Though the term "enemy of the state" could theoretically be

---

[1] As Hardwick 2006: 212 elucidates ("Murmurs"), there are actually *two* political impulses for the creation of *The Burial at Thebe* (Heaney 2004a). The first is Eibhlín Dubh Ní Chonaill's eighteenth-century poem "Caoineadh Airt Uí Laoghaire," a woman's lament for an Irishman killed by the English; the second—in a more specifically post-colonial context—is Bush's invasion of Iraq.

[2] Though ambivalent about the success of Heaney's translations of Greek tragedy, Wiles 2005: 23 notes that "Creon speaks a political language that is chillingly recognizable." Michael Billington's review in the *Guardian* (Apr. 7, 2004) argues that the text's parallels with the Bush administration are muddled by an inaugural production that emphasizes instead a "standard-issue, theatricalised tyranny."

applied to citizens of any political situation, it's telling that conservative FOX-TV host Sean Hannity's *Hannity's America* once featured a segment entitled "Enemy of the State." Actor and activist Sean Penn was deemed the first such enemy.[3]) Antigone even makes fun of Creon's Bushlike swagger, mocking his accent as she imitates (what amounts to) a State-of-the-*Polis* address: "'I'll flush'em out," he says. / "Whoever isn't for us / is against us in this case" (7). Though a "new king" (or President), Creon/ Bush, is in fact "right for the city at this moment" (15). Critics—like Creon's son Haemon—charge that Creon/Bush, convinced of his own ethical superiority, becomes agitated by any whispers of dissent from "a poisonous minority" (22): therefore, "people shield" him from criticism (a reference, perhaps, to Bush's notoriously tight-knit political cabinet (43)).

Such metaphors and allusions are deliberate on Heaney's part. On Creon's brutal edict to leave his traitorous son Polyneices unburied, Heaney himself notes that "basically Creon turns Polyneices into a non-person, in much the same way as the first internees in Northern Ireland and the recent prisoners in Guantanamo Bay were turned into non-persons."[4] And yet there is an occasional moderation to Heaney's version. Surprisingly, Heaney keeps intact Antigone's famously problematic assertion that "Not for a husband, not even for a son / would I have broken the law" (54); this declaration tempers Antigone's extremism, and glances at the psychological, rather than political, underpinnings of the central conflict. Elsewhere, however, Antigone argues that she is persecuted "for practicing devotion, / for a reverence that was right" (55), a position that flirts with religious fundamentalism, in which faith is married to ethical certainty. But unlike *The Burial at Thebes'* "real-world" referent, Heaney's Creon experiences a change of heart, as he confesses: "But I am beaten. / Fate has the upper hand" (63). This Theban Bush thus rewrites and re-imagines his own metaphorical referent: America's 43rd President.

If Heaney saves his most intemperate condemnation of the Bush administration for his afterword, fellow Irish poet and playwright Conall Morrison leaves little doubt that his adaptation of the *Bacchae*—the *Bacchae of Baghdad* (2006)—refers explicitly to Bush's invasion of Iraq in 2003.[5]

---

[3] As noted by *Media Matters*, the "Enemy of the State" segment was quickly retitled "Enemy of the Week": apparently the specific accusation of treason was a bridge too far, even for Sean Hannity. See: http://mediamatters.org/research/2007/01/16/hannitys-enemy-of-the-state-now-enemy-of-the-we/137740. Accessed Apr. 18, 2014.

[4] Heaney 2004b: 422.

[5] I thank Jessica Traynor (of Dublin's Abbey Theater) and Conall Morrison for generously sharing the full unpublished script with me via email. Excerpts have been published in Morrison 2009.

Though there is nothing particularly new about transforming Pentheus into a military leader (in this case into George Bush, as America's chief-of-military), Morrison's version explicitly recasts Dionysiac religion as Islamic and fundamentalist. Indeed, the first line of the play is transformed from "I have come to this land of Thebes, the child of Zeus" (ἥκω Διὸς παῖς τήνδε Θηβαίων χθόνα / Διόνυσος) into "There is no god but God ... My father Zeus." Morrison thus translates the first line of the Greek into the language of the Koran (37:35 and 47:19), as he substitutes Zeus for Allah: this is the first of many such provocative transformations in the play. Likewise, Morrison transplants the play from mythical Thebes to an Iraq simultaneously ancient and modern: "come here to this palace, / here by the waters of the Tigris" (1). Unlike Heaney's Thebes, Morrison's *mise en scène* is explicitly Middle Eastern; the seer Tiresias enters, for instance, "dressed in a combination of festive Arabic gear and old military fatigues" (5). (His companion, Cadmus, likewise sports "old army trousers, a loud Hawaiian shirt and Arabic robes" (6).) It's a measure of these characters' incomplete conversions to Islam/Dionysus that American and Arabic garb rest uneasily on these elders' shoulders: the confused visual imagery thus reinforces Cadmus' fateful lack of *sophrosyne*, 'balance.' But if Cadmus and Teiresias are merely confused, Pentheus *aka* George Bush is positively misguided. Sweeping onto the stage amidst his entourage of Secret Service, Pentheus clearly expresses his distaste for Bacchism—it "has no part in the culture of this land"—by summoning a fantasia of torture: "Let me find this man [the priest of Dionysus] inside these walls... / I'll cut his throat and burn his balls! / I will make his dick stick fall / and his long hair lose its lustre" (9). Pentheus' predilection for torture clearly expands upon the Greek original, and gestures towards the abuses at Abu Ghraib in central Baghdad, perpetrated by American soldiers on predominantly Muslim prisoners.[6] In fact, Pentheus even orders the recreation of the most infamous image of American abuse: the leaked photo of a hooded prisoner forced to stand while hooked up to electrical wires. As Pentheus fulminates in wrath: "Go scour this city, every souk and alleyway– / you must bring this man-girl freak to the light of day.... Chain him, hood him, bring him here to me" (14). Dionysus indeed makes his entrance "chained, hooded, and wearing an orange jump-suit" (16): it's Abu Ghraib on the Greek stage. The costume design of Dionysus exactly replicates a leaked image from the

---

[6] Pentheus later continues this charming line of inquiry: he crows that he will "make [Dionysus' followers] wipe my toilet with their tongues" (22).

Figure 4.2. One of the infamous leaked images from Abu Ghraib.

Abu Ghraib scandal: the attack of a dog on a hooded, jump-suit-clad prisoner (see leaked image, Figure 4.2). It's Dionysus as accused terrorist.

As several reviewers noted after the play's premiere at Dublin's Abbey Theatre in 2006, the equivalences between Pentheus and Bush—and between Dionysus and an Islamic cleric—seem compelling on one level, but ultimately founder on *The Bacchae*'s fundamental premise: that Pentheus is in fact defending his homeland from invasion, however ineptly and disastrously. As we've seen in the analysis of the film *300*, the Bush administration's argument that an invasion of Iraq is a *defensive* maneuver —responding to the invasion of New York City and the Pentagon—aligned Iraq and Al-Qaida as foreign intruders on American soil. (The infamous boondoggle over Iraq's purported "weapons of mass destruction" was part and parcel of a larger discourse of American defense.) Contemporary anti-Bush sentiment largely attempted to deconstruct or subvert that argument; to the extent to which *The Bacchae in Baghdad* aims to criticize American foreign policy, it struggles in that it (inadvertently) reinforces the Bush administration's central contention: that Iraq attacked the United States. Pentheus, after all, *is* being invaded by Dionysus and a horde of funda-mentalist women, and it is unclear why Bush is king of Baghdad at all. It would be more consistent for Morrison's argument if Pentheus were tyrant of, say, Manhattan; otherwise, the play posits a world in which homebody Americans are in fact under attack by those who brand them as "infidel unbelievers" (16).

Still, there are pleasures to be found in Morrison's no-holds-barred indictment of American excess and colonialism, as filtered through Greek tragedy. The famous dissolution of Pentheus' Palace—which must have been a *coup de théâtre* even in antiquity—is here transformed into a royal residence of quite another sort: a Burger King. ("Stage direction: *The Bacchae climb and attach the ropes to the neon/fluorescent Burger [King] sign; with a huge effort, they pull it down. It explodes...,*" 25). This victory for the Bacchae—as well as *haute cuisine*—segues to the famous central scene of cross-dressing, as Pentheus/Bush is ensorcelled into a dress; from this point on, the script follows the original play fairly literally, with little overt reference to the American foreign policy decisions that flavor the evening's opening scenes. Still, there are touches: Agave's recognition scene —centered on her son's dismembered head—is accomplished not through Euripides' sky (*Bacch.* 1264) but through a shining panoply of stars (52): a reference, perhaps to America's "Stars'n'Stripes." Dionysus' concluding theophany reinforces the modern religious underpinnings of the adaptation: imperiously, the god commands the helpless Americans to "read the Book, attend the play, learn about hubris" (58). (The book is presumably the Koran, not the Bible.) The Americans did not learn the lesson—that "there is no god but God" (58).

In a foreword to an excerpt separately published, Morrison expands on the insights—and metaphors—of *The Bacchae of Baghdad* to include a whole host of geopolitical disasters: "Demeter is weeping huge tears at the polar caps; Poseidon is lashing water at New Orleans and the Maldives; Antigone is strapping bombs to herself in Palestine and Iraq; Dionysus has come from the east to strike back at an arrogant, incomprehending West."[7] In a sense, this is pantheistic allegory. The Greek gods are here again, appearing as forces beyond our control: global warming, tsunamis, terrorism, cultural collision. The arrogance of the West is a type of impiety towards Demeter, Mother Earth. Of course, the use of Greek tragedy to illuminate the clash of (modern) East and West runs the risk of reinforcing the very stereotypes that an adaptation seeks to illuminate. For instance, Bill T. Jones—a Tony Award winning choreographer and Macarthur Award recipient—explains the choices behind his May 2001 production of *The Bacchae Project*, which, though pre-9/11, uncannily prefigures the post-9/11 production of *The Bacchae of Baghdad*: "The notion of the chorus dressed in chadoor also takes its cue from Euripides' instructions, when they are described as Asian women .... I thought, making a play for a contemporary audience, why couldn't I use an image [i.e. the chadoor] that resonates more with us when you think of that which is Other, foreign, exotic .... And one of the most ... piquant and poignant images in our popular imaginations, I believe, is the image of fundamentalist Islam" (as quoted by Powers, 9–10).[8] As in Morrison's adaptation, Pentheus is a U.S.

---

[7] Morrison 2009: 151, "The Future of Ancient Greek Tragedy."   [8] Powers 2009: 9–10.

soldier befuddled by Islam and the mysteries of the East; such mysterious-ness—symbolized by the Islamic veil, or chadoor—earns the ire of critic Melinda Powers. On her view, Jones, far from exposing or mitigating American military folly, actually anticipates the "orientalist discourse surrounding the U.S. invasion of Afghanistan";[9] thus *The Bacchae Project* inadvertently contributed to the discourse that led to America's subsequent invasion. Bill T. Jones' push to "unveil" the east in his *Bacchae* found a military reflex in the United States' drive to "unveil" Afghanistan in war; his *Bacchae Project* didn't just expose Afghanistan: it ravaged it.

One can understand the attraction of mapping the machinations of the Bush administration on to tragedy, particularly for left-leaning artists: there's more than a bit of wish-fulfillment in seeing a towering figure—a Pentheus or a Creon or a President—tumble into ruin. There is also the inherent and time-tested attractions of Greek tragic structure: Dismemberment! Deoculation! Shattering irony! But what happens if an artist turns classical narrative on its ear, mapping contemporary events not on to kinetic Greek tragedy but contemplative Roman philosophy? The result is Richard Nelson's strange brew of politics and antiquity, *Conversations in Tusculum*, a drama that premiered at the Public Theater in Manhattan in March of 2008.

Like the versions of Greek tragedy by Heaney, Morrison, and Jones, *Conversations* clearly had the Iraq war and the upcoming American presidential election as its subtext; putatively a fantasia on Cicero's retreat from politics in the spring of 45 BCE, *Conversations in Tusculum* allegorizes the figures of Cicero, Brutus, and Cassius as American Democrats longing for the overthrow of Bush-as-Caesar. In this respect, Nelson continues a distinguished tradition of comparing American political figures to Roman ones: George Washington-as-Cincinnatus is a familiar, even comforting trope[10] and Nelson fills out the evening with various allusions to American political crises, including citizens' rights and the war on terror. Though a talky, even static piece, *Conversations in Tusculum* demonstrates how even "fringe" classical texts can function as metaphors for American political upheaval during—perhaps *especially* during—the administration of George W. Bush.

Cicero's *Tusculan Disputations*—or, less grandiloquently, *The Conversations in Tusculum*—would not seem an obvious choice for dramatization.

---

[9] Powers 2009: 15.

[10] See Wills 1984: 20–4 on the similar ways in which the Roman soldier–farmer Cincinnatus and George Washington juggled multiple roles as landowners and statesmen; see Wills 1984: 137–8 on the perils of comparisons to Caesar.

Unlike, say, the Aquila Theater Company's *Iliad: Book One* (2009), which includes the built-in drama of the Great Quarrel between Achilles and Agamemnon, Cicero's original *Disputations* are almost entirely plot-free. Even the title *Disputations* is something of a misnomer: though the disputations mimic the form of a Platonic dialogue in very broad outline, they are mostly soliloquies intoned by M.—presumably shorthand for Marcus Tullius Cicero—with only occasional and meager interjections from the mysteriously named interlocutor, A. (In fact, A. is so colorless that "stooge" is a possible interpretative spin.[11]) In essence, the five books of the *Disputations* form a primer of Greco-Roman philosophy, beginning with the fear of death; continuing through to physical pain, emotional suffering, and the importance of moderation; and concluding with a ringing endorsement of *virtus*, 'virtue,' as the be-all-and-end-all of human happiness. Throughout, Cicero scatters passages and endorsements from various Greek and Roman poets, tied together with his characteristically elegant prose. It makes for fine philosophy, but not particularly riveting drama.

What Nelson attempted to do, then, is to map the *inactivity*, the contemplative staticness, of the *Disputations* onto modern political debate, thereby indicting modern-day American Democrats as thinkers rather than doers.[12] Reviewers of the play were generally unimpressed—"tedious" is a much-bandied epithet—though Ben Brantley's *New York Times* review praised the acting of its high-powered cast, including the formidable Brian Dennehy as Cicero, Aidan Quinn as Brutus, and David Strathairn as his fellow conspirator Cassius.[13] Constructing a drama around stasis, is, of course, nothing new: Beckett's *Waiting for Godot* upends Aristotelian precepts of a beginning/middle/end by presenting an extended episode in which characters simply wait for a plot—*any* plot—to begin. Likewise, Tom Stoppard's *Rosencrantz and Guildenstern Are Dead* (which *Conversations in Tusculum* occasionally resembles) explores the interiority of characters caught "off-stage": accidental interlopers on plots both narrative and political. While Cicero's original *Disputations* includes some knotty philosophical exposition (a typical insight: "Happiness and lust are predicated on the expectation of future good, since lust is kindled and enflamed by the

---

[11] Gildenhard 2007: 22.
[12] Meineck 2008: 180. "In creating an atmosphere of immobility, [Nelson] was trying to tell us something about the political inertia of our own times."
[13] http://theater2.nytimes.com/2008/03/12/theater/reviews/12conv.html?ref=theater. Accessed May 6, 2009.

expectation of what seems good, while happiness is borne aloft by the possession of a coveted object," 4.6.13), Nelson tends to keep Cicero's philosophical ruminations to a minimum. (Nevertheless, some Ciceronian language bubbles through into the modern play, sometimes in the form of a letter: "Grief is not a condition of the senses, but of the soul. And the physician need put away his tools before administering to such a patient," 27).

Conversations really only gains traction as it draws ever-increasing parallels between George W. Bush and the megalomaniac Julius Caesar; in fact, Caesar's storied history of drinking provoked a knowing laughter at the performance I attended, apparently in recognition of Bush's battles with alcohol (83). One important leitmotif of the play is the apparent *necessity* of a Caesar/Bush: he's the last line of defense against the barbarism of the (Middle) East. As Cassius explains, the ill-treatment of Crassus by the Syrians—in which the general's decapitated head is used as a sort of hand puppet—"was the first real hint that these 'people' weren't just out to kill us, defeat an army, but—to show contempt and hatred for a whole civilization" (64–65), a reflection, one might say, of Al-Qaida in the wake of 9/11. Cassius continues with a famous episode preserved in Suetonius' *Life of Caesar* and Plutarch's *Life of Crassus* 33.2–4: "Crassus was butchered in sight of us ... and his head, after feeding his brains to the dogs, it's been reported, was sent to a local theater performance where it was used to publicly drink from and piss in" (65). Plutarch's account, however, focuses only on the strange metatheatrical resonances of Crassus' head being used in a scene from *The Bacchae*; Nelson exaggerates the grotesque elements of the beheading in order to stress the savagery of the punishment: the East gruesomely defiling the West. As Cassius sorrowfully concludes: "no matter how disgusted or angry or personally hurt I become—it always comes back to: if we lose Caesar—do we lose everything else?" (65). Caesar's other front—a war against "barbarism" in Spain (62)—likewise becomes a touchstone for political considerations, as Brutus elucidates: "The war in Spain has gone well for 'us.' 'Them.' They have no one else to fight. 'We've' won. And so without a war, perhaps Caesar will—" Cicero glumly interjects: "He won't" (32).

Nelson's play thus piles upon Caesar an overdetermination of modern political subtexts: it's the mighty Roman leader versus the savage East, with Caesar/Bush as the sole bulwark against brutality and barbarity. Of course, the price for obeying such a leader is the diminution of personal liberty, a theme that Cicero, Brutus, and Cassius explore almost endlessly in *Conversations*. In the play's second scene, for instance, we discover that Brutus has written a small playlet in which Cato the Younger, defender of the traditional Roman republic and a foe of Caesar in the civil wars, chooses to kill himself rather than live under Caesarian rule (a true story, as recorded in Plutarch's *Life of Cato* 70). Thus Nelson's "Cato" declaims: "It is Caesar that ought to be looked upon/ as one surprised and vanquished, / for he is now convicted and found guilty/ of those designs against my country" (25). In Cato's world-view, the consolidation of executive power into one leader indicts that leader of treason: the enemy is not the East, but *us*. Cato cannot abide such a world, and so kills (even better, *disembowels*) himself: a possible avenue of escape for every character in the play. And, perhaps, every American in 2008.

Conversations in Tusculum thus presents three political choices for the trio stuck at Tusculum: to remain as "slaves" to Caesar (albeit generally docile, self-sufficient slaves); to kill themselves flamboyantly *à la* Cato (as Cicero admits, "I've held a knife to my throat as least five times these past few months," 40); or—perhaps, most daringly—to fight back. At first, the definition of fighting back is, at best, modest: Brutus' marriage to Cato's daughter, Porcia, for instance, is figured as an act of political confrontation:

CASSIUS: Caesar couldn't help but see that as a slap in his face. [Brutus] did
    something.
BRUTUS: (over the end of this, to Cicero): What did I do?!! What did I do?!! What
    can we do?!
CASSIUS: (shouting at the same time, to Cicero): He did something!!! He did
    something!!! (29)

Nelson's exuberant punctuation emphasizes the excitement of Cassius at the same time as it ironically underscores just how pathetic Brutus' acts of resistance actually are: though politically intriguing, wedding bells aren't exactly cloaks'n'daggers. Later, Brutus explores the possible "action" of political compromise: "Two days ago I wanted to kill him …. I think I was wrong. He's an old man, Cassius… We can have a significant influence. We can do something" (62). For Brutus, "influence"—or shall we term it lobbying?—is a possible avenue towards political rapprochement, and both Cassius and Brutus are later tricked by Caesar into becoming cogs in his bureaucratic machinery, the one as "Chief Administrator of all of Rome," the other as chief administrator for Central Rome (86–87). In other words, they have been absorbed into a Bush-style, Harvard Business School cabinet, along the same lines as Colin Powell and Condoleezza Rice, Bush's twin Secretaries of State. In the meantime, Caesar/Bush continues his imperial machinations, just "looking for an excuse" (89) to invade Syria; or, as Cassius paraphrases, "War, he says—it's best for Rome. We need a war—to keep us focused" (90). Brutus is yet more succinct: "Perpetual war—that is his philosophy" (90).

Things come to a head when an off-stage Caesar compares his pragmatic philosophy—a philosophy of doing—with his apparent condescension towards thinking: "'You people,' he says, 'The problem with you people is you think too much. You think about it this way, then that way—until you don't know which way... Argue with a man for five hours, or take five seconds and slice through his left nostril—which gets the man's attention better?... People like our friend Cicero—they sit in comfort and complain. They sit on their hills in Tusculum and have—conversations. But they are in comfort—because of men like me... I know that there are those out there who wish to kill us. And so we must never stop—trying to kill them" (93–94). Several stereotypes of George W. Bush are apparent here: his Texas-bred braggadocio and "swagger" (an idea actually propagated in his own Republican acceptance speech of September 2004)[14]; Bush's perceived anti-intellectualism (when Tucker Carlson interviewed Bush for the September 1999 issue of *Talk* magazine, he asked the Texas governor to name his weaknesses. Bush replied, "Sitting down and reading a 500-page book on public policy or philosophy or something");[15] and Bush's transparent warmongering, a theme apparent throughout his post-9/11 administration. As reviewers of Nelson's play noted, it was impossible *not* to think of Caesar as Bush at the play's climax; one reviewer goes so far to as to label Nelson's "Caesar-Bush bashing" as simply "unbearable."[16] The heavy-handedness of the metaphor also backs the playwright into a corner, so to speak: the logical extension of the metaphor of Caesar-as-Bush is, ineluctably, Bush-as-perforated-leader. Surely Nelson wouldn't go so far?

Fortunately, metaphor is a more malleable medium than a political manifesto, and *Conversations in Tusculum*'s last scene explores theater itself as the conduit of covert discourse, or, as Brutus puts it, "You can

---

[14] "Some folks look at me and see a certain swagger, which in Texas is called 'walking.'" Sept. 2, 2004. Transcribed at the Washington Post online at www.washingtonpost.com/wp-dyn/articles/A57466-2004Sep2.html

[15] See, for instance, Michael Hirsch's ecstatic declaration that with President Obama in the White House, "Brains are Back!": an implicit rebuke to George W. Bush's "politics of ideological rigidity, religious zealotry and anti-intellectualism." www.newsweek.com/id/168032. Orig. Nov. 7, 2008. Also, Colleen J. Shogan 2007, "Anti-Intellectualism in the Modern Presidency: A Republican Populism." The quote concerning Tucker Carlson's interview is from a revealing footnote (#34).

[16] Leonard Jacobs, for Backstage Online. March 11, 2008. www.backstage.com/bso/news_reviews/other_news/article_display.jsp?vnu_content_id=1003723424&inp=true

say things in a play that—you can't or dare not say in life" (98). In the
play's final act, then, Brutus scripts a playlet for the actor Syrus in which
both Nelson *and* Brutus blur the lines between metaphor and reality. Syrus
begins this playlet with a short preamble by Prologue, a character
borrowed from traditional Roman comedy, especially from Terence:[17]
"Along the gentle hills of a town, one much like this one, Tusculum. But
of course it's not Tusculum but has another name" (101). There are
multiple levels of irony and metaphor here: Prologue is insisting that the
playlet's *mise en scène* of a Tusculum-esque locale is not Tusculum—but in
fact, it couldn't be more like Tusculum. It *is* Tusculum. The playlet thus
reaffirms its "real-world" referent even as it coyly (and disingenuously)
denies that reality. Next, Syrus dons a mask: a mask that bears "some
resemblance, maybe hair color or hairstyle or eyes—to Brutus himself"
(96). Brutus has thus obliquely written himself into his own play, allowing
him to "say things" that he dare not utter in real life. This pseudo-Brutus
next orates the final lines of the play: "He who takes away our country. Our
Republic. Pits us against ourselves. He who takes away our freedoms and
our rights. He who takes away our pride in ourselves and in each other,
takes away our moral purposes and resolve. He who corrupts what we
cherish. Who divides us to conquer, who attempts to crown himself and
his family 'name.' He—must die." (101–102).

The play concludes with a bravura moment of metafictionality. Brutus-
as-"Brutus" calls for Caesar's assassination—a moment, finally, of action!!!
—but it's a moment occluded by the fictionality of the playlet: this is all
make-believe. But it's also a hermeneutical life-preserver for Nelson, who, by
creating Brutus-as-playwright, has, in addition, metaphorically written *himself* into the play: Brutus-as-Nelson, theatrical *provocateur*, calling for political action through the medium of drama. Obviously, Nelson wasn't calling
for presidential assassination (or so I trust), but he *was* calling for the
deposition of Bush and heirs to his "name," including the contemporary
(to 2008) slate of Republican presidential candidates. By constructing Caesar
as the destroyer of a Republic (rather than the savior of it), Nelson (fairly or
unfairly) channels contemporary liberal frustration with George W. Bush
into ancient form, thus continuing a decades-long fascination with the
possible metaphorical antecedents of America's Republic (and Republicans).

A glance at classical drama's production history over the past thirty
years reveals that certain plays possess obvious possibilities for

---

[17] See Duckworth 1994: 211–18.

contemporary political commentary, particularly plays that touch upon the friction of the East–West divide.[18] On some views, even ancient plays that would seem to include a strong pacifist element—Euripides' wrenching threnody *The Trojan Women*, for instance—aren't calls for peace at all: they only articulate, in complex and lyrical form, William Tecumseh Sherman's more pithy dictum that "War is hell." For ammunition in the debate, scholars have turned to even more peripheral plays—like Euripides' Trojan War fantasia *Helen*—as they join the scrum. Modern interpretations of this particular play couldn't be more antithetical: in response to mid-century pacifist readings of the play, commentator A. M. Dale tartly dismissed scholars who would interpret the play as a "romance-coated anti-war manifesto";[19] this was met with the provocative counterblast of Erich Segal, who claimed that ". . . the *Helen* is a far more vehement anti-war statement than *The Trojan Women*."[20] (Ironically, these are, as they say, fighting words.) In the most recent volley, William Allan generally follows a Dale-esque line of interpretation: "The various anachronisms at the heart of 'anti-war' interpretations of *Helen* have their roots in equally inappropriate models of what fifth-century Attic tragedy is doing and what it is for."[21]

But what *is* the *Helen* for? And how do modern artists capitalize on the *Helen's* ideological slipperiness? Certainly, all great texts can—and should —support multiple interpretations, but few can support such *diametrically opposed* interpretations. In part, it's because *Helen* famously defies categories; formally a "tragedy," it begs the question of what is *essentially* tragic. As a plot, *Helen* takes its cue from the famous recantation of the poet Stesichorus, preserved in Plato's (much later) *Phaedrus* (243a): "That story was not true; you [=Helen] never sailed in the well-oared ships; you never went to the city of Troy."[22] Instead, a phantom Helen, an *eidolon*, journeyed to Troy with the eloping prince Paris, while the real Helen languished in Egypt, in thrall to (but not enthralled by) the domineering Egyptian king, Theoclymenus. In Euripides' version, King Menelaus— Helen's husband—has succeeded in rescuing the illusory (but apparently convincing) Helen from Troy, but has crashed in Egypt en route to Sparta. In Egypt, he meets the real Helen (in a delightful scene of mutual

---

[18] Among Euripides' plays, Walton 2009: 81 singles out *Rhesus, Trojan Women, Suppliants,* and *Iphigenia in Aulis*.

[19] Dale 1967: ix.

[20] Erich Segal 1983: 248n8. For a structural reading of *Helen*—as a play that fitfully glues together binary opposites—see C. P. Segal 1969, "The Two Worlds of Euripides' *Helen*."

[21] Allan 2008: 5.

[22] Stesichorus' blindness—for blasphemy against Helen—is recorded in Isocrates, *Helen* 64.

befuddlement, ll. 557ff.) and together they concoct an escape from the fantasy world of the play into the "real" world of the *Iliad* and *Odyssey*. Theoclymenus is himself thwarted by a devious fiction—Menelaus "plays dead"—and grants Helen the use of ships for Menelaus' "burial"; the wily Greeks use the ships instead for an escape, and are rewarded with a swashbuckling messenger speech straight out of a good pirate movie, as they ambush the unsuspecting Egyptians:

> The son of Atreus (=Menelaus) shouted out to his allies: "Why do you delay, choicest of the Greeks, in slaughtering and killing the barbarians (*barbaroi*), and dumping them from the ship to the sea?" ... Everybody sprang into action—the barbarians with ship's oars in their hands, the Greeks with swords. The ship positively ran with blood. And even Helen encouraged from the prow: "Where is the glory (*kleos*) from Troy? Display it now towards these barbarians! (*barbaroi*)." (1592–1604)

This is exciting stuff: deception, slaughter, barbarians. From this passage, at least, it would seem *Helen* in fact reifies the East–West divide that we've seen in other ancient works, and in other modern receptions: the ineluctable victory of the West over the cruel and barbarous East. Triumphant Queen Helen and King Menelaus literally ride off into the sunset, while the wicked Theoclymenus reconciles himself to loss.

How, then, can *Helen* be interpreted as a vehement anti-war statement? For many, the clue lies in the unreal—even surreal—nature of Menelaus' predicament: he has just fought an entire war—at the cost of countless lives —for literally nothing. There was no Helen, and thus no point. It's an irony not lost on an old Greek servant, one of the many marginalized characters in Greek tragedy who nevertheless provide an alterative view of the "reality" of the heroic world: "What are you saying? Did we vainly suffer all this toil (*ponos*) just for a shadow (*nepheles*)?" (706–707).[23] It's a concern echoed by a chorus of captured Greek women, even on the level of word choice; they too ruminate over the struggles engendered by Troy: "I sing of the woeful struggles (*ponoi*) of Helen and the sorrowful struggles (*ponoi*) of the women of Troy, forced to the spear... Many Greek men breathed their last, by spear or by sling, embracing then the underworld of Hades; their wives, in sorrow, crop close their hair; and the bedchambers

---

[23] Again, a tart dismissal from Dale (1967: xvi): "But it is surely hardly justified to claim as critics sometimes do that the *Helen* gains in profundity, or qualifies as 'tragic' (in our sense), because it concerns the interplay of illusion and reality. This is to allow oneself to be mesmerized by abstract nouns ... [T]here is no metaphysical or psychological depth here." This last phrase sounds rather like a police officer moving things along at the scene of an auto wreck.

lie widowed" (1113–1116; 1122–1125). The chorus, though of Greek women, in fact blurs the distinctions between friend and barbarian: whether Greek or Trojan, women are left desolate by war. The ode concludes with the play's most straightforward indictment of the folly of belligerence: "How brainless are those who seek excellence in battle, with the mighty spear: they stupidly end their troubles (*ponoi*) by dying. If every quarrel is to be settled by blood, never will *Eris* ('Strife') leave the cities of men" (1151–1157).

So there are certainly seeds of an anti-war interpretation within the *Helen*, even as the "tragedy" itself concludes with an (ironically?) rollicking battle at sea. And it's to such seeds that Ellen McLaughlin—the original Angel in Tony Kushner's *Angels in America*—finds herself drawn, in contradistinction to at least one prevailing strain of Anglo-American scholarship. As her friend and admirer Kushner puts it, McLaughlin is a quintessentially "political playwright," one who rejects "docudrama" and who instead composes plays out of the belief that "writing [a play] will make an actual difference, for the better, in this terribly troubled world, or, rather... in the hope that it will...." (vii). McLaughlin is thus attracted to the Greeks because—again in Kushner's words—their plays "were written by war veterans for war veterans" (x) and so appeal to McLaughlin's sense of urgency and social import: these aren't just plays, they're wartime documents. McLaughlin's introduction to the *Helen* (2003/2005) clearly shows her allegiance to the "anti-war" interpretation of the *Helen* and, even more, to the *Helen's* capacity to provoke specific changes in wartime policy. McLaughlin notes that the original performance took place shortly after the Athenians' disastrous expedition to Sicily, an attack made under illusory (indeed, delusional) pretenses: a phantom menace. (In this respect, McLaughlin clearly sides with scholars who see in the original play *specific* references to Athenian military policy.) But McLaughlin also draws parallels to contemporary— to 2005—American military policy: "To find that a ghastly war was fought under false pretenses makes the war almost unthinkably obscene—a truth Americans are all too familiar with at this moment in our history. Consequently, this play becomes one of the greatest, if strangest, antiwar plays ever written, and it continues to disturb centuries later" (124). Though McLaughlin doesn't mention the Bush administration's famously touted Weapons of Mass Destruction (WMD) in Iraq, she doesn't need to: Secretary of State Colin Powell's address on February 5, 2003 to the United Nations made clear that such weapons were a principal motivation for an American invasion: "Indeed, the facts and Iraq's behavior show that Saddam Hussein and his regime are concealing their efforts to produce more weapons of mass destruction."[24]

Though originally produced in April 2002, the text of *Helen* means *differently* after its publication in 2005—and after America discovers that the pretext for its own, recent war was, like Helen's shadow, an illusion. Though Euripides' text principally refracts such disillusion through its marginalized characters, McLaughlin substitutes a more startling transformation: the general *himself* realizes the awfulness of the error. The end of the play thus concludes with a wrenching exchange between the real Helen and real Menelaus:

MENELAUS: CAN'T YOU GET IT THROUGH YOUR HEAD WHAT
    HAPPENED? A generation of men threw down their lives in that hellhole for
    the sake of you. My god, the dead. They rise up in terrible armies every night
    in my dreams... IF YOU WEREN'T THERE, THEY DIED FOR
    NOTHING....
HELEN: THEY DIED FOR NOTHING. IT'S THE TRUTH.

(*Menelaus is in agony.*)

MENELAUS: It's unbearable. All those boys. I must have written ten thousand
    letters. Ten thousand reorderings of the same tepid lies: "He left his world
    shining in the wake of his glory," not "Your son died as he was trying to stuff
    his entrails back into his belly." Or, "He gave up his body with characteristic
    nobility of spirit," not "His head was shattered like a pumpkin under his own
    wheels." All for some schmuck of a husband whose whore of a wife threw her
    dress up over her head for a houseguest.
HELEN: But that didn't happen.
MENELAUS: What does it matter when everything else did?

(*Pause.*)

HELEN: Take me home. (pp. 186–187)

Like Harold Pinter, McLaughlin is a master of the *pause*: all the futility of wars past and present, Trojan and Iraqi, compressed into a single nothingness. As Menelaus and Helen quit the stage—and soon, the play—McLaughlin's servant states even more baldly the famous line from the Euripidean original: "A war fought for nothing and costing everything" (189).

A later broadcast of a more straightforward version of Euripides' *Helen* on BBC Radio 3 likewise advertises itself as a contemporary piece: "[This

---

[24] The *Guardian*. www.guardian.co.uk/world/2003/feb/05/iraq.usa. Accessed Feb. 24, 2011.

is] Don Taylor's translation of the savage tragicomedy by Euripides about a war in the Middle East fought for the flimsiest of reasons. . ... This story of a war in the Middle East fought over dubious claims now has contemporary resonance."[25] Taylor's version originally dates from 1990 but was subsequently adapted/directed for radio by Ellen Dryden in 2011. For the broadcast, Dryden reads out brief excerpts from Taylor's introduction, concerning the play's probable effect on its original, war-weary Athenian audience. She continues then in her *own* words: "And for a modern audience? Well, a viciously destructive war in the Middle East, fought on a false premise, the bodies coming home, so much public and private grief, and anger. *Helen* ends with hope and with reconciliation. So let's forget Greek tragedy for a moment, and enjoy the rich comedy, the irony, the bitterness, and the poetry of this marvellous work." There's some deft doublespeak, here: on the one hand, the BBC—and Dryden—is *explicitly* describing the play as a metaphor for the Allies' invasion of the Middle East, at least partially brought about by the illusory Weapons of Mass Destruction. It's a tendentious statement. On the other hand, Dryden uses the fairy-tale ending of the *Helen*—everything wrapped up neatly with a bow—as an escape from contemporary partisanship: yes, the play can be read as a metaphor for a colossal multinational military blunder, but also as a blueprint for healing and hope, if only we "forget" the tragedy and focus on the comedy. (Responses on the online forum for BBC radio exhibit mixed feelings about the radio production as a whole; for instance, "Russ" opines: "I tend to think [it doesn't have contemporary resonance], although the BBC blurb might like us to think so, presumably on the grounds that the play's portrayal of the entire Trojan War being waged over a silly mistaken premise ... makes it equivalent to the now infamous absence of Saddam's weapons of mass destruction."[26] Others were fascinated by the play's weird mix of the campy and the tragic.)

The adaptations of McLaughlin and Taylor, though composed before the WMD-fiasco, took on new and unexpected resonances *after* the policy disaster: contemporary events *forced* a re-interpretation of the text, whatever the impulses or intentions of the modern author. A particularly spectacular example of compulsory re-interpretation took place immediately after the events of 9/11 and demonstrates how social and political context can—indeed, must—affect the "meaning" of particular piece of art,

---

[25] www.bbc.co.uk/programmes/b00yy948
[26] www.for3.org/forums/showthread.php?1410-Do3-Euripides-Helen&s=403e6c80c1ff467d0b7965b9dd48fd7d

regardless even of an author's (or adapter's) original intent.[27] (The episode thus gives further point to Martindale's assertion that meaning is constituted at the point of reception, not origination, as we saw in the introduction.) Mary Zimmerman's theatrical adaptation of Ovid's epic *Metamorphoses* had a "proto-version" workshop in 1996 and a Chicago premiere in 1998; its genesis was therefore in the pre-2001 days of the second Clinton adminis-tration.[28] For Zimmerman, adapting the myriad tales of the *Metamorphoses* into one play was, in some aspects, a fool's errand: after all, Handel created an entire opera just from the *Acis and Galatea* episode of book 13, and Ovid has several dozen more myths intertwined throughout his fifteen books. Often envisioned as a sort of anti-*Aeneid*—a literally flesh-and-blood jour-ney through war and adversity—the heroic protagonist of Ovid's *Meta-morphoses* isn't flesh at all, but the abstract idea of change itself: change perpetrated by and to the gods and humans of Ovid's fluctuating, frequently dystopic world. Zimmerman's selection of about nine tales from Ovid, therefore, represented—even at the most mechanical level of editing—a "reading" of Ovid: in her case, a reading of Ovid that focused more generally on tales of love and desire than on rape and carnage (or on teleology or vegetarianism—two possible, if rather more *outré*, choices). It is this version of the *Metamorphoses* that was planned for an off-Broadway run in the fateful month of September, 2001.

Obviously, the timing could not have been worse; as Zimmerman elucidated in a later interview with Bill Moyers on PBS, the show entered technical rehearsals just two days after the attacks in New York City, and opened on October 9th. As Zimmerman herself explains, the dramatically altered landscape of New York unexpectedly, and irrevocably, altered the *meaning* of the play:

MOYERS: This play was in rehearsals during the World Trade Center attack.
ZIMMERMAN: Yes, it was. We were in rehearsal September 11th and we went into
     technical rehearsals on the 13th. And you know, it felt sort of strange going in

---

[27] A striking example in contemporary music is offered by Laurie Anderson's provocative revival of her 1981 song "O Superman" the evening of 9/11 in Chicago, followed by a concert in New York: "The show was one week after 9/11, and as I sang, 'Here come the planes / They're American planes,' I suddenly realized I was singing about the present." Further verses chillingly ask: "They're American planes. Made in America. Smoking or non-smoking?" See a review of Anderson's work (and album *Big Science*) by Joshua Klein: http://pitchfork.com/reviews/albums/10455-big-science/. Accessed Feb. 2, 2012. Clearly, the verses have an entirely new (and political) resonance in their post-9/11 context.

[28] Farrell 2002. Farrell offers a positive assessment of the production, with a focus on the play's editing of the text into a type of new, moralizing Ovid.

to rehearse a play at that time, but on the other hand, the play suddenly had all of these very profound resonances.[29]

It's Zimmerman's use of *suddenly* that merits attention: the terrorist attacks created meaning—or, perhaps, *metamorphosed* meaning—in Zimmerman's splicing of Ovid's text. Much of Zimmerman's (celebrated) staging took place around a pool: Zimmerman wisely focused on a potent Ovidian literary symbol—the fountain or spring—as a unifying device. This meant that in addition to some of Ovid's "greatest hits"—such as the curse of Midas' touch (cured by water), or Orpheus' descent past the river Styx—Zimmerman also included lesser-known tales, such the affecting fable of Alcyone and Ceyx, in which water (the ocean) features prominently. As so often in Ovid, water here accomplishes its metamorphoses through dissolution and destruction; yet, as Segal notes, in the tale of Ceyx and Alcyone, the sea, though unsurprisingly dangerous, is also "potentially kindly."[30] (We will see both aspects of this symbol in the story.)

In Ovid's original tale, the tale is—like many in the *Metamorphoses*—aetiological: it explains the origins of the mythical halcyon bird. King Ceyx, happily married to Alcyone, must travel to an oracle; he chooses to travel by sea. Alcyone has premonitions of disaster and begs Ceyx not to brave the fickle waters, but Ceyx is resolute: he promises that if the fates should allow it (*si me modo fata remittant*, 11.452), he will soon return. Clearly, these are platitudinous words, meant as solace for an over-anxious wife: he cannot know how pregnant with meaning they really are. The voyage meets with disaster; a mighty storm overwhelms the crew. The tempest is so terrible that Ceyx doesn't even know where to look as he yells out the name of Alcyone: he can't tell the direction of either his homeland or his home (11.547). Ceyx drowns; his unknowing wife prays daily to the gods for his return; Juno at last sends Morpheus, god of sleep, to Alcyone in a dream, in the guise of her dead husband. Alcyone wakes, despondent and disconsolate; she rushes to the shore, only to find her husband's lifeless body bobbing towards the sand. ("Thus you return to me (*redis*)?" she laments (11.718)—her husband's promise is thus kept, though grisly in effect.) As Alcyone races towards the corpse, she is transformed into the halcyon bird; in pity, the gods likewise transform

---

[29] Interview with Bill Moyers, March 22, 2002. www.pbs.org/now/transcript/transcript_zimmerman.html

[30] C. P. Segal 1969: 33.

her husband, and the two remain devoted to each other, as a pair of halcyon birds in their halcyon days.[31]

As Elaine Fantham has noted, this is, within the wider context of Ovid's *Metamorphoses*, an unusual myth: a "tender love-story" narrated with "special sensitivity," and devoid of the baser human motives that so often appear in the epic.[32] Indeed, the episode's poignancy *depends* on the innocence of the lovers: unlike any other tale in Ovid, the death isn't caused by betrayal or treachery or malice. It's narratively non-necessary; it's arbitrary; it's natural. It's thus *realistic*. Brooks Otis traces the literary history of such epic storms, and remarks that unlike the famous episodes in the *Aeneid* and the *Odyssey*—tempests whipped up by an elaborately contrived divine machinery—this particular storm has no apparent reason for being.[33] From the point of view of the bereaved, and even the gods, the death of Ceyx is entirely pointless; it furthers no perceptible goal. Ceyx is alive, and then he isn't; and his body is nowhere to be found.

In retrospect, it is unsurprising that this episode, above all, resonated with a post-9/11 Manhattan. In a city inundated with debris and ash—with bodies missing, and missing still—the narrative of a lost corpse, and of a grieving widow, hit local theater audiences hard. Indeed, Zimmerman was worried that the play's narrative would find *too* contemporary, and painful, a resonance: "There are at least two stories in the play where someone goes away, off to work basically, and is suddenly taken from the earth — just destroyed. And I remember on our first public performance, which was [September] 18th, just sort of shaking and trembling off stage about showing this and dragging the audience through this story, including the dying prayer of a man saying, I only pray my body is found. Just let my body be found."[34] The impact of the piece is enhanced by Zimmerman's spare, poetic adaptation; when Ceyx goes under the waves, he states only, "Alcyone, my treasure, Alcyone." To which a narrator adds: "And this is the end of the world" (24)—a line now eerily prescient. Alcyone's final reunion with Ceyx takes place in the stage's pool, with Ovid's all-important water as *antidote* not only to the textual world of disaster but the extra-textual world of Ground Zero, with its ubiquitous dust and detritus. Critic

---

[31] The mythical halcyon bird was regularly associated with the kingfisher in antiquity; Gresseth 1964: 93–5 argues that the origin of the halcyon myth revolved around the possibilities of birth and rebirth (like a Phoenix), and that later mythographers later romanticized the myth as a fable of marital devotion.

[32] Fantham 1979: 330.   [33] See n. 29 above.   [34] Otis 1970: 233.

Ben Brantley's review in the *New York Times*—significantly and almost prosaically entitled "How Ovid Helps Deal with Loss and Suffering"—focuses most particularly on Zimmerman's staging of anguish: "[T]he final glimpse of a loved face, the moment that swallows a life. ... In another context, it might have registered as too precious, perhaps, too arts-and-crafts for Eastern urbanites. But for now it is speaking with a dreamlike hush directly to New Yorkers' souls."[35]

Indeed, preview audiences apparently dissolved into tears—adding water to water—as Ground Zero remained a terrible reminder of the reality of the devastation, just some blocks south of the theater.[36] As an entirely unintentional metaphor for 9/11, then, Zimmerman's *Metamorphoses*—especially its episode of *Ceyx and Alcyone*—"reads" the attacks less through the lens of Orientalism (as we have seen, a common response), and more specifically through the lens of shared, communal grief: a tragedy in a profound and suitably classical sense. The text's emphasis on *senselessness* resonated with New Yorkers' own sense of incomprehension: a disaster with no easily apprehensible cause. There is nothing accidental, however, about Craig Lucas' post-9/11 play *Small Tragedy*, which, in the first of its many ironies, refers explicitly to the recent Great Tragedies in American history. If Zimmerman's "classical" play became a post-9/11 reception by terrible luck, Lucas' play takes no chances as it combines a sweeping exploration of American politics with the granddaddy—so to speak—of all tragedy: *Oedipus Tyrannus*.

Sophocles' original *Oedipus the Tyrant* was, of course, a political play, as its name might indicate. For many of the ancient city–states of Greece, the term *tyrant* was morally ambiguous, a signifier of an autocratic political position that may be used for good or ill. In a specifically Athenian context, however, the term took on decidedly sinister connotations: tyranny was despicable to the radical democracy of Athens, which cherished the tyrannicides Harmodius and Aristogeiton as rescuers of the Attic *polis*, and which indeed honored them with nothing less than hero cult.[37] In contradistinction to a *basileus*, 'king,' a *tyrannos* sought and gained power through extra-constitutional or non-hereditary means, frequently through violence[38]; thus

---

[35] Brantley, Ben. "How Ovid Helps Deal with Loss and Suffering." www.nytimes.com/2001/10/10/theater/theater-review-how-ovid-helps-deal-with-loss-and-suffering.html. Oct. 10, 2001.

[36] See Garwood 2003.   [37] Podlecki 1966: 129.

[38] For the classic formulation, see Knox 1957: 57: "For the word [*tyrannos*] meant more to the fifth-century audience than a usurper who replaced the hereditary king: the *tyrannos* was an adventurer who, however brilliant and prosperous his régime, had gained power by violence and maintained it by violence."

the incorporation of *tyrannos* into the title of the play—as opposed to something neutral like *Oedipus the Ombudsman*—signals a text that concerns, at some level, the nasty intersection of power and politics. Indeed, one of the most famous lines of the play—"hubris breeds the *tyrannos*" (873)—reads like a primer on the proper institution of government. Maladministration is its own punishment.

The contemporary fascination with the *psychology* of Oedipus has spawned both deeply political and, paradoxically, deeply *a*-political readings of this central figure. Freud's famous analysis of the play's central character provided the foundation for his taboo-laden "family romance," in which "it is the fate of all of us, perhaps, to direct our first sexual impulse towards our mother and our first hatred and our first murderous wish against our father."[39] Oedipus thus becomes a cipher for the psychological foibles of *every* man, even the lowliest citizen, though the implications are rather woollier for a tyrant. So in French postwar dramaturgy and thought, the psychological and the political become hopelessly intertwined, as France refracts the figure of a power-hungry and delusional Oedipus through Germany's occupation.[40] Anglo-American interpretations of the same myth tend to focus less on the political/psychological aberration of Oedipus than on the tyrant's considerable skills as epistemological sleuth: in this vein, *Oedipus*—on many readings, and famously, on American scholar Charles Segal's—is filled not with "a sense of total chaos and despair, but a quality of heroism in the power of self-knowledge." As Segal neatly puts it, "the tragic hero is both anomalous individual and universal mythic paradigm."[41] In a later, essentially New Critical work, Segal expands on the humanistic reception of Oedipus as a text for deepest contemplation: the play possesses a "private, psychological dimension" that "remains rich with insights for the modern reader," one that explores the "inner reality of the emotional life." Sophocles, as an artist and thinker, thus "probes the dark side of life and the hidden depths of the soul," making us "see what we would rather not see and know what we would prefer not to know."[42] Here, the emphasis on the "private" dimension of *Oedipus Tyrannus* implicitly displaces other, more public dimensions.

---

[39] Freud 1967: 296. Pucci 1992: 2–3 marvels at the "extraordinary richness" of a Freudian reading, though believes it misses the "one question essential in *Oedipus Tyrannus*. The central question is, What is a father?" For the centrality of the "Theban Paradigm" to Freud's work, see Armstrong 2005: 47–62.

[40] Leonard 2005: 22–95, "Oedipus and the Political Subject."   [41] Segal 1981: 247–8.

[42] Segal 1993: 156–7.

In his deft 2004 reworking of the Oedipus myth, *Small Tragedy*, play-wright Craig Lucas turns Segal's lofty, humanistic reading on its head, crafting a tendentious play that torpedoes Segal's interpretation on its way to a surprisingly geopolitical climax. Lucas thus crams the politics back into *Oedipus*, Freud and Segal be damned. The set-up: a washed-up but previously promising stage director, Nathaniel, is mounting a shoe-string adaptation of *Oedipus Tyrannus*. Jen, a desperate actress, lands the part of Jocasta, Oedipus' wife and sister; the uneasily gay Christmas (a nickname for Chris Massaccio) doubles as Teiresias and a messenger; Paola (Natha-niel's wife) and Fanny play the entirety of the chorus of Elders. A mysterious, talented Bosnian named Hakija lands the part of Oedipus. Much of *Small Tragedy* revolves around the theater company's fraught rehearsal process and concomitant infighting—there's not only a clash of personalities (and an inevitable backstage romance), but deep disagree-ment about the role of interpretation in the production of classical drama, particularly of *Oedipus Tyrannus*. Politically conservative director Nathan-iel would prefer a "hands-off" approach to interpretation, allowing the audience access to the original play without a heavy-handed *auteur* at the helm (*à la* the European *Wunderkinder* Peter Stein and Peter Brook). Nathaniel even mocks "topical" productions of Sophoclean plays: "I hate ... productions where you can see the goddamn point of view of the director like handprints from a blind Person feeling their way around the set." He thus rejects—as common and facile—approaches to the play that appear too modern or presentist, such as (a) "the Riddle of Human Identity" (i.e. Segal's approach) (b) repression (c) Freudianism and (d) homelessness (67). That last approach, he sneers, would be especially appealing to social workers and socialists. Instead of "limiting" interpret-ations, he prefers an open-ended *Oedipus* in which many interpretations are valid: "[Y]ou don't have to pick one over the other" (110).

To this end Nathaniel would prefer to focus on a grand, putatively non-ideological approach to the idea of tragedy. He thus compels his wife Paola to read excerpts from Charles Segal's *Oedipus Tyrannus: Tragic Heroism and the Limits of Knowledge*, which, in the context of *Small Tragedy*, is meant to illumine for the characters the Idea of Tragedy writ large:

PAOLA (*READS*): "it is precisely by showing Oedipus' life against its earlier success
    and power that Sophocles defines it as tragic and thus creates the form of the
    'tragic hero' in literature: a figure whose force of personality and integrity—
NATHANIEL: *Integrity.*
PAOLA: "—set him. (*Or her.*) apart for a special destiny of pain and struggle—"

NATHANIEL: Special destiny.
PAOLA: "—and enable him to confront that destiny with clarity and courage . . . after a difficult journey to self-knowledge." (88–89)(= Segal's *Tragic Heroism*, p. 120)

Nathaniel's interruptions focus on the essence of masculine heroism: a personal integrity shattered by a destiny filled with dramatic *peripeteiai* ("reversals of fortune"), yet concluding with the saving grace of self-knowledge. This is, for lack of a better term, a sublime interpretation, with roots, ultimately, in Aristotelian literary criticism. Roommates and actresses Jen and Fanny arrive at a similar conclusion, though in considerably less highfalutin language:

FANNY: I mean, I don't know why we're supposed to like [Oedipus], seriously. . ..
JEN: You don't have to like him, you have to feel terror and pity.
FANNY: Well, okay, then, why pity? Where's the pity? What's it for? He kills people who get in his way.
JEN: Yeah, but the gods shit all over him. (20)

Here, Jen applies—with a trowel—Aristotle's concepts of *phobos* and *eleos* (*Poetics*, 53a1) to *Oedipus Tyrannus*; Fanny seems to understand the notion of terror, but only concedes some pity after Jen explains Aristotle's tragic reversal (*peripeteia*, 52a22) as the "gods shit[ting] all over" someone. This is an effective, if unorthodox, application of Aristotle's *Poetics*.

Both of these "off-stage" scenes feature a resolutely *non*-political reading of *Oedipus Tyrannus*, a positive endorsement of Charles Segal's humanistic interpretation of the play. In rehearsal, however, an argument breaks out among the actors about the value of perhaps "Americanizing" the play, with Oedipus himself signifying a deluded, if still notionally democratic, America. The confused chorus would thus signify a pre-mass-media American populace; Jocasta (who is afraid of probing questions) would stand in for a reactionary or center-right politician; and Teiresias would assume the role of an outspoken dissident (49–51). This generally left-wing interpretation infuriates director Nathaniel, who pleads with his actors, "[C]an we just agree we're going to not try to make the fucking play *relevant* if it isn't already?" (50). In a deft and richly educational gesture, Nathanial spins the metaphors like a top: why can't Oedipus be an America rich "in natural resources," "money," and "military might," for whom "the use of power is inherent" in America's very existence? "If America were really smart," Nathaniel argues, "we would just blow up

anybody who doesn't get that"—precisely as Oedipus unleashes his physical might on the hapless party on the road to Daulis. On Nathaniel's view,
the left-wing interpretation of Teiresias, in particular, is misguided: "If
anything, Teiresias is the Wall Street Journal telling everybody what is
completely obvious if they would get their heads out of their buttholes:
America is fated to be an Empire. That's our true fate" (51).

So, at the director's behest, the play-within-the-play remains resolutely
"apolitical," even if aesthetically challenging. The beauty part of *Small
Tragedy* is that playwright Lucas refuses to let this *Oedipus* remain her-
metically sealed from the rest of his narrative: *Oedipus* as an *internal
production* might be apolitical, but as *a metaphor*, it controls the narrative
absolutely, and with a definite political spin (even as the hapless director
denounces ideologically-driven interpretations of *Oedipus*). At first, playwright Lucas toys with his characters—and his modern audience—by
crafting a compelling and straightforward parallel between the actor
Hakija and Oedipus, as Hakija relates to a cast-mate the unusual circumstances of his upbringing: as a native Bosnian reared in Vermont, he is
"abandoned," he is told, by his mother, and sequestered from the outside
world by his father. At a friend's house, however, he is discovered to be the
missing child advertised on a milk carton; Hakija's "father" is arrested and
exposed as a kidnapper (even if a well-meaning one) who had rescued
Hakija from an abusive, drug-addled mother. Hakija considers this man,
even in prison, to be "[his] true father": his childhood is thus revealed—
and in a sense wrecked—by a freak, Oedipal revelation (17).[43]

At the conclusion of this astounding, affecting tale, Hakija exits the
rehearsal stage, adding the marvelous curtain line that the entire story is
"horseshit." Thus a possible, even probable, Oedipal parallel is established
and demolished in the same stroke. Lucas flirts with a neatly crafted
domestic parallel to Oedipus' private life, and then shatters it: Hakija is
no more baby Oedipus than baby Moses.

Later, however, Hakija reveals his *true* adolescence as the victim of
Serbian aggression, of power run amok. Angry at his fellow American
actors' ignorance of the ethnic strife in former Yugoslavia, he pointedly
compares Americans to Oedipus, "Blind to your own tragedy, not to
mention … anybody else's …. Our Christian neighbors … *indistinguishable* from you or me if you were to see them—which you couldn't or
refused to, I won't speak for you, Americans refused—these people, friends,

[43] It is hard to know what to make of Lucas' own Oedipal childhood: as a baby, he was abandoned
by his birth mother in a car, and later adopted by an FBI agent and his wife (Nelson 2003: 272).

colleagues, simply because they had Serbian ancestry and we were Muslims, came into our home, murdered many of the men, raped the women and drove the survivors into camps where most starved to death.... The only people in the world capable of putting a stop to any of this [i.e. America] left an embargo on all weapons to one side, ours, and stood by, using so-called Humanitarian Efforts to excuse themselves from doing anything" (45). Hakija furiously applies Sophoclean metaphors to a geopolitical crisis: America-as-Oedipus is singularly powerful and yet unable to tell friend from foe (a distressing combination that resonates with Sophocles' Oedipus-at-the-crossroads). This composite Oedipus is a well-meaning but ultimately destructive nation/hero, one that is "willfully blind" to its power, one that "can't afford to see that [it] is making the world unliveable" (112). Hakija himself is a casualty of this wayward power: he saw his whole family murdered, his mother shot, his father and brother tortured and beheaded (82–83). Metatheatrical nomenclature to the contrary, Hakija's tragedy is anything but small. As at Sophocles' massacre at the crossroads, "all [were] killed save one" (96).

But what is metatheater without a twist—particularly metatheater based on the most famous literary *peripeteia*, 'reversal,' from antiquity? The *Oedipus Tyrannus*—as a play-within-a-play—is something of a hit, with Hakija giving a standout titular performance. There's a troubling note, however: before stepping on stage, Hakija "*crosses himself in the fashion of a Serbian Orthodox Christian*" (107), a detail that does not quite jibe with earlier self-presentations of his adolescence. In an extended epilogue, after the close of the play-within-a-play, we discover that Hakija's career as an actor is now going swimmingly; that he and Jen—who played Jocasta—are living together with a newborn baby; and that other members of the cast are pursuing other careers, with varied degrees of success. Three of the former cast members unexpectedly drop in on Jen/Jocasta, which prompts from her a telling exclamation: "I can't believe it. The Messenger, the Prophet, the Elders!" (121). The arrival of a messenger, prophet, and elders isn't likely to herald joyful news in any drama, particularly for a version of *Oedipus*. Christmas/Teiresias springs a revelation on Jen/Jocasta: that, while on a peacekeeping mission to Bosnia, he discovered that the *real* "Hakija" was dead, and that a photo of Jen's Hakija/Oedipus proved that Hakija/Oedipus was ... a Serb, one who had participated in the ethnic cleansing: "one of the ringleaders, one of the most brutal, a rapist" (128). As in the Sophoclean original, Jocasta is horrified by the sudden revelation.

The play is at its *dénouement*. Jen confronts Hakija with proof of his origin (this would be a *symbolon* in Greek); in this case, it is a videotape of his participation in a gang-rape. Hakija confesses: "There was no choice for us. When the Serbs came through, it was clear that we either participated or we were killed. . .. One was either one of them or one was dead, those were the two choices . . . You have no way of imagining. It was worse than a nightmare. I know . . . you see me on the tape, but that's, if I didn't . . . if we didn't all play along . . . There were only two choices" (132). It turns out that Lucas has created a far more powerful parallel with *Oedipus Tyrannus* than the soap-operatic tale of childhood abandonment with which he had started *Small Tragedy*: Hakija is Oedipal not in his birth, but in his *re-birth*, his desperate attempt to escape a hideous crime of violence by the assumption of a new identity. Of course, the original Oedipus' re-birth was a direct consequence of his own ignorance: his "Segalian" moment of self-realization the result of his single-minded pursuit of a murderer. Hakija's re-birth is, by contrast, quintessentially modern: the Protean metamorphosis of a war criminal, fleeing across borders under an assumed identity. Hakija's tragedy is not at all the turn from ignorance to knowledge that we see in the Sophocles, but rather Hakija's *inability* to escape the consequences of violence: a violence directed, Oedipally, at his own community.

In the end, the most affecting parallels between *Small Tragedy* and *Oedipus* coalesce around the character of Jen, who, like Jocasta, must endure a harrowing *anagnorisis*, a Greek "recognition" scene. The ancient Jocasta discovers at once her husband and son (*OT* 1071–1072); the modern Jen discovers spouse and ethnic cleanser (128–129). Jocasta, in the way of all despondent Greek heroines, commits suicide and breaks her neck;[44] Jen, however, breaks the fourth wall. She ends the play and ends the parallels.

Even within the admittedly circumscribed genre of twist-Oedipus-endings, Jen's curtain speech comes as a surprise. Other modern adaptations of *Oedipus* frustrate audience expectations by fashioning a novel response of the hero Oedipus to his existential predicament. In Berkoff's play *Greek*, for instance, Oedipus decides that sex with one's mother isn't, in the larger scheme of human foibles, particularly distressing. ("Yeah I wanna climb back inside my mum. What's wrong with that."[45]) In Neil LaBute's one-act *Wrecks*, Oedipus is not only agreeable to the idea of mother-fornication, but actually seeks her out for that express purpose:

[44] See Loraux 1987: 8. "[Suicide] was a woman's solution and not, as has sometimes been claimed, a heroic act."
[45] Berkoff 1983: 53.

the surprise to the audience is that it's no surprise to Oedipus.[46] Lucas, extraordinarily, gives the final words to Jen *aka* Jocasta, who rejects the ancient heroine's choice—suicide—and, with it, the entire frame of *Small Tragedy*:

> JEN (*to us*): I don't believe in tragedy. Did you know that there is no other word for it in any other language, it is always a variant of the Greek word: tragedy. It belongs to them … I choose to be happy. … Hak still always says that Americans don't understand tragedy, and I hope that could always be true. Don't you?" (134)

The play's internal, thematized argument—whether the myth of Oedipus's blind devotion to power can be "Americanized" as an international tragedy—finds no real resolution; paradoxically, Jen hopes that Americans will remain blind to tragedy even when that very blindness *constitutes* the tragedy. She thus yearns for a return to a world of simply small tragedies: to a world before Jen, like America, opened her eyes.

[46] LaBute 2007:33. Edward, on his path to finding his mother and soon-to-be-wife: "Took a long time to gather that info, trust me, lots of letters and begging and shit … Oh yeah, I finally did do it. Found my way here. Home. To her. Mary Jo."

5 | From the borders: Contemporary identity, community, and the ancient world

In 1993, at the height of the so-called culture wars (and after the publication of such fulminating, *Zeitgeist*-defining works as Allan Bloom's *The Closing of the American Mind* (1988)), classicist Bernard Knox provocatively dubbed his own book-length salvo *The Oldest Dead White European Males*;[1] he thus proudly claimed this derogatory label as a mantle for classicists and antiquity-lovers everywhere. Striking back against contemporary attacks on the canon, Knox located in such protests an exquisite irony: "Advocates of multiculturalism and militant feminists, among others, have denounced the traditional canon of literature that has so long served as the educational base for Western societies, repudiating it not only as sexist and racist but even as the instrument of ideological *Gleichschaltung* used by a ruling class to impose conformity. . . .. Yet . . . it is strange to find the classical Greeks today assailed as emblems of reactionary conservatism, of enforced conformity. For their role in the history of the West has always been innovative, sometimes indeed subversive, even revolutionary" (12, 15). For Knox, there's nothing *intrinsically* racist, misogynistic, or reactionary about the Greco-Roman canon as a *canon*: books, and the ideas contained there, are to be employed for contemporary *ends*. Thus, in a strange and circuitous way, Knox anticipated the primary thrust of classical reception studies. Unfortunately, his tendency towards demonization was polarizing; it's hard to imagine that any otherwise open-minded feminist would warm to the adjectives "militant" (12) and "radical" (26), for instance. And surely, there was something to be said for the drive to include writers of every stripe in the modern canon.

The next two chapters of *Antiquity Now* explore communities and groups not often glossed as historically favored or privileged, and which —out of pique or genuine admiration—have grappled with their marginalized status by (paradoxically) engaging with the tools, texts, and myths of the oldest, deadest, Europeanest males. Indeed, any contemporary impulse towards multiculturalism necessarily depends on the notion of a

1 Knox 1993.

monoculture—and that monoculture has often been figured as Greco-Roman antiquity and its legacy. The paradox—and fun—of contemporary reception studies is that some of the most dazzling and effective meditations on antiquity have been predicated on what seems to most classicists a distorted or hackneyed idea of the original text. Philosopher Simone Weil's powerful anti-war essay *The Iliad, or the Poem of Force*, written during the German occupation of France, is a lovely reflection on oppression in general, but few classicists would recognize the essay as mainstream Homeric scholarship.[2] Instead, Weil's ethically charged reading of Homer remains a clarion call for pacifism composed under extremely trying circumstances. So even as the cultures of Greco-Roman antiquity are constructed as hopelessly white, militaristic, capitalist, etc., that construction can itself be used as a springboard for improving our contemporary world, as antiquity is refracted through the sensibilities (and metaphors) of historically marginalized groups.

Race and classics – and musical theater

In my analysis of the afterlives of the Persian War film *300*, I argued that the orientalism inherent in that particular reception of Herodotus' *Histories* managed to persevere in whatever form it was cast, whether in comics, film, or board games: classical reception is a study of ideology, not of medium per se. This multiplicity of media sometimes makes reception a particularly slippery field of study: one never *quite* knows when, where, and how the classical world will make a startling contemporary appearance. For instance, a recent episode of the occasional series *In Performance at the White House*, a musical variety show on America's Public Broadcasting channel, featured a particularly eclectic selection of songs for its "Broadway Celebration," starring luminaries from the Great White Way.[3] Though there were some familiar standards in the mix—such as "What I Did for Love" (from *A Chorus Line*) and the Irving Berlin favorite "Blue Skies"—the evening tended towards songs that spoke to a specifically American experience, especially concerning matters of race. Thus the production included songs from the musical *Memphis* (about interracial romance in 1950s Tennessee);

---

2 For an appreciation of Weil's work and the essay's own varied reception among classicists, see Holoka 2003: 1–17, esp. 8–9.

3 The episode originally aired on Oct. 20, 2010, and is still currently available as a streaming video on pbs.org.

"America" from *West Side Story* (about the Latino immigrant experience); and "Gonna Pass Me a Law," from Tony Kushner's reflective musical on race and class in Civil Rights-era Alabama, *Caroline, Or Change.*

In this context, the little-known song "Free," specifically introduced as originating from the Roman playwright Plautus, might seem a strange fit. But like the original stage adaptation of *A Funny Thing Happened on the Way to the Forum* (1963) in which it appeared, the song "Free" is as much a commentary on contemporary social forces as a "straight" adaptation of Roman comedy. As Monica Cyrino has argued, *Forum* tackled, if only obliquely, America's civil rights movement, with a particular emphasis on the slave Pseudolus' potential liberation from slavery;[4] manumission is a theme that gallops throughout the corpus of Plautus, himself (presumably) descended from slaves. For instance, towards the end of Plautus' *Menaechmi*—an hilarious farce of doubled slaves and doubled masters— the slave Messenio begs for manumission from (the character he thinks is) his master:

MES: By Pollux, if you really mean it, master, then set me free (*med emittas manu*) . . .. Even if you don't think I'm yours, let me walk free (*liberum*).
MEN1: Certainly, then. By my power, May You Go Free (*liber esto*) and wherever you wish.
MES: Really?
MEN1: Yes, if I have that sort of authority.
MES: Hail, my patron (*patronus*)! (*Speaking to himself, as if comically supplying witnesses.*) I'm so thrilled, Messenio, that you are free (*liber!*). (*Men.* 1023–1031)

The official, ritual language of manumission shoots through this passage: Messenio includes the idiom *emittere manu*, 'to release by hand,' in his request, and Menaechmus grants his wish with a formal, archaic imperative: May You Go Free.[5] This speech-act *instantly* changes the social status of both men, from slave and master to patron and client: this is "freedom," Roman-style.

Sondheim's song "Free" originates in Plautine dramatic principles, but takes the form of the highly stylized song'n'dance numbers of vaudeville

---

[4] Cyrino 2005: 172. Cyrino mostly analyzes the film version of *Forum*, of course, but her observations are more generally applicable to the original stage musical.

[5] Gratwick 1993: 242 notes the phrase's formalism, and notes too that it usually accompanied by ritual: "saying which, the master turned the slave around and gave him a symbolic slap on the face (*alapa*)." For an excellent book-length study on the construction of slavery in Plautus, see McCarthy 2000.

and Broadway. But "Free" is hardly one of the great, free-standing standards of the American theater; indeed, the script of *In Performance at the
White House* is forced to include a great deal of introductory patter in
order to make the song intelligible to the White House (and television)
audience. As actor Nathan Lane explains: "Plautus [is] the father of the
situation comedy. Set in ancient Rome, [*Forum*] tells the story of a wily
slave, Pseudolus, who will stop at nothing to win his freedom. In this song,
he strikes a bargain with his master, Hero. If he can win for him the girl he
loves, he (= Hero) will free him." Brian d'Arcy James and Nathan Lane
then perform a particularly long segment from the show, prefaced by the
following exchange:

JAMES-AS-HERO: Pseudolus, people don't just go about freeing slaves.
LANE-AS-PSEUDOLUS: Be the first. Start a fashion.

As a rendition of the song within its original artistic context, this version
of "Free" is perfectly straightforward, with suitably Plautine and clownish
gestures from Lane's slave while James plays the straight man. (The song
even includes lines concerning "the house of Lycus," a reference to a
brothel that remains completely opaque outside of the context of the
original script.) What's extraordinary about this particular performance is
not the allusion to the house of Lycus, however, but its pointed reference
to a very different type of house: the White House, now inhabited by the
Obamas. To emphasize this point, the camera *twice* cuts away from the
performance to the smiling Obama family: once after Pseudolus fantasizes
about the freedoms of a free life, and once again during the concluding
bows. The song's inclusion in *In Performance at the White House* both
connects Plautus to other overtly political artists on that evening's program—Kushner, Bernstein, *et al.*—but also specifically to *this* White
House: it's no accident that Pseudolus' paean to manumission is juxtaposed with panning shots of America's first black First Family (see
Figures 5.1 and 5.2). To the camera's eye, this First Family is the obvious
result of America's multiple attempts at "freedom"; Michelle Obama is
herself the descendant of a manumitted slave, Melvinia Shields.[6] The
broadcast thus repoliticizes Plautus in a surprising new context, and
contributes to the ongoing discourses of America as a new—and perhaps
freer—Rome.

---

[6] Swarns 2012. *The Story of the Black, White, and Multiracial Ancestors of Michelle Obama* see
www.nytimes.com/2012/06/17/books/review/american-tapestry-by-rachel-l-swarns.html?_r=1&
pagewanted=all.

Figure 5.1. Brian d'Arcy James (as Hero) whispers "freedom" into the ear of Nathan Lane (Pseudolus).

Figure 5.2. The Obamas enjoy a scene from Sondheim/Plautus.

With this performance of "Free," one dead, white, European male—Plautus—is made to comment on the lived experiences of generations of black Americans: it's a provocative intersection of classics and race, and Plautus' sheer antiquity lends a timelessness (and, paradoxically, an urgency) to the call for social justice. Indeed, PBS' complex juxtaposition of race and classical antiquity caps several decades—indeed, three or four centuries—of classical reception concerning the African and African-American experience, a legacy now explored in an ever-increasing number of scholarly studies, including William W. Cook and James Tatum's *African American Writers and the Classical Tradition* (2010) and Patrice D. Rankine's *Ulysses in Black: Ralph Ellison, Classicism, and African American Literature* (2006). Such receptions (and such receptions of such receptions) move us past, in a sense, one of the more vexing periods in classical reception studies, when Cornell Sinologist Martin Bernal issued the confrontationally titled *Black Athena: The Afroasiatic Roots of Classical Civilization* (1987). (Later editions added the tendentious subtitle *The*

Fabrication of Ancient Greece, 1785–1985.)[7] It was intended by Bernal to be a multi-volume exploration of the persistently racist rewriting of history by European (and American) academics, a rewriting that literally denigrated the contributions of (Black) Egypt to Western culture. As a scholar, Bernal seems to revel in his iconoclasm: in the conclusion to the second volume, he happily notes that for many critics, that particular volume will seem even "more outrageous than the first" (522).

The scholarly response to *Black Athena* was a flurry of equally impassioned tomes, including *Black Athena Revisited* (a collection of sharply negative essays and reviews, 1996, edited by Wellesley College professors Mary Lefkowitz and Guy MacLean Rogers); Lefkowitz's *Not Out of Africa: How "Afrocentrism" Became an Excuse to Teach Myth as History* (1997); Walter Slack's *White Athena: The Afrocentrist Theft of Greek Civilization* (2006), and Ron Fritze's *Invented Knowledge: False History, Fake Science, and Pseudo-religions* (2009), which includes a retrospective of the *Black Athena* controversy. (It also includes chapters on the contemporary mania for ancient extraterrestrials, a fascinating viewpoint that, sadly, we cannot delve into here.) Lefkowitz produced a particularly ardent demolition of the evidence for a "Black" Cleopatra, Pharaoh of Egypt, whose lineage was certainly Greek and only dubiously Afro-Egyptian.[8]

Surprisingly, this scholarly debate over the Afroasiatic roots of Egypt—roiling for years in one segment of American intellectual discourse—again pops up in that most unlikely of contemporary media: the American musical theater (!). The original production of Henry Krieger and Tom Eyen's *Dreamgirls* premiered on Broadway in 1981; it told the barely disguised story of the African-American girl group *The Supremes* and its breakaway star Diana Ross. In the critically hailed film version (2006) by Bill Condon, the breakaway star, Deena (Beyoncé Knowles), dreams of a film career centered upon small, independent roles; her domineering husband–manager (Jamie Foxx), however, has contracted her as the lead in a blockbuster version of *Cleopatra*. In a feud that anchors the film's second act, Deena argues that she's too old for this teen-aged role, but the manager steers things back not to age, but to *race*: "And it's more than you. Think about all the beautiful black women who ain't even born yet. When they grow up, they're going to say: 'I can play any part I want to: look at Deena Jones.'" For Jamie Foxx's character, Cleopatra is a *racial* as well as cinematic role, one that signals to African-American girls that the most

---

[7] Bernal passed away in 2013, leaving *Black Athena* ultimately incomplete.
[8] Lefkowitz 1996: 34–6.

famous queen in antiquity was (or at least could be) black *like them*.
Deena's choice—whether or not to star as a black Cleopatra—thus has
sociopolitical as well as personal consequences, particularly for a film set
during the civil rights era in the United States. The afterlives of this black
Cleopatra are numerous and surprising: in 2010, American producer Scott
Rudin discussed his plans to shoot a big-budget *Cleopatra* starring Angel-
ina Jolie (who is white).[9] This announcement generated the impassioned
Essence online essay "Another White Actress to Play Cleopatra?" by Shirea
L. Carroll. Carroll argues that "while historically there is no concrete
confirmation that Cleopatra was of a darker complexion, there is more
evidence than not that she was Black, and not entirely of Macedonian
Greek ancestry... [I]t remains that she was in fact an African queen."[10]

Fortunately, the bulk of contemporary reception in race has shied from
the ugly and fractious Culture Wars that characterized the 1980s and
1990s, and again towards sophisticated treatments of metaphor, society,
and identity. Will Power's recent musical theater adaptation of Aeschylus'
Seven against Thebes, "The Seven" (2006), retells an ancient tale of fraternal
conflict through the medium of hip-hop, with a largely African-American
cast and subtext, this time of American urban gang warfare.[11] In an
appearance on the satirical *The Colbert Report*, the faux-conservative host
Stephen Colbert interrogates Power about this potentially confusing socio-
artistic fusion of hip-hop and Aeschylus. "The ancient Greeks were not
black, so how is it possible to do that?" Colbert deadpans, with perfect
irony.[12] (As a parody of fulminating right-wing talk show hosts, Colbert
embodies, in a sense, the old Culture Wars ethos of the 1980s.) Power
patiently explains that though Greeks were not black, their myths weren't
exactly Greek; or rather, their myths drew on a number of sources,
including Egyptian and Phoenician traditions. In a separate interview with
Bill Moyers, for PBS, Power further explains how he sees in the figure of
the fallen Oedipus—the most famous figure from tragedy—a new and
decidedly contemporary American parallel: "He used to be a pimp. He
used to have that power. But he's lost it. It's like a fall from grace. And
in my community, a lot of the old hustlers from the seventies, that used to
be, what we call, 'high rollers,' are now kind of, you know, of lower

[9] www.mtv.com/news/articles/1676183/girl-with-the-dragon-tattoo-david-fincher-director.
jhtml. Interview by Josh Horowitz. Dec. 19, 2011.
[10] www.essence.com/2010/06/14/commentary-angelina-jolie-to-play-cleopa/#ixzz21f3IJeg0
[11] See Dorota Dutch 2010 for a brief overview of the social implications of Power's work.
[12] Aired Sept. 18, 2006. Available on the Colbert Report's website at: www.colbertnation.com/the-
colbert-report-videos/75584/september-18-2006/will-power

stature."[13] For Power, Oedipus the King translates easily and powerfully to Oedipus the Pimp, a "community" figure who embodies the battle-scarred generation of urban warriors from the Jimmy Carter years. Oedipus used to be "hip"; but now he's sadly "old school," as another generation learns to live, and to die, on the streets of Thebes—or San Francisco.

Alfaro's Chicano/Greek Trilogy

In Power's re-envisioning of the Oedipus myth, Oedipus the King maps easily (and powerfully) onto a specific figure in a specific type of contemporary American community, and thereby taps into the power of *metaphor*: of drawing connections between (seemingly) disparate societies and social structures. The bulk of this chapter examines a trio—better yet, trilogy—of recent Greek tragedies by Chicano playwright and activist Louis Alfaro, who specifically and intentionally "receives" both Euripides and Sophocles through the prism of American race and ethnicity. He then metaphorically maps these texts onto a new and exciting intellectual geography: the *barrio*.

We begin with Alfaro's version of *Elektra*. In a tour-de-force essay on the operatic reception of Sophocles' version, classicist Simon Goldhill explored how that text's combination of psychological complexity and dramatic structure helped create the conditions for a perfect storm of avant-garde receptions, up to and including Richard Strauss' famously experimental version of 1909.[14] If the artists at the beginning of the twentieth century saw in *Elektra* a reflection of current trends in psychology (particularly Freudian analyses of hysteria and interiority),[15] twenty-first-century artists, however, are apt to see in the text quite different trends and interpretative paths. As in Euripides' later version, Sophocles' *Elektra* goes a long ways towards demythologizing its homicidal protagonists, Elektra and Orestes, as they slaughter their mother and her paramour; indeed, it strips from them the comforting reassurances of an Aeschylean world-view (one buttressed by law courts and beneficent deities) and leaves them as agents of cold revenge. Thus the end of *Elektra*—like the beginning

---

[13] http://www.pbs.org/moyers/faithandreason/print/lppower_print.html

[14] Goldhill 2002: 108–77.

[15] Breuer and Freud's *Studies in Hysteria* was published in 1895, the same year Hofmannsthal enrolled in courses on art and psychology; Hofmannsthal's version of *Elektra* premiered in 1903. This was then adapted by Strauss for a famous, and scandalous, 1909 premiere. For the two-way street between the study of psychology and antiquity see especially Armstrong 2005.

of the *Elektra*—presents a world ruled by the very forces that Aeschylus' previous *Oresteia* tries so strenuously to suppress: for all of the action in the play, this world is ultimately static, unmoved, unchanging. It thus provides fodder for contemporary playwrights, like Alfaro, who see in *their* own world—a world informed by ethnicity and class—similar questions (and perhaps similar non-answers) concerning fate, agency, and change.

Luis Alfaro's *Electricidad*, the Chicano version of Sophocles' play, first opened at the Borderlands theater in 2002; Borderlands is a community-based, "activist" theater in Tucson, Arizona. As its name implies, the mission of the theater is to examine borders of every stripe, including the physical and metaphorical borders between Mexico and the United States. The theater is a thus perfect fit for Alfaro, a politically engaged artist with an impressive roster of accolades, including productions at some of America's most highly regarded theaters: in 1997, Alfaro even nabbed a prestigious Macarthur "Genius" Grant for playwriting. In an interview in *American Theater*, Alfaro explains he was drawn to *Elektra's* world because of its uncanny parallels with the sorts of communities on whose behalf he agitates: "I work a lot in 'youth authority programs' for teen felons, and I met a young girl who had killed her mother. Shortly afterward, [I came across] a collection of the Greeks on sale. I thought, I should read this. And you know, you're reading *Electra* and it's basically the same story. Nothing's changed. Why do we still have a need to avenge?"[16] On the one hand, Alfaro discovers, on the level of *theme*— vengeance—a parallel to a specific American phenomenon: youth who battle against the law (*nomos*, in the Greek), in the name of personal retribution. In *Electricidad*, that community is a gang community, which abides by social codes at odds with the rest of society; the friction generated between the two systems produces tragedy, then as now. At the same time, Alfaro needs to translate the play on the level of *space*: what real-life American community corresponds to mythical Argos? Alfaro hits upon a solution: "In Chicago you have Pilsen, in L.A., you have East L.A., in Tucson the Southside is where all the gang culture is. . . . [I]n the Southside it's the *barrio*. Everything runs differently in these communities; *there's a different kind of justice*" (emphasis added). Again, we see Alfaro struggling with the idea of appropriate translation: to the extent to which *Elektra* is about interrogating the idea of justice and "payback," the best *physical* space for this topsy-turvy world of

[16] Alfaro: 2006.

alternative justice is a *barrio*, in which a community has developed its own, idiosyncratic *nomoi* ('laws') regarding honor, insults, and vengeance.

Finally, Alfaro translates the Sophoclean characters themselves, often adding suggestive descriptions in the text's *dramatis personae*. Electra is transformed into Electricidad, "an old-school *chola*" or gang member, and Alfaro wittily puns on her name: she's indeed a live wire. Elektra's father, Agamemnon, is now Agamenón, or, more affectionately, "El Auggie"; his rotting corpse is the centerpiece of the set. Clytemnestra, "a total *veterana*," emerges as Clemencia; the son Orestes remains Orestes, "a peewee," now in exile in Las Vegas, land of new beginnings. Elektra's sister Chrysothemis is translated—surprisingly—as Ifigenia, a nod to that character's rebirth as a committed, reformed Christian, after a symbolic death. A chorus of local women wields brooms instead of *thyrsoi*, but still provides an identical function to its ancient counterpart: they comment on the action, and offer up the communal voice of the city–state, or as Alfaro rather more jauntily terms it, "the 'hood."

Throughout the play, Alfaro constantly juggles his analogies between the old world and the new. Indeed, as the chorus describes the fallen leader Agamenón, the citizens provide a sort of interpretive road map, demonstrating how the play slides between Greek and American tragedy:

LA CARMEN : A father.
LA CONNIE : El rey.
LA CUCA : Yes, the king.
LA CARMEN : Even if he was a *cholo*.
LA CONNIE : A warrior.
LA CUCA : A parolee. (67)

Agamenón is a warrior and a king—in Sophoclean terms—but also a *cholo* and parolee in Alfarean terms. Semantically, he's overdetermined: a literal king of Argos, a metaphorical king of the *barrio*. Likewise, the startling translation of Clytemnestra is even commented upon by the chorus:

LA CARMEN : She killed him.
LA CONNIE : Who?
LA CUCA : The mother.
LA CARMEN : La Clemencia.
LA CONNIE: What kind of name is that?
LA CUCA: Texas, I bet. (67)

La Cuca's tart observation signals that two things are happening here. First, the chorus is drawing attention to the *mis*-translation, in effect, of

Clemencia's name: she's arguably the least clement person in the play, if not on the planet. At the same time, Alfaro deftly reminds the audience of the play's *physical* translation: from fairy-tale Greece to the fraught and restless borderlands of the south-west United States.

Having translated the characters from Greece to the *barrio*, Alfaro now translates the play's (timeless) ethical concerns into culturally specific language. For instance, here is Electricidad's definition of the *barrio's nomoi*, its code of the street: "You are the old ways, papa. You are the history and the reason we know how to live. I want to live the old *cholo* ways, papa ... You shoot. I shoot back" (70).[17] In the original Greek, such calls for vengeance are buttressed by appeals to gods of vengeance—Zeus and the Furies among them (ll. 209, 276). Alfaro has translated such invitations for vengeance from ancient Gods to Aztec gods, at whose altar Electricidad prays. The character of Chrysothemis/Ifigenia becomes Sophocles/Alfaro's mouthpiece for the more "civilized" values of the law-abiding polis or city–state: "Listen, *hermana*, your loyalty to Papa has always been deep and kind of creepy ... But it's time to call a truce and let the House of Atridas mourn and move on" (73). (This commentary on Elektra's apparent "creepiness" could be a nod towards the Freudian reading of Elektra's antisocial hysteria.)

Within the play, Ifigenia is the voice of compassion, the voice of wisdom, the voice, quite nearly, of God. She is also entirely unheeded.[18] Unlike in Sophocles' version of the play, there's only one murder at the end: there is no murder of Aigisthus, Clytemnestra's new bedmate and fellow corpse. But *Electricidad's* single, terrible matricide is enough to bring home Alfaro's point—the *barrio's* ultimately destructive code of ethics—with frightening intensity. Here is Sophocles' version of the death of Klytemnestra, accomplished by Orestes at the urging of Elektra.

KLYTEMNESTRA: My son, my son, have pity on your mother!
ELEKTRA: But he had no pity from you, nor did his father before him.
KLYTEMNESTRA: I am struck! (ll. 1411–1412, 1415)

And here is Alfaro's *barrio* version:

(*Orestes is crying. He holds her down, but he cannot do it.*)

[17] For a sociological analysis of these new American "codes of the street," see Anderson 1999.
[18] Powers 2011: 197 aptly compares this interpolated figure to the "born-again" heroines of Euripides' *Iphigenia in Aulis* and *Iphigenia in Tauris*, and points out that her inclusion undermines one (potent) reason for Elektra's revenge.

CLEMENCIA: *Por favor*, no. You don't know. How hard it is. I'm just like you.
  Nobody showed me shit. Nobody gave me . . . nothing.

At first, it seems that Alfaro is going to change radically the arc of the myth: that Orestes will sacrifice not his mother, but his warrior code. Indeed, Clemencia appeals to the common social bond, not just between a mother and son, but between citizens of this blighted *barrio*, each living hardscrabble lives of poverty and neglect. As she sees her son waver, Clemencia continues the hard sell: "All I wanted was to make it better . . . forgive me" (85). As in the ancient text, however, the daughter Electricidad conquers any sort of reasonable approach with unbridled rage, as she screams "Orestes! Do it!" Alfaro's subsequent stage direction clinically observes: *And with that, [Orestes] cuts his mother's throat.*

An American watching *Electricidad* might have expected the murder to take place off-stage: that is the Greek norm. By translating the murder from off-stage to on-, Alfaro completes his physical transformation of the Greek text from a mythical *polis* to a modern gangland; a mythical *polis* might obey the niceties of Greek dramatic convention, but there's nowhere to hide in a *barrio*, even a mimetic one. It's hard to put into words the reaction of an audience watching a son slit his mother's throat but the atmosphere at a San Antonio, Texas production was—to pun—electric.[19] As the chorus laments in the play's epilogue, we are now back to the beginning: "What is to be done, we never learn. Ai. . .." (85). And it's hard not to hear in that lament the voice of not only of Alfaro, but of Sophocles himself: that contrary to some interpretations of this play, this is not an "optimistic tragedy," of vengeance rightly pondered and executed, but a bleak examination of a moral code that knows only retaliation—with no trial scene, as in Aeschylus's *Oresteia*, to arrest that unending cycle.[20] It's a dissection, then, of a particular community—an ancient *barrio*, so to speak —that takes pride in the *exact* thing that causes its dysfunction. In Alfaro's play, one can perceive the author's outrage that girls like Electricidad have a choice, and that they *choose* to be chained, as Alfaro observes, to ritual and history. Alfaro also relates the effect that *Electricidad* had on several thousand high-school kids in the Los Angeles area. For them, the corpse rotting in the front yard had its own cultural translation: "It was

---

[19] For my review of that production, see www2.sacurrent.com/arts/story.asp?id=66797. The production was directed by Marisela Barrera.
[20] See Segal 1981: 249–91 for a "dark" reading of the play, in contrast to a century's worth of "affirmative" interpretations.

unbelievably thrilling to have only kids that age in the audience, and the body was a big part of it. They saw it differently, maybe because rap stars get killed every day. The symbolism for them was present; they were glued to this idea that Electricidad would be there protecting her father's body. She became kind of like a rock star."[21] Electricidad is thus a hero in the modern sense of a celebrated local star—while fulfilling her grimmer, mythic function as the site of contested cultural values.[22]

Alfaro's *Oedipus El Rey*—a Chicano version of *Oedipus*—similarly transplants a Sophoclean myth to the *barrios* of East Los Angeles, and, just as in *Electricidad*, employs ancient myth for trenchant sociological analysis. In *Small Tragedy*, we saw how one playwright—Craig Lucas—emphasizes the *violence* of Oedipus, a capacity for social disruption that no amount of rewriting can entirely erase (even as Oedipus stands for, among other things, American foreign policy and America's own suspect history of muscle-flexing). In *Oedipus El Rey*, Alfaro tackles, in some senses, the most Greek-like aspect of the original play: Sophocles' emphasis on the ineluctable *fate* of Oedipus. His is a destiny far beyond the power of ordinary mortal control.

This Greek concept of *moira*—'fate'—does not translate easily to modern Western contexts, particularly given the contemporary cult of individuality. Indeed, clumsy undergraduate attempts at analyzing Sophoclean *moira* nearly always equate this term with a vaguely Calvinist doctrine of predestination, itself a process destined to produce the unfortunate and un-Greek observation that "Oedipus is a puppet in the hands of fate."[23] Though brilliantly and pithily eviscerated by classicist E. R. Dodds, this argument—that Oedipus-as-puppet somehow lacks free will—has exerted an impossibly pernicious influence over popular interpretations of the play.[24] It is to Alfaro's credit, then, that the playwright transforms this concept of *moira*—the *least* "American" aspect of Sophocles' play— into its *most* "American" aspect, as Oedipus the King becomes, in effect, Oedipus the Kingpin: a small-time crook doomed to livin' large on crime. The constraints of "fate" envisioned by Alfaro are not the cosmic bonds

---

[21] Interview with Alfaro, "Electric Youth," *American Theater*, Feb. 2006.

[22] Foley 2012: 24–5 reads Alfaro's *Electricidad* through the lens of several contemporary (American) Elektras, and notes this version's particular emphasis on the *dissolution* of bonds between women, a dissolution occasioned by the *barrio*'s peculiar (and destructive) social codes.

[23] For my own undergraduate classes, students automatically receive a failing grade on any paper that mentions both fate *and* puppets. The pedagogical rewards have been astounding.

[24] See Dodds 1966: 42–4.

explored by Sophocles, but the mundane social institutions and customs that promote an inevitable, tragic recidivism. As in *Electricidad*, Alfaro's implicit critique of *barrio* culture outlines the gangland traditions that "doom" its young men (and even women) from the very start.

Alfaro's command of the play's inherent alterity, of its "Greekness," is impressive. The first scene—of a deserted highway—presents an empty stage, and Alfaro notes this deserted space's solemnity: "its emptiness should feel religious" (7).[25] Here, we've a modern translation of the ancient *orkhestra* at the theater of the god Dionysus in Athens: just a bare platform for a chorus, one that reveals "time, nothing but time" (7). Next, Alfaro plays with time itself, as he imposes on this space a new and fresh concept: "Suddenly the highway is interrupted by the loud sound of prison doors slamming shut" (7). The prison is, of course, a quintessentially *modern* institution—an innovative social mechanism for the control and regulation of the body, as Foucault famously argued. (Foucault thus links prisons to other evolving institutions of control, including factories and schools.[26]) Even before the first word of *Oedipus El Rey* is uttered, Alfaro makes clear that this modern prison will be the overriding metaphor of the play: Oedipus is "doomed" not to a life of violence *per se*, but to a life defined and confined by gang culture and society's futile attempts at reform. As David Simon argued concerning his Baltimore street-life TV show *The Wire*, Greek tragedy is the tragedy of a *system*, not the individual hero.[27] Its title notwithstanding, *Oedipus El Rey* is the tragedy of entire East Los Angeles, from the lowliest to the kingliest.

Alfaro takes liberties with the general plot of Sophocles' play in order to emphasize the play's critique of *barrio* culture and prison as conjoined systems. King Laius, the *barrio*'s crime lord, discovers through the agency of a divinely inspired healer, *El Sobrador*, that the King will be killed by his only son. As *El Sobrador* explains, "[This son] will grow up to be *un Rey*. And like *todos los Reyes*, he will be ruthless. . . . To your son, you will be the only obstacle in this *barrio* and its territories. . . . *Es* destiny. *Esta* willed and your son must follow it" (26–27). As in the original Greek play, the political position of Oedipus is paramount: tyrants and *Reyes* may embody

[25] Page numbers from the Woolly Mammoth Theater Company's locally produced edition, 2011.
[26] Foucault 1979: 77, 174–5.
[27] "We're stealing [not from Shakespeare but] from an earlier less traveled construct—the Greeks —lifting our thematic stance wholesale from Aeschylus, Sophocles, Euripides to create doomed and fated protagonists who confront a rigged game and their own mortality. . . . *The Wire* is a Greek tragedy in which the postmodern institutions are the Olympian forces." (Alvarez 2009: 384).

the people, but their ascension to the position is often—to put it mildly—extra-constitutional. Laius, as it happens, exhibits a particularly nasty streak: after doping up his post-partum wife Jocasta on drugs (a perk of the job, it seems), Laius hands over the child to Teiresias, with instructions to hang the baby from a tree until coyotes harvest the corpse (33). As an added precaution, Laius scores the bottoms of Oedipus' feet: "I don't want him chasing me in the afterlife," he explains simply, in Alfaro's fresh twist on the origins of Oedipus' name. (Later, Oedipus will acquire the street name of *Patas Malas*: a Spanish translation from the Greek that means both "wretched feet" and—oh-so-presciently—"bad luck.") A kind-hearted Teiresias instead rescues the boy and rears him in another part of L.A.

The next few scenes take place in prison, and Alfaro only gradually reveals Oedipus' backstory throughout the rest of the play. As a young hoodlum, Oedipus dabbles in petty theft and drug dealing, with stints in juvenile detention (39): he thus shuffles constantly between *barrio* culture and the comparative comfort (!) of incarceration. Indeed a young Oedipus finds he is terrified of life beyond the reach of "The Youth Authority": "I didn't know how to live on the outside. So for my 17th birthday—I robbed a Costco. . . .. I didn't want the money or anything. I didn't even have a gun. I just went outside and waited for the cops. And they put me in the big house. A place I knew" (94). Here, Alfaro indicates that "life" for Oedipus has been, and is still largely, an existence between institutional walls—and Oedipus' transition to adulthood is spectacularly thwarted by his own self-demolition. (There's also a sly glance at Sophocles, here, in that even as a hoodlum Oedipus is constructed as a creature of knowing, of knowledge.) In a touching gesture, Teiresias, who has been posing as Oedipus' father, "robbed every 7–11 in the Central Valley, just so that he could be in here [=prison] and raise me. Fathers sometimes do that" (43). Primal ties of *kinship*—like fatherhood—are now assimilated to the tyranny of the county prison; the cellblock has replaced the hearth.

Oedipus' eventual release from "adult" prison terrifies him. "What if I don't want to go?" (48), he wonders, even as "destiny" and "fate" conspire against him: it seems the parole board has—like the Fates—"set a date" for his release. This, then, is Oedipus' destiny: to discover that the rules of the world *outside* the prison will lead him back—ineluctably, it seems—to *inside* the prison. Teiresias prophesies that Oedipus must head to the Pico-Union *barrio* of L.A.; en route, he encounters (the unknown) Laius in a moment of modern road rage. This encounter is famously related as an off-stage event in the original Sophoclean play: Jocasta asserts that the *moira* (*OT* 713) predicted for her husband never came true because random robbers slew Laius at a crossroads, not his son. In Alfaro's play, we see this *moira* in action: father and son square off against each other, obeying the laws of the street, not the family. "Let me tell you something, asshole, I have a problem with my temper," Laius growls (59). Laius, noticing Oedipus' prison tattoo, immediately taunts the man for his inexperience with the "outside," non-prison world, even as Oedipus attempts to hide his terror. "You're so obvious, *pendejo*. . .. You got convict written all over you, *baboso*" (see Figure 5.3).

Alfaro's play continually constructs and explores the tension between the Oedipus' identity as an independent man and as a product of postmodern social institutions. Laius is eager to press his advantage: "Ah, you don't know the outside, do you? Wow, *ese*, you threw me for a *momento*. I thought you were an *hombre*, but you're just a little boy." Indeed, Laius threatens Oedipus with the *barrio* equivalent of social retardation: "Wouldn't that be crazy if you went right back in? I could do that. Make a call—Highway Patrol—tell them you got some sort of road rage. . ." (60). The play's terrible conflation of inside/outside reaches its apex in this pivotal scene: at this literal and metaphorical crossroads, Oedipus "punches [Laius] in the face repeatedly, with an absolute savagery and lack of emotion. It's hard and quick, like in a prison yard" (60). Even *outside* of the prison yard, Oedipus seals his fate as if *inside* a prison yard: there is no outside, outside.

And so Oedipus kills his father and continues on his merry way to his native *barrio*, just as in the Sophoclean original. Oedipus' fling with his mother receives a steamy, extended treatment (even *I* was shocked when Jocasta and Oedipus coupled at my feet during the Dallas Theater Center's production) but the metaphor of imprisonment continues to make surprising reappearances: Jocasta's bereavement over Laius is described as "doing time" (67), and Alfaro's Pinter-esque dialogue pirouettes around the idea of stasis and repetition. When Jocasta and Oedipus' mating dance eventually hits upon the topic of theology, Jocasta pointedly asks Oedipus what he believes in; Oedipus replies, "I believe in my own power" (78). This is a metaliterary comment on the entire reception history of *Oedipus*: Oedipus' noble belief in his self-determination and his concomitant denial of *moira* may be gloriously humanistic but they're also gloriously tragic.[28] And in Alfaro's most wrenching monologue, Jocasta disabuses Oedipus of

---

[28] See Charles Segal 1981: 248: "Oedipus' tragedy . . . asks whether human life is trapped in a pattern of its own or others' making or is all random . . . [Oedipus] asks, in other words, whether the sources of such suffering lies in an overstructured or an unstructured universe, absolutely necessity or absolutely chance. That question can have no ultimate answer."

Figure 5.3. Romi Dias, Joshua Torrez, Marc David Pinate in *Oedipus El Rey*, Magic Theatre.

his folly: "In this *barrio* . . . we haven't changed. This ain't downtown—it's the borderlands. This is the way we live. You might think you have the power to make the world you want to make, but there's someone upstairs pulling your strings. You think you got here on your own? We all got destiny. . .. Our story has already been told. We're fated" (79).

In Sophocles' original play, Jocasta is a keen skeptic of *moira*; here, the Chicana Jocasta redefines fate and destiny through the prism of *barrio* culture and the borderlands. (Even the phrase borderlands seems ironic, here: less a border than a *terminus*.) Nevertheless, Jocasta is attracted to Oedipus' determination to rewrite history (80–81): this is free-will-as-seduction, as Oedipus convinces his (unknowing) mother that he freely, willfully, and carnally aspires to King. Oedipus and Jocasta seal the moment with sex (85), even as Creon carps about Oedipus' unfair shot at the throne. (Indeed, Alfaro sometimes outdoes Sophocles in terms of wordplay and sheer awkwardness: for instance, Jocasta remarks to the postcoital Oedipus that "You fill the space that was his" (97).) But as in the original play, knowledge will out: a suspicious Creon announces his intention "to go do a little Sherlock Holmes" (113), which happily re-inscribes the play within the long reception history of *Oedipus* as detective fiction, and which only highlights the criminal undercurrents of the play's *mise en scène*.[29] A forced *rite de passage*—in which Oedipus must solve the riddle of the *Esfinge*—is only an *apparent* victory over *moira*: indeed, the chorus comments that "Prison may have set you free / but freedom will imprison you forever" (124). This quixotic *mot* encapsulates Alfaro's play in a nutshell: Oedipus' victories in his post-prison life are illusory, not real, and his ascension to drug-lord will lead him into a far greater, if more existential, trap. *All* of *barrio* life is a prison, not just the walls.

In the original play, Thebes famously suffers from a demoralizing plague, and discontent swirls too in Alfaro's *barrio* even as Creon runs a background check on Oedipus: Creon's fact-finding mission thus replicates the revelations of the herdsman and the messenger in Sophocles, both of whom straddle the worlds of Thebes and non-Thebes. Oedipus' tussle with Creon is delayed until nearly the climax of the play, when Creon reveals that Oedipus has slain his father; a confused Oedipus believes that Teiresias has been killed. Teiresias, just now out of prison, appears and confesses that he has already told the truth to Creon about the "man in the

---

[29] As Moddelmog 1993: 61–2 notes, classical scholars tend to downplay interpretations of *Oedipus* as detective fiction, while more popularizing critics and authors emphasize precisely that element. Alfaro's in-joke about Sherlock Holmes seems popularizing, here.

middle of the road." Oedipus misunderstands and explains that he simply had no choice but to kill: Teiresias then taps into the dominant metaphor of the play: "My son, even here you are still in there. . ... [Teiresias points to Oedipus' head.] You are still inside, *mi hijo*" (139). Here Alfaro crafts an iron-clad correspondence between the inside of *Oedipus*, and the inside of *prison*: every aspect of Oedipus's selfhood is linked to incarceration. He is not a free agent within the context of *barrio* and prison culture, but rather its most perfect, peerless subject.

Indeed, our Chicano Oedipus eventually realizes he's a subject in multiple senses, including contemporary, pedagogical ones. "I did exactly what [the gods] wanted, didn't I? I played out their version. My weakness was their plotting. . ... Am I the way their lesson looks? Am I? AM I THE WAY THEIR LESSON LOOKS?" (142). Not to put too fine a point on it, but, yes, he *is* the way their lesson looks; and it's not a pretty sight. A second *anagnorisis*, or 'recognition scene,' reveals Oedipus and Jocasta to each other: each is naturally horrified. Oedipus begs Jocasta to scoop out his eyes; she does; and as she kisses each bloody socket, Oedipus executes Alfaro's final twist: *Jocasta pulls back as Oedipus pulls out a small prison-made blade and shanks her with it* (152). Whereas the Sophoclean Jocasta's desperate death-by-noose dovetails with Greek conceptions of feminine vulnerability[30], Oedipus' shanking of his mother—besides the obvious sexual overtones—reinforces the play's central conceit: Oedipus is *always* a prisoner, even when "outside" prison. As the chorus intones typically Greek gnomic statements—such as "No man is *feliz*/ until he is six feet under"[31]—Oedipus dons a pair of old *cholo* shades, and walks with a blind man's cane. He meets Tiresias—his "father"—as Oedipus places his hand on his shoulder for balance. The end of the play? "Tiresias slowly leads him back to prison. We hear the prison doors opening as they enter, and closing as they leave" (153).

Alfaro's brilliant adaptation of *Oedipus* concludes with an effective ring composition: the prison soundscape reinforces the playwright's argument that lives in the *barrio* are Oedipal not in the Freudian sense, but in a far more devastating *narrative* sense. As in the original play, the plot of Oedipus' life is determined by the circumstances of his birth: this isn't fair and isn't just, but neither is Los Angeles. Told with verve and compassion, Alfaro's *Oedipus El Rey* thus lays bare the complex system of economics

---

[30] Loraux 1987: 13–17; 50–3.   [31] A version of the last line of the play, 1529–1530.

and ethnicity that dooms America's youngest citizens to a life of crime: for many Chicanos, it's a mix that's fatal to any deliverance from fatalism.

With *Bruja*—Alfaro's recent re-envisioning of Euripides' *Medea*[32] —the playwright again takes an ancient play and concentrates on what might seem the most difficult aspect of the original text: Medea's strange "otherness," her barbarian-ness as a Colchian from the Black Sea, and thus foreigner in the (highly self-regarding) "civilization" of the greater Panhellenic world. As in *Oedipus El Rey*, Alfaro maps this "otherness" onto a contemporary issue of particular urgency, this time of immigration and undocumented citizenship. As a native speaker of Nahuatl, an indigenous Aztec language, Medea is clearly marked (as in the original Greek text) as *barbarē*, 'barbarian,' albeit a barbarian happy to follow her lover Jason to the land of the civilized (that is to say Corinth ... or California). Alfaro complicates the ideological bases of the original play by equating Creon— king of Corinth—with American entrepreneurism: Jason abandons Medea not so much for a shot at political power as for the realization of the American Dream. Medea's terrible vengeance—the slaying of their children—thus signals a rejection not just of Jason, but of all that Jason signifies: a capitalist system that rewards exploitation in the name of "family." Alfaro's play exposes the contradictions in American constructions of immigrant labor at the cusp of the twenty-first century.[33]

Euripides' version of *Medea* has been so influential that it is easy to forget that the main plot point was, in fact, a shocking twist: as far as scholars can tell, this is the first version in which Medea intentionally slays her children.[34] This distressing ending might help account for the play's poor showing—an embarrassing third place prize for poor Euripides—but perhaps also because the ending emphasizes all too graphically the play's political critique of Greek society. After all, the play famously includes Jason's paean to the glories of Greek law and culture: the hero reminds Medea that she left a barbarian land for wonderful Greece, with its justice (*dikē*), and the rule of law (*nomoi*), and the opportunity for renown

---

[32] Many thanks to the playwright Luis Alfaro and literary manager Dori Jacob for providing me with a production copy of the script. *Bruja* premiered at San Francisco's Magic Theatre in May 2012. Subsequent productions are planned regionally.

[33] The bibliography on *Medea*, and its reception, is vast. For specifically postcolonial receptions of the play see the five essays that constitute "Appropriation and Exile" in Heike Bartel and Anne Simon 2010. Especially germane is Paula Straile-Costa's analysis of Cherríe Moraga's Xicana-Indígena version of the myth.

[34] William Allan 2002: 22–3. Other versions record Medea's accidental killing of her children, or their slaying by Creon's relatives.

(a renown that could never be secured at the edges of the world, ll. 538–540). Jason continues to stress that his present arrangement—of securing the throne of Corinth by marrying into the local royal family—will only benefit Medea's children economically and socially: Medea is trading up. Medea, perhaps unsurprisingly, rejects Jason's rhetorical arguments through some no-nonsense *praxis*—she kills the kids—and thus shines a searchlight on Jason's ideological sureties. Medea's final proclamation that she is escaping to Athens (ll. 1384–1385) only reinforces the play's political dimension: citizenship matters.

Alfaro's version of the play changes the character of Creon into a business mogul, whose power is predicated on unscrupulous real estate dealings: as Jason explains, "He's the biggest contractor in the city. Every wall, every kitchen, every parking lot—he's built it. And now I do" (23). An immigrant from Zamora, Michoacán, Creon has been perhaps *too* thoroughly assimilated into the American way of life—Jason admits that Creon is now "ruthless" as a businessman. Part of that assimilation is a terrible conflation of business and family: Creon will only support Jason if Jason is his adopted son and heir – otherwise, he is merely labor. Medea is horrified by Jason's ambitions and recoils from further association with either Creon or even other assimilated Mexican-Americans. Jason is furious: "Dress like them. Learn to talk like them. Be like this place" (23). Here, Jason outlines three essential prongs of assimilation: habit, language, and culture. Medea rebels against such assimilation, and continues her life as a *curandera*, 'native healer', with incantations in her native tongue—even as her neighbors whisper that she's a *bruja*, 'witch' (see Figure 5.4).

In both the original play and in Alfaro's re-envisioning, Medea treats the neighboring nobleman Aegeus for impotence: her therapy for his childlessness sows the seeds (so to speak) for her later vengeance on Jason. One of the many effects of this exchange is to position Medea as either an agent of family-making—a nurturer of the family—or family's deadliest opponent.[35] In Alfaro's version, Aegeus, himself an immigrant to America, reveals an ambivalence about the choices necessary for success in his adopted homeland: "I came to this country like everyone—to survive. I didn't realize you had to become a new person to do that. . . .. I put my head to the ground and I worked and I worked. To build something that would live longer than me. I didn't realize that you can't buy your success—you have to pay for it. Big difference" (44). Alfaro's Aegeus, though a

[35] For Medea as the sworn enemy of "familial *trophē*, 'nurturing'" see McDermott 1989: 91–2.

Figure 5.4. Sabina Zuniga Varela as Medea in *Bruja* by Luis Alfaro at Magic Theatre.

successful businessman, realizes the crucial distinction between "buying" and "paying for" success in America: the actual price is always far greater than the initial calculation. In the case of American immigration, that payment seems to be brutal work conditions in a hostile neighborhood, with an accompanying nostalgia for the world (and country) left behind.

Still, Jason pursues his American Dream with the tenacity and the determination of the truly evangelical, including the courtship (and even marriage) to Glauce, daughter of Creon. In Greek, *glaukē* means 'gleaming,' particularly with a blue-green tint; it is the (appropriate) name of a water nymph in Hesiod (*Theo.* 244) and the name of a spring in Corinth into which Glauce threw herself during her death throes (and which then took its name from this legendary death). As Jennifer Larson notes, Glauce, as a mythical figure, thus combines characteristics of both heroine and nymph;[36] she is set apart from the ordinary rabble by the connotations of her extraordinary name. (It's worth noting Creon's daughter is never named within the play itself; the name comes from other sources, such as Hyginus *Fab. 25* and the hypothesis to the play. Variant traditions name her Kreonta.) Alfaro, however, runs with both the name and the very *idea* of Glauce: as Creon explains, he realized he could only get ahead in America by marrying a *gabacha*—that is to say, an Anglo-American—and when it came time to name their only child, he took his inspiration from the mass media equivalent of the American Dream: "I used to hear about all these shiny magazines, 'glossy' magazines, and that is where I got the idea, but I didn't know how to spell it...." (29). As constructed by Alfaro—and Euripides before him—Glauce is the political and social antithesis of Medea: a secure, native-born citizen, financially protected, and with a predilection—in Alfaro's version—for glossy high fashion. As a wealthy *gabacha*, Glauce could not be more unlike Medea—or more desirable to Jason, who sees in Glauce the social path towards citizenship and a new, "American" family. Medea's terrible vengeance puns on the Greek connotations of Glauce's name, a visual quality that can be applied—as in Pindar *Olymp.* 8.49—to the silvery sheen of snakes. Glauce is in awe of the very implement of her death, as she contemplates the gift of Medea's snakeskin robe: "The snakeskin was so delicate and vibrant. Hundreds of threads, sitting side-by-side, shimmering like rain on a sidewalk" (69). As the snakes spring to life, Glauce, 'she who shimmers,' is shimmered to death.

[36] Larson 2001: 148.

To the extent to which Glauce is constructed as the most literally visible person in the play—always wearing eye-catching dresses at swanky parties, for instance—Medea comes to realize that she is, politically and socially, the *least* visible person in the play. As an "undocumented" immigrant, without even a marriage license, the powerless Medea is derided as a "ghost" by Creon (58), who then turns the play's powerful visual imagery against her. In the original play, Creon declares Medea a "fugitive" (φυγάδα, l. 273), cast from the land of Corinth; if he finds her and the children alive in Corinth after a day, she will be put to death. Alfaro transfers the power of exile from a tyrant to a rather more insidious institution: "If you are not out in a day, I'll have the INS [=Immigration and Naturalization Service] pick you up. You are one of the invisible ones now" (60). The difference in (probable) fortunes between Jason and Medea could not be more stark: Jason marries into a conspicuously "American" family, while the invisible Medea faces deportation back to Mexico, a country that her heart has never really left. (As Aegeus puts it, "I never felt like I was in exile until I met you. If someone like you, so much of the old country, can't go back, how can I?" (64).) The interfamilial problems of Jason and Medea mirror the political entanglements on both sides of the border.

Medea's slaughter of the children—Acan and Acat—is not just an act of vengeance; as in the original play, the murder is overdetermined as, paradoxically, an act of mercy. In Euripides' version, Medea views the murder of her children as a kinder, gentler version of the execution the boys will inevitably face if they stay in Corinth as unwelcome "barbarian" children: as Medea puts it, they would necessarily meet their end by an even *more* unfriendly hand (δυσμενεστέρᾳ χερί, l. 1239). Alfaro's Medea— while obviously pleased that she destroys Jason—has less to say about the probable fate of her children in America, but it's clear that her attack on the children—and Glauce—is an attack on Jason's newfound American Dream. The children are not just biological Progeny—the name of Aegeus' new baby daughter (15)—but symbols of the success and wealth that Jason plans (however ineptly) to foster in his new family business, with a *gabacha* on his arm. As the play concludes—with Glauce and the children dead, and with Creon as collateral damage from the snakes' poison—Alfaro steers the play into the world of memories: in a previous exchange, we discovered that Jason once saved his family and community during a terrible hurricane, and as he struggled, disconcerted and disheartened, in the mud and debris, he heard a call—*Gwa Gwa Gwa*—of the *guaco* bird, which he figured must be safe on high ground (33). The "bird" turned out to be

Medea, and he alludes to Medea's role as a guide throughout the play: "This bird got us across the border. We migrate and even El Guaco follows us." At the play's end, Jason kneels to Medea and squawks a call—*Gwa Gwa Gwa*—but receives no response: Medea is already "levitating" (71), taking flight, migrating to a new home and a new identity across old borders.

Alfaro's deft reworking of Euripides' play manages the nifty trick of preserving the play's "Greek-ness" while simultaneously teasing out the text's applicability to contemporary social issues. During the fraught exchange, Creon and Medea bandy about a term of particular interest:

CREON: Oh come on. This is pathetic.
MEDEA: I am pathetic. You said it yourself. I am a woman. There's nothing more pathetic in this world. (58–59)

The word 'pathetic' leaps out of the text: *pathos* is one of the three components of tragedy identified by Aristotle in his *Poetics* (the other two—'reversal' and 'recognition'—have also received buckets of scholarly ink).[37] For Aristotle, *pathos*, 'an action bringing pain or suffering' is one of the mechanisms by which a playwright might arouse "fear and pity" (*Poetics* 53b), but it is not necessarily related to the current stage action (unlike plot reversals and recognitions). Indeed, a *pathetic* moment or experience can occur off-stage, "before" the action of the play—such as Oedipus' murder of his father Laius. Alfaro's use of pathetic is, of course, modern—meaning something like 'pitiable'—but catches something of the flavor of the ancient usage as well: Medea has *already* killed her brother (an off-stage *pathos*, adapted from the earlier play) and will soon kill her children (on-stage *pathos*), provoking in contemporary San Francisco audiences the very ancient, and indeed universal, emotions of fear and pity. (At the performance I attended, audience members openly gasped at the *vieja*'s grisly messenger speech, which details Medea's snaky murder of Glauce. Rarely have I seen fear and pity so expertly provoked by a playwright, ancient *or* modern.) So Alfaro's Medea is clearly pathetic in the sense that she's a borderless woman, obviously disenfranchised, and increasingly shunted to the margins of *two* societies; but she is also pathetic in the richer, Aristotelian sense, of a character who's an inherent catalyst for communal suffering—the terrible consequences of a woman, and a migrant, scorned.

---

[37] B. R. Rees 1972: 1–11. See also Pietro Pucci 1980: 169–74, "Pity and Fear."

Knox's *The Oldest, Dead White European Males* argued that resistance to the canon was largely a failure of imagination, of the unwillingness to look past the race, gender, and geography of the ancients, and to engage with what truly matters: social and artistic thought. After his accidental perusing of Greek tragedy in a bookstore, the proudly Chicano Alfaro seems to have taken Knox's advice to heart: he looks past the original temporal and ethnic background of both Sophocles and Euripides, and grapples with their *ideas*: of the "fate" of the individual *vis-à-vis* the state, of the paradox and tragedy of non-normative social codes, of the apparently limitless human need for constructing borders and barbarians. Alfaro's "Greek" trilogy works because of, and not in spite of, its classical pedigree: it grounds its analysis of contemporary Chicano concerns in the political and social enquiries of the West's oldest—and, yes, whitest and deadest—men.

6 | Power, the canon, and the unexpected voice

As we saw in Chapter 2, the case for homosexuality—even homosexuals—in antiquity is a controversial one, and so the reinscription of homosexuality into the distant past is necessarily an ideologically freighted maneuver; to the jaundiced eye, it may even smack of cheap anachronism. In the previous chapter, we similarly turned our gaze to appropriations of the ancient world—famously characterized as the province of dead, white, European males—by emphatically *non*-dead, *non*-European cultures, including African-American and Chicano: these are appropriations that appropriately engage such hot-button issues as immigration, religion, and identity. But we are missing still further "voices" that speak, often unexpectedly, through the texts and ideas of antiquity: what, for instance, of receptions that reinscribe *women* into the world of dead (and only coincidentally white and European) males? Such reinscription necessarily constructs as well a previous *erasure* or ellipsis; indeed, feminist (or feminizing) adaptations often stress the *suppression* of women's voices from the ancient world, in sources both mythological and historical. Two contemporary versions of ancient heroic epic— *Lavinia* (2008) by Ursula Le Guin and *The Penelopiad* (2005) by Margaret Atwood—not only rewrite a "masculine" text from a female point of view, but spring from an interpretative crux or problem in the original text. In each case, the original poem's problematic construction of gender relations provides the impetus for a new, "corrective" version, one that redresses the ancient's poem's flawed depiction of female subjectivity.

In the case of Virgil's epic *Aeneid*, the "flaw" is that the Italian princess Lavinia—the "Helen" figure of the second half of the epic—simply does not possess the presence or personality of her Homeric counterpart; indeed, few characters in Virgil are so apparently presented as ciphers. She is, however, integral to the plot: the hero Aeneas, fleeing the destruction of his native Troy, is fated to marry her in Italy, thereby ending his exile and founding the Roman state. Lavinia is thus the lynchpin to the plot, even if her physical presence in the poem is reduced to just a few dozen lines. (In)famously, and although her very life is at stake, Lavinia never speaks in the poem: as she overhears a potential suitor, Turnus, quarrel with her mother Amata over her marital possibilities, she fantastically *blushes*:

> accepit vocem lacrimis Lavinia matris
> flagrantis perfusa genas, cui plurimus ignem
> subiecit rubor et calefacta per ora cucurrit.
> Indum sanguineo veluti violaverit ostro
> si quis ebur, aut mixta rubent ubi lilia multa
> alba rosa, talis virgo dabat ore colores. (12.64–69)

> > With tears cascading down her burning cheeks, Lavinia heard the voice of her mother; a redness cast its fire under her skin and ran through her warm face. Just as when someone stains Indian ivory with blood-red dye—or when white lilies grow red when mixed with roses—such colors did the maiden display on her face.

Though soon to be the wife of Aeneas (and thus progenitor of the Latin kings), Lavinia expresses herself exclusively through blushing; the blush, therefore, acts as Lavinia's sole narrative "voice," the only moment that readers catch a glimpse of her (possible) interiority. Moreover, as R. O. A. Lyne wryly phrases it, "it seems a tremendous amount of heat to attribute to a blush,"[1] and scholars since antiquity have sought the psychological or narrative bases for the extended simile. (Lyne helpfully catalogues the main threads of interpretation: that the blush reflects Lavinia's erotic impulses; that the blush is filtered through the fevered vision and wishes of her fiancé Turnus; that the blush stresses Lavinia's virginal *ethos*; that the blush is directed at Lavinia's mother rather than at Turnus.[2]) A recent stab at the problem, by Crescenzo Formicula, argues that Lavinia lacks speech largely because Lavinia, as an *idea*, belongs outside of time-limits of the poem: paradoxically, she's an essential part of the *Aeneid* and an outcast from it.[3] Her position thus precisely reverses the status and characterization of Dido, Aeneas' paramour from the first half of the poem. On the one hand, Dido, Queen of Carthage, is a detour on the way to greater things: she is not a *necessary* part of Aeneas' heroic conquest of Italy. On the other hand, Dido, as a *character*, threatens to devour the entire first half of the *Aeneid*, due in no small measure to her soaring speeches of staggering complexity

---

[1] Lyne 1983: 57.

[2] Lyne 1983: 61–2. For the conflation of blushing and violation in Latin poetry, Dyson 1999.

[3] Formicula 2006: 93. Cairns 1989: 151–76, through a reading of Lavinia's predecessors in lyric poetry, rescues the princess from earlier dismissals of her character as a passive, poorly characterized plot device.

and power. Lavinia is thus figured as a Dido-in-reverse: she's ontologically necessary—for Rome, she is a *sine qua non*—but dramatically opaque.

From a "feminist" point of view, then, Lavinia does not exactly make the grade as a role model for emulation; in fact, none of the *Aeneid*'s women do, though the "Amazon" Camilla comes closest. In the main, the *Aeneid*'s women are relegated to the periphery of Aeneas' relentless will-to-conquer, or, worse, are figured as impediments to his manifest destiny. Creusa, Aeneas' first wife, faithfully obeys her husband's orders to "stay a few steps behind" (*Aeneid* 2.711) during the frantic escape from Troy, and perishes in the subsequent holocaust.[4] The Carthaginian Queen Dido distracts Aeneas from his duties as the founder of the new Roman race, and, with her dying curse, prefigures the future Punic wars. Lavinia's distressingly delayed marriage (through no fault of her own) is nevertheless the primary narrative obstacle of the second half of the *Aeneid*. Though her story encompasses six books—more than Dido's episodes in Africa—Lavinia's silence looms large as a metaphor for the suppression of contrary voices. Even Aeneas' father Anchises receives multiple speeches of many lines, including an extraordinary prophecy of Rome's greatness (6.710–886)— and Anchises is *dead*. For Lavinia, however? Just a blush.

Ursula Le Guin's novel *Lavinia* (2008) owes its genesis to this extraordinary blush. As Le Guin revealed in an interview with *Kirkus* magazine, Virgil (on Le Guin's reading) ignored the character of Lavinia because she fit uneasily into the scope of the *Aeneid*'s second half:

> In the *Aeneid*, Lavinia is a mere convention, the blond maiden, a background figure barely sketched ... She so evidently has a voice, and Vergil knew how to listen to women; but he didn't have time to listen to her. He's in the war part of his story and has to get all the battles fought. So all Lavinia gets to do is blush.[5]

If Virgil was sincere in calling books 7 through 12 "the greater part" of his work (7.45), its greatness did not, it appears, extend to Lavinia. And so Le Guin's *Lavinia* is part of a project to reinscribe women into the poem's historical narrative, particularly the Italian books. Indeed, in Le Guin's view, *Lavinia* is a corrective to popular receptions of Rome as a "sick, luxurious Empire"; for her, the Roman republic is a place of "extended families," of women running farms and integrating themselves into the life

---

[4] Schleiner 1975 notes how the flight from Troy has been historically interpreted as an act of Aeneas' filial piety towards Anchises.

[5] As quoted by Ursula Le Guin on her website at: www.ursulakleguin.com/Index-Lavinia. html#Interviews

of the family. Unlike in Greece, women were "not set apart as chattel"; to Le Guin, they had subjectivity, agency, voice.[6]

Thus Le Guin turns the *Aeneid* inside out, showing the reader the voices and actions of lives lived "off-stage," so to speak. Indeed, *Lavinia* begs comparison, in its postmodern reconfiguring of an established, authoritative narrative, to Stoppard's *Rosencrantz and Guildenstern Are Dead*, which likewise takes a minor character from a masterwork (in this case, the Tweedle-Dee/Dum duo from *Hamlet*) and focalizes the narrative from a new and disconcerting point of view. Stoppard's play becomes a rumination on boredom, among other things: Rosencrantz and Guildenstern are so constrained by the logic of Shakespeare's master narrative that their off-stage actions are over-determinedly useless: no matter how many games they play—flipping coins is a much-beloved pastime—the two *can't* change fate. Rosencrantz and Guildenstern *are* dead because they *will* be dead: their fates are indissolubly wedded to Hamlet's story, and Hamlet's subsequent revenge. It cannot be otherwise. Lavinia, likewise, cannot and will not change the plot of the *Aeneid*; indeed, the *Aeneid* exists in large part *because* she cannot—or will not—change the story. So Le Guin's meditation on Lavinia begins with Lavinia's metaphysical fictionality: a "real" person who may or may not exist.

> No doubt someone with my own name, Lavinia, did exist, but she may have been so different from my own idea of myself, or my poet's idea of me, that it only confuses me to think about her. As far as I know, it was my poet who gave me any reality at all. (3)

This is already philosophically intriguing stuff, figuring the author as a godlike creator, and Lavinia as his female creation, who only exists because "written." (Specialists in Roman literature will recognize this as a *scripta puella,* most particularly from Roman love elegy.[7]) But Lavinia next introduces a surprising, narrative swerve: "But he did not write [the events of my life]. He slighted my life, in his poem. He scanted me, because he only came to know who I was when he was dying" (3). From Lavinia's point of view—and perhaps also from Le Guin's point of view—Virgil did not take an adequate interest in *her* story, concentrating too much on the male characters, on Turnus, Aeneas, Ascanius, and Pallas. Virgil realized his mistake, Lavinia intuits, only when it was too late: Lavinia only came to life when, ironically, the author passed into death. Lavinia laments—like some

[6] Le Guin 2008: 278–9.
[7] See for instance, Maria Wyke 1978: 47–61, "Written Women: Propertius' Scripta Puella."

subsequent scholars—that "the life [Virgil] gave me in his poem, is so dull, except for the one moment when my hair catches fire—so colorless, except when my maiden cheeks blush like ivory stained with crimson dye—so conventional, I can't bear it any longer. If I must go on existing century after century, then once at least I must break out and speak. He didn't let me say a word. I have to take the word from him" (4).

Le Guin's Lavinia emphasizes the two moments of the poem in which she displays any sort of subjectivity: her flaming hair and flaming cheeks. Both instances are visually stunning but sonically wordless; Lavinia might be a striking presence, but in Virgil, she is a mute one. So Le Guin's feisty Lavinia turns the violence of Virgil—who denied her speech—back on her creator: now Le Guin/Lavinia writes *Virgil* as a character, who appears not in the flesh, but as a melancholy ghost in a series of oneiric encounters in a wood (beginning at pp. 38–47). In *Lavinia's* world, magic has been displaced onto gender, and it is apparent that Lavinia—as priestess and as girl —has access to the supernatural by dint of her piety and femininity. An altercation between Lavinia and the ghost of Virgil demonstrates Lavinia's strong sense of right and wrong (she is angered at the miserable dead babies of Virgil's underworld: a "misinvention," she claims, that was morally "wrong", or *nefas*, 61); the passage demonstrates, as well, Lavinia's considerable pluck and will-to-correct. Finally, after a series of interviews, Virgil realizes the deep paradox of his subsequent "writing" *by* Lavinia: "You're almost nothing in my poem, almost nobody. An unkept promise. No mending that now, no filling your name with life, as I filled Dido's. But it's there, that life ungiven, there, in you. So now, at the end, when it's too late, you have it to give to me. My life" (63).

And so Le Guin has one-upped Virgil; the historical Virgil never lived to correct, even to notice, Lavinia's near-nothingness, her state of being "almost nobody." (Virgil could not even see Lavinia's true hair color, much less her soul.) Le Guin, more charitably, not only includes Virgil in her novel, but gives him the life, and the interiority, that he denied his own creation: Le Guin thus corrects (and implicitly chastises) Virgil through her own fiction. Hers is a correction, however, full of generosity, displaying the true love of Le Guin *aka* Lavinia for *both* her heroes, Aeneas and Virgil: "I am not the feminine voice you may have expected. Resentment is not what drives me to write my story.…" (68). This confession is especially surprising since both Lavinia—as a wisp of a character—and Le Guin—as a modern female reader—have fair claims to resenting Virgil's original work. *Lavinia* thus vacillates between two different types of loves: Lavinia's love for the hero who overshadowed and nearly obliterated her; and Le Guin's love for the poet who could create such a being. As Lavinia terms it:

> My question is which of them did I more truly love? And I cannot answer it. One was my husband, the beautiful man whose flesh my flesh enclosed to make my son in me, the author of my womanhood, my pride, my glory; the other was a shadow, a whisper in shadows, a virgin's dream or virgin, yet the author of all my being. How can I choose? I lost them both so soon. I knew them only a little better than they knew me. And I remember, always, that I am contingent.
> So, of course, were they. (68)

Le Guin here juggles issues of gender and authorship with uncommon grace: Lavinia, figured as "real," loves Aeneas because through Aeneas, she is metaphorically "authored" as a woman: she is thus gendered (even impregnated!) by the embodiment of Roman masculinity, and in that relationship there is love. Lavinia, as *truly* "authored" by Virgil, loves him as well: as a god-substitute who literally fashioned her being in the first place. To each man, Lavinia remains (sadly?) contingent: a wife to a husband, a character to an author.

Lavinia's final comment, however, reverses the thrust of her contingency: yes, Lavinia is contingent, but so is Aeneas, and so is Virgil; so is Le Guin, and so too, one might add, are we all. In the final analysis, we are, all of us, contingent on death; and thus Le Guin expands her feminist reading of the *Aeneid* into a more-ranging rumination on human mortality, and the limits of life. Indeed, within *Lavinia*, both Virgil and Aeneas encounter the limits of their respective lifespans; Aeneas dies shortly after marrying Lavinia, and Virgil—who dances between death and life, anyhow—fades for the final time.

The female-authored *Lavinia* thus "completes" the male-authored *Aeneid*. Le Guin is scrupulous about preserving the major events of the *Aeneid*, including Lavinia's voiceless blush ("I could not move or speak," she admits (159)), though the events are often told in paraphrase. The end of Virgil's *Aeneid*, featuring Aeneas' sudden and furious execution of the suppliant warrior Turnus, has become something of a battleground in scholarly interpretation: it brings to the fore Virgilian readings of Augustan virtues; the proper place of anger in ancient philosophical systems; the futility, or the necessity of war; and the inevitability of Roman imperialism and advancement. Though the end contingently concerns Lavinia—in admitting his defeat to Aeneas, Turnus concedes that "Lavinia is your wife; do not extend any further your hatred" (12.937–938)—Lavinia is present only as an exogamous link between native Italians and foreign Trojans. She is trafficked as property between two warring clans, and so the original poem ends. *Lavinia*, by contrast, absorbs this "male" ending within its own narrative (175): in fact, the novel really only comes to life in its final hundred pages, when Le Guin proffers a distinctly *female* version of the early Republic. Lavinia comes to terms with living "as a woman in exile," discovering that in casting off her girlish self and by "taking on the obligations of womanhood," she finds herself "freer than [she] had ever been" (184).

The final act of the novel thus presents the "classical world"—or its early Italian incarnation, at any rate—through the eyes of a mother, and so completes or supplements our modern knowledge of female experience in the ancient world. After all, the evidence for female-authored Roman literary texts is notoriously scanty: we have a half-dozen poems from the poetess Sulpicia (sometimes attributed to her contemporary Tibullus, instead); we have (possibly spurious) letters by Cornelia, mother of the tribunes Gaius and Tiberius Gracchus; and little else.[8] (It's a dispiriting haul.) So Lavinia's travails with her children—including her showdown with her "stepson" (192) Ascanius—reveal the modern concerns of a woman marrying into a new home.[9] This includes Ascanius' jealousy of "his baby half brother" Silvius (192); Lavinia's joys at breast-feeding (193); and Lavinia's own resentment of Ascanius' behavior, particularly towards his father (203). Her husband's death is narrated in the unblinking, dry manner of a woman looking back on life; in an ironic re-enactment of Aeneas' dual with Turnus, Aeneas once again has a suppliant at his sword's edge—but this time, he lets the suppliant live. Once freed, the suppliant grabs a weapon and spears Aeneas through the back (223)—so much for an heroic end. It's the sort of deflationary maneuver that Le Guin employs through the novel: there's nothing lofty about Lavinia's account of Grand Roman Myth. Lavinia's later widowhood plays out in a power struggle with Ascanius, as Lavinia strives to protect her biological son Silvius from danger; another self-imposed exile finds Lavinia at the loom and gardening (259).

Finally, Le Guin inserts a surprisingly homoerotic twist into the afterlife of the *Aeneid*. Ascanius' failure to produce an heir by his Rutulian wife, Salica, is at least implicitly tied to his undying affection for Atys, his "boy

---

[8] Conte 1994: 326 clearly attributes the Sulpicia poems of Tibullus 3.2 – 3.6 to Tibullus; other scholars continue to see in the "Sulpicia" poems a genuine female authorship.

[9] For Lavinia's grappling with exogamy in *Lavinia*, see the postcolonial reading of Rea 2010.

lover" (262); and Ascanius' inordinate weeping for Atys' death is tied to a lovers' spat between the pair. Lavinia admits that this is all "sad and shameful gossip," but it makes for a good story. It also jibes uneasily with ancient, historical attitudes towards sexuality; phrases like "Ascanius' sexual discomfort with women" (265) would not appear to have much basis in ancient sexual practices. (Perhaps such discomfort, Lavinia offers, drove him "to seek the tender simplicities of his first love" (265–266).)

The novel, as an anti-epic, fittingly ends with mundane, even banal, slices of daily life. It features scenes of sweeping the hearth, of preparing salted meal, and of sundry domestic matters, including the rearing of four grandchildren: Lavinia was now the "grandmother queen" (269). Only at the very end of novel do we again approach any measure of grandilo-quence: Lavinia imagines that she oftentimes hears an owl, crying into the night, *i, i,* the Latin command for '*go, go.*' "Only sometimes my soul wakes as a woman again, and then when I listen I can hear silence, and in the silence his [i.e. Virgil's] voice" (272).

It's too early to prophesy the scholarly and artistic fortunes of *Lavinia*, but initial reviews suggest that Le Guin's rewriting/re-feminization of the *Aeneid* has resonated strongly with some readers, particularly female ones; the *Boston Globe*'s Amanda Katz praises this "compelling" novel's "stew of feminism and pop-Buddhist philosophy" and ends with a ringing endorse-ment of Le Guin's central conceit: "This neglected queen may owe her place in legend to Virgil, but it is in Le Guin that she has finally found her poet."[10] By the same token, this same sense of reinserted interiority may also be seen as a fault: for instance, the *New York Sun's* Sam Munson complains of the title character's "flaccid introspections" and general passivity:[11] though rewritten as the star of her own novel, Lavinia is still in many ways trapped by Virgil's original narrative. She remains eternally circumspect—and circumscribed.

In *The Penelopiad*, which antedates *Lavinia* by only three years, Marga-ret Atwood likewise takes as her starting point a short, problematic passage from *another* "male" authored epic—only this time, it's the *Odyssey* that receives a radical re-gendering. The return of Odysseus to his homeland of Ithaca, and his subsequent, terrible revenge on his wife's suitors, consti-tutes the stuff of high adventure: the massacre is as visceral and bloody as anything in the *Iliad*. (The massacre even provides an occasion for the darkest of Homeric irony; Odysseus beheads the traitorous soothsayer

---

[10] *Boston Globe*, Aug. 2, 2008.   [11] *New York Sun*, Apr. 9, 2008.

Leiodes, who obviously didn't see him coming (*Od.* 22.302–305).) In the interlude between slaughter and marital reunion, however, lies a difficult, often neglected episode, one that doesn't exactly redound to the glory of either Odysseus or his son Telemachus, at least in the modern imagination. After the suitors' slaughter, Odysseus interrogates Eurycleia, his former nurse, about the extent of treachery among the household's female staff. Eurycleia replies that twelve of the fifty handmaidens were disloyal; she then asks to notify Penelope of Odysseus' arrival. Odysseus, however, wishes first to deal with the handmaidens; he commands, therefore, the women to be punished by sword for their secret liaisons with the suitors. First, the women are forced to clean up the remnants of the battle; then Telemachus, intriguingly, changes the punishment from death by steel to death by hanging, denying the women "a clean death" (22.462). Instead, he strings up all the women with a ship's cable and hangs them:

> Thus he spoke, and he tied the cable of a dark-prowed ship to a mighty pillar, and threw it around the rotunda: he stretched it aloft so that none of the women would be able to touch the ground with her feet. And just as when long-winged thrushes or doves are caught in a snare set in a thicket—just going to roost!—and receive instead a hateful resting-spot, even so did the women hold their heads all in a row, and around their necks were thrown nooses, so that they would die most piteously. The women jerked awhile with their feet, but not for long. (22.465–473)

As Laurel Fulkerson has argued, to the ancient mind, this death-by-hanging better fits the crime than the "clean," honorable death by sword proposed by Odysseus. For the Greeks, hanging constituted a particularly ignominious end: besides its spectacular nature, it was a slow, painful death (in contradistinction to the efficient dispatch of a sword).[12] In a sense, then, the perfidious handmaidens received a punishment even *worse* than that of the suitors, who at least were killed in a martial setting: the death of the handmaidens is calculated to inspire pity, mixed with contempt.

It is hard to believe that this wrenching incident is often skipped or omitted in retellings of the *Odyssey*. On the level of the poem's later reception, however, the reasons for its omission are not hard to fathom: it is difficult to square the grisly punishment of the maidservants with more positive appreciations of Odysseus's humanity or his sense of justice throughout the *Odyssey*. In fact, in his delightfully named *The Odyssey for Boys and Girls* (1906), Alfred J. Church goes out of his way to

---

[12] Fulkerson 2002.

whitewash the *Odyssey*—and specifically Odysseus—of any troubling ethical considerations. For the edification of the young and impressionable, Church's Odysseus refrains from stealing the Cyclops' cheese (4); accepts the seductress Circe's enthusiastic invitation to "Come now, let us be friends" (11) with no apparent sexual *quid pro quo*; and, after the death of the suitors, Odysseus simply bids the women to "come and wash the hall and the tables with water and smoke them with sulfur," as if this were just another day of bourgeois housekeeping. The death of the handmaidens is thereby elided, in accordance with Church's focus on the sort of stories appropriate to boys and girls. But even paraphrases intended for grown-ups may be complicit in such whitewashing, such as Thomas Cahill's gooey appraisal in *Sailing the Wine-Dark Sea: Why the Greeks Matter*. For Cahill, the *Odyssey* is the "world's first comic novel—and first romantic comedy" (72–73), and he sums up books 12–23 as if a scene from *The Honeymooners*: "Odysseus makes it home in the end, is reunited with his son, clears his home of interlopers, and once more sleeps with his faithful wife Penelope in the great rooted bed." Not only are the handmaidens not mentioned, but even the suitors are literally marginalized in a footnote: the massacre "can only be called a comic, even a ghoulishly humorous, episode. Such rough comedy, not quite to our taste, is nonetheless not far from the comic violence of Saturday morning cartoons and movies made for teenage boys …. [W]e are not to take it too seriously" (73). Instead, we should appreciate the violence for what it is: "zany" (73 fn. Δ). For Cahill, the "romance" of the *Odyssey* precludes extended rumination on the morality—even the inclusion—of the epic's concluding murders and executions.[13]

Margaret Atwood's *Penelopiad*, like Le Guin's *Lavinia*, proceeds from a very different reading of the *Odyssey*, one informed by Atwood's generally feminist ideology, and by her sense that previous readings of the *Odyssey*—such as Cahill's—ignore the disquieting narrative implications of the hanging scene.[14] Indeed, Atwood remarks in her introduction, "What led to the hanging of the maids, and what was Penelope really up to? The story as told in *The Odyssey* doesn't hold water; there are too many

[13] For a dark reading of the end of the epic, in which Odysseus reasserts his identity as an active agent of suffering, see Cook 2009: 130–4.
[14] For an examination of the ways in which Atwood's *Penelopiad* dovetails with some contemporary feminist critiques of the *Odyssey*, see especially Suzuki 2007: 269. For a quick overview of Atwood's acerbic protagonist as an example of "post-feminism at its most cynical," see Hall 2008: 125–6. For a reading of *Penelopiad* as a cautionary tale concerning "mutual betrayal among women," see Braund 2012: 206.

inconsistencies" (xv). In *Lavinia*, Le Guin uses Lavinia's "voice" to explain, or flesh out, the interiority of a silent character; though the *Odyssey's* Penelope is not exactly silent, Atwood senses, however, a similarly occluded narrative voice. Penelope—and her maidens—have a story, and Homer, like Virgil, refuses to tell it. Thus the matter is left to Penelope herself, even if her voice is (surprisingly) *post mortem*. Again, as in Le Guin's *Lavinia*, there's a blurring of identity between protagonist and author; Atwood confesses that she's "always been haunted by the hanged maids; and, in the *Penelopiad*, so is Penelope herself" (xv).

The title of Atwood's novel, then, confirms that we're now reading an epic told from the "wrong" point of view; or at least an epic told from a *female* point of view. Indeed, the suffix *-iad* lends a grandiose air to what is, after all, more of a novella than an epic. (In a similar move, poet Richard Howard employed the term as a specifically female parallel to Homer's work: "the loom's my odyssey—/ dare I call it my penelopiad?"[15]) Something of the novella's *modus operandi* can be gleaned from Penelope's explication of the famous dream of the geese from the original *Odyssey*.

> I have twenty geese in my house, that come from the water and eat wheat, and I am full of joy when I watch them. But a great eagle, with his crooked beak, swooped from the mountain and killed them all; in a heap, their carcasses lie in the great halls, while the bird is again borne aloft into the bright sky. Although in a dream, I wailed and lamented, surrounded by Achaean women with their fair locks: I was grieving in a most piteous way, because the eagle had killed my geese. (19.536–543)

As Penelope indicates in her preamble to Odysseus-as-beggar (19.535), the dream needs an auditor and interpreter: the dream is transparently symbolic, though symbolic of *what* is a more vexing issue. The dream even adverts to its own dreaminess with the curious Greek particle περ, 'although' (19.541): *although* in a dream, Penelope weeps—as if the dream-Penelope were aware of her own oneiric surroundings, her own fictionality. Indeed, the *real* Penelope does not even require the dream to end in order for the symbolism to be made pellucid. Returning to the scene of the crime, the dream-eagle reports to the sobbing dream-Penelope:

> Take heart, daughter of far-famed Icarius: this is not a dream, but a noble vision that will come true for you. For the geese are the suitors, and now in turn I am come as your husband, who will unleash a shameful death on all the suitors. (19.547–555)

[15] Howard, Richard. "Ithaca." *Grand Street*, Vol. 2, No. 4 (Summer, 1983), pp. 15–17. Pg. 17.

In a poem otherwise abundant with oblique symbolism and fantastic passages, the "dream of the geese" stands out as the rare Homeric passage that—amazingly—posits its own hermeneutics: within the *dream itself*, the eagle explains its function. We do not need an "Interpretation of Dreams" because the dream is self-interpreting: Odysseus is the eagle; the geese are the suitors; the dream itself is a harbinger of Odysseus' return. But commentators on the passage have noted the troubling incongruity between the "obvious" (even heavy-handed) symbolism, and Penelope's reaction: if the geese are indeed suitors, why weep for them at all?[16] A solution from the 1960s—that Penelope in fact harbors affection for the suitors, and that Odysseus' return "is rather a matter for apprehension than joy"—has received a host of scholarly responses, from cautious acceptance to outright dismissal.[17] (Marilyn Katz, for instance, has steered a middle road, arguing that the dream reflects, on an unconscious level, an affection for, or a least a comfort, with the suitors, however awkward the particulars of the situation: Penelope's weeping thus reflects her "divided state of mind."[18]) The real-Odysseus' own interpretation of the dream, predictably, mirrors that of the Eagle-as-Odysseus. According to him, the interpretation is both elementary and univocal: Odysseus will return and slay the suitors (19.555–556). Neither the eagle-Odysseus nor the hero-Odysseus make a stab at interpreting dream-Penelope's weeping, however. Within the poem's *own* hermeneutics, the passage is elided; within modern scholarly exegesis, the passage remains an interpretive crux.

We may add now a third Penelope to this *Odyssey*-Penelope and dream-Penelope: the Atwood-Penelope, who provides yet another iteration of the dream, and a radically different solution:

---

[16] Russo 1992: 102 points out that the geese's eating (within the dream) only reinforces the identification with the similarly eating suitors, and thus makes more Penelope's reaction all the more puzzling. Heitman 2005: 74 argues that the dream-eagle's own explanation does not work, since the twenty geese are thoroughly domesticated and the suitors are—shall we say—absolutely not. Instead, the twenty geese represent the twenty years of Odysseus' absence, and signal Penelope's distress and premonition over the change in her household circumstances: after twenty years, the dream-Penelope realizes that she must take another husband and change houses.

[17] Rankin 1962: 622. For a review (and dismissal) of similar interpretations, see Rozokoki 2001: 2–3. The debate obviously continues.

[18] Katz 1991: 146–7. A possible reflection of this line of interpretation can be found in Penelope's admission in the *Penelopiad* that she harbored some reveries about sex with the suitors: "I have to admit that I occasionally daydreamed about which [suitor] I would rather go to bed with, if it came to that" (105).

> ... I then related a dream of mine. It concerned my flock of lovely white
> geese, geese of which I was very fond. I dreamt that they were happily
> pecking around the yard when a huge eagle with a crooked beak swooped
> down and killed them all, whereupon I wept and wept.
>
> Odysseus-the-beggar interpreted this dream for me: the eagle was my
> husband, the geese were the Suitors, and the one would shortly slay the
> others. He said nothing about the crooked beak of the eagle, or my love
> for the geese and my anguish at their deaths.
>
> In the event, Odysseus was wrong about the dream. He was indeed the
> eagle, the geese were not the Suitors. The geese were my twelve maids, as
> I was soon to learn to my unending sorrow. (139–140)

Atwood has taken her central interpretative concern—the execution of the
maids—and cleverly linked it to *another* interpretative concern, again
related to gender. Atwood-Penelope has noticed the elements that the
Homeric-Odysseus (and the Eagle-Odysseus) chose *not* to interpret: the
crooked beak of the eagle (a Homeric epithet never explained) and dream-
Penelope's weeping. Finally, we receive an explanation for Penelope's
lamentation, straight from the horse's mouth, so to speak: "male" interpretations of the passage have misconstrued the gender of the geese.
Penelope's weeping is a prescient manifestation of her sense of bereavement, but not bereavement concerning the suitors: by the end of the poem,
it is her *sorority* who shall be slaughtered.[19] Towards the end of the
Penelopiad, Penelope herself links together the avian metaphors of these
controversial Homeric passages, mourning the loss of her "snow-white
geese. My thrushes, my doves" (160).

Of course, Atwood fudges the problem of numbers—there are twenty
geese in Homer's original, and apparently only twelve handmaidens. But
this is Penelope's story; and if she claims an unspecified "flock" of geese,
then, the reader must follow her lead. (As we saw in Merlis' *An Arrow's
Flight*—in which Philoctetes snaps the bow of Heracles—it is the preroga-
tive, perhaps even imperative, of adaptors to surprise the reader.[20]) In fact,
Penelope records a series of dreams that never made it into the *Odyssey*,
including premonitions of the Cyclops, the death-singing Sirens, and a
seductive mixture of Calypso-and-Helen (123). For the most part, however, Atwood hews closely to the Homeric original, with a minimum of
original, interpolated episodes. It's in the *backstory* that the *Penelopiad*
takes its liberties: the plot of the novella arcs to the same *conclusion* as the

---

[19] Indeed, Penelope nearly labels it a sorority: "We were almost like sisters" (114).
[20] See *supra* p. 77.

Odyssey, but through a completely different emotional map. Atwood's Penelope defines herself not through Odysseus—or at least not exclusively through Odysseus—but through her lived experience as a member of a sorority. Penelope is, we discover, the product of a broken home: her father tried to drown her as a girl (9); and her mother, a water nymph with appropriately "rippling laughter," was at best "chilly at heart" (10). Penelope's forced, exogamous marriage into another clan impressed upon her the strong relationship between gender and economics: the successful suitor "obtained wealth through the marriage – gold cups, silver bowls, horses, robes, weapons, all that trash ..." (26). Suitors of Penelope, then, didn't want Penelope: they wanted "only what comes with me—the royal connection, the pile of glittering junk" (29).

Though unceremoniously traded to Odysseus "like a package of meat" (39), Penelope and Odysseus do reach a level of intimacy, but one laced with distrust: "I myself had developed friendly feelings towards him—more than that, loving and passionate ones—and he behaved as if he reciprocated them. Which is not quite the same thing" (48). It's tough, it seems, to be married to a trickster king; and Odysseus' long absence at Troy does not exactly strengthen the union. Instead, Penelope bonds with Eurycleia (62–64), Odysseus' nurse and a maternal figure to both king and queen. In addition, she takes a keen interest in the slave girl Melantho—she of the Pretty Cheeks—one of many handmaidens that Penelope rears from infancy herself (88). Disappointed in her obnoxious son Telemachus—a characterization and a temperament expanded from sharp exchanges at *Odyssey* 1.356–359, 21.344–53, and 23.97–103—Penelope creates in effect a surrogate, substitute family of women: from the mother-substitute of Eurycleia to the daughter-substitutes of her handmaidens. With Odysseus far afield, Penelope takes on, as well, the economic tasks usually left to men, including inventory and animal husbandry (87–88).

In Homer's *Odyssey*, there is clearly cause for the handmaidens to be punished, if not executed; they have indeed been carousing with the suitors, and so have, in a sense, aided and abetted the enemy. Even in the *Odyssey*, Melantho's betrayal is figured as the most unseemly: Penelope raised her from childhood and gave her toys to delight in (18.322–323), but when asked by Odysseus-as-beggar to help ease the grief of Penelope as she cards the evening's wool (18.315–316), we discover that Melantho has no concern for the sorrow, *penthos*, of Penelope, but instead sleeps with and adores (in that order) the suitor Eurymachus (18.324–325). She responds to Odysseus' request with a hair-raising catalogue of the beggar's offenses, including his unwelcome presence in the company of noble suitors, and his mental impairment, whether through drunkenness or as his permanent condition (18.327–336). Odysseus' terse response encapsulates the Homeric ideology of punishment and gender: "Soon I shall leave and tell to Telemachus, you bitch, such things *you have announced in public* (ἀγορεύεις), so that he may, on the spot, slice you limb from limb" (18.339–340). The frightened maidens scatter at the threat.

Especially notable is the *public* nature of Melantho's insolence. As we have seen, Atwood never *contradicts* the public, narrated events of the original *Odyssey*, only their motivations or backstory. In fact, Penelope has secretly ordered her handmaidens to fraternize with the suitors, "to hang around" and "spy on them" (115):

> "You must pretend to be in love with these men. If they think you have taken their side, they'll confide in you and we'll know their plans. It's one way of serving your master, and he'll be very pleased with you when he comes home." That made them feel better.
>
> I even instructed them to say rude and disrespectful things about me and Telemachus, and about Odysseus as well, in order to further the illusion. They threw themselves into this project with a will: Melantho of the Pretty Cheeks was particularly adept at it, and had lots of fun thinking up snide remarks. (117)

Homer's *Odyssey*—the *Odyssey* of over two millennia—is here constructed as an "illusion"; because Homer has suppressed the interiority of Penelope, her own machinations are ignored by the dominant narrative voice. The insolence of the maids therefore seems just that: insolence. Melantho's rebuke of Odysseus (even if ironic and conspiratorial in Atwood-Penelope's world) earns the threat of execution in Odysseus' world, a threat subsequently made good. From the underworld, Atwood's Penelope admits her terrible error in judgment: she first endangered the girls by urging them to associate with the suitors (with resulting assaults and rapes), and next by failing to include Eurycleia as a co-conspirator, thus able to vindicate the maids at an appropriate moment (115). Instead, Homer-Eurycleia offers to inform Odysseus of the maids' malfeasance (19.495–498), and soon the maidens are hanged.

As we have seen, the bulk of the *Penelopiad*—appropriately—replays the major incidents at Ithaca through the focalizing lens of Penelope, thereby "correcting" the gender bias of the original epic. But Atwood has as well another trick up her sleeve: the voices of the maidens themselves, heard in music-hall choruses and parodies throughout the *Penelopiad*. The first, a "rope-jumping rhyme" (a macabre joke, considering that the maidens die from swinging from rope), directly upbraids Odysseus for his inhumanity: "We are the maids / the ones you killed / the ones you failed / we danced in air / our bare feet twitched / it was not fair." As the maids elaborate, Odysseus—the "you" of chant—slept with "every goddess, queen, and bitch" across the Mediterranean; yet, Odysseus "had the spear" and the "word": he combined masculine authority and voice into one, overpowering force (5–6). Justice is nowhere to be found. In a subsequent idyll, the maidens complain that they were birthed at the same time as Telemachus, "helpless as he was helpless but ten times more helpless as well" (66): Telemachus, in the heroic poetics of the *Odyssey*, "was longed for and feasted" as a "princeling" and rightful heir of the house, while the mothers of the maids merely "spawned, lambed, farrowed, littered, / foaled, whelped, and kittened, brooded, hatched out their clutch" (67). Again, Atwood emphasizes the arbitrary perks of both birth and gender: a male prince, born to a kingdom and a king, as opposed to the wretched, inhuman treatment of the infant maidens, "bought, traded, captured" and enslaved to that same king.

Having "problematized" key passages of the *Odyssey* through an interrogation of the collision of power and gender, the *Penelopiad* truly leaps off the rails in its climactic chapter "The Chorus Line: The Trial of Odysseus, as Videotaped by the Maids." Atwood's Penelope is forever chained to the outline of the Homeric story: even in death she ruminates on the tragic, haunting events of her days on Ithaca. The dead maids, incensed as they are by the injustice of the cosmos, feel no such compunction about sticking merely to Homer: their own diatribe against gender discrimination encompasses Aeschylus' *Oresteia* as well. The *Oresteia* (in)famously mythologizes the creation of the jury system through the trial of Orestes, ordered by Apollo to slay his mother, Clytemnestra, who had herself slain his father, Agamemnon. The Furies, ontologically furious at Orestes for his matricide, hound him throughout the Greek world; finally, a prepared trial at Athens pits Apollo and Orestes, exemplars of male privilege, against the Furies, female spirits of vengeance. Apollo's defense of Orestes includes the argument that mothers are not blood-related to their children, but are, rather, vessels for the father's seed; whether or not that particular argument holds weight, a split jury votes to acquit Orestes. The Furies are only mollified by promises of future cult offerings in Athens.

Critical commentary on the *Oresteia* is voluminous, particularly the troubled (and troubling) trial scene.[21] Atwood's decision to include the

---

[21] Gagarin 1976: 87–118, "Sexual and Political Conflict in the *Oresteia*" remains a lucid account of the conflict between blood-ties (supported by the females in the trilogy) and marriage-ties

themes of *Oresteia* in the *Penelopiad* replicates a rhetorical maneuver in the original poem. Throughout Homer's *Odyssey*, Odysseus encounters tell-tale signs of a disastrous homecoming: Agamemnon's return to his murderous, adulterous wife.[22] Within the design of the *Odyssey*, Agamemnon is figured as an anti-Odysseus: all brawn, no brains, and with little understanding of the potential perils of a *nostos*, 'homecoming.' Aeschylus' subsequent dramatic version of the aftermath foregrounds the notion of gender: the justice of Orestes' revenge hinges as much on gender as on any "objective" criteria. In Atwood's novella, Odysseus—like Orestes, on trial for the murder of the suitors—cops a plea of "self-defence" (177); the judge immediately agrees. Only after the angry ghosts of the maids appear does the court consider *their* deaths as well: the maids' complaint that they were "forgotten" is both a judicial *and* literary–critical grievance. The judge rectifies matters by "leafing through [a] book: *The Odyssey*" and reading of the maids' rapes; however, the judge deems this to be a crime of the maidens, rather than of Odysseus since they were being raped "without permission" (181) of their master. The judge therefore dismisses the case against Odysseus: it is a "regrettable but minor incident" and in any case, the judge does not want to be guilty of "anachronism" in the application of the law (182). As in Aeschylus' *Oresteia*, the Furies appear in order to exact vengeance: in Atwood's version, there are twelve – one for each maiden. Pandemonium ensues, as the judge screams for the Furies to cease their "barking and hissing" (amusingly, he also asks Athena to cover her chest, 184). Unlike Aeschylus' *Oresteia*, this conflict has no resolution: Athena whisks away Odysseus in a cloud.

By rewriting the end of the *Oresteia*, Atwood declares war on the muzzling of women's voices—even powerful women's voices, such as those of the Furies. Atwood's mini-*Oresteia*, like the *Penelopiad* that encompasses it, not only adapts and transforms a central, canonical text from antiquity, but takes aim at gender-biased interpretations of that same text. The maids implore the Furies not merely to "inflict punishment" on Odysseus and "exact vengeance" for their execution, but, in a startling turn of metafiction, to haunt the hero throughout centuries of subsequent scholarship: "Dog his footsteps, on earth or in Hades, wherever he may

---

(supported by males) (101); the male argument holds. Zeitlin's influential "The Dynamics of Misogyny: Myth and Mythmaking in the *Oresteia*" (Zeitlin 1978) analyzes the *Oresteia* as a self-conscious and powerful version of the myth of female matriarchy, eventually replaced by the (superior) political structure of a patriarchy.

[22] For a full list of Odyssean references to Agamemnon's death—as well as their structural purpose within the macronarrative of the *Odyssey*—see Olson 1990.

take refuge, in songs and in plays, in tomes and theses, in marginal notes and in appendices!" (183). The goal of the maidens—and by implication, the goal of Atwood—is not just to prove the iniquity of the original *Odyssey* and *Oresteia*, but the iniquity of the classical canon's later readers, adapters, and scholars, who continue to lionize Odysseus at the expense of Penelope specifically and women more generally. And while the *Penelopiad's* Odysseus is indeed upbraided as unjust, Atwood's *Penelopiad* is more concerned with constructing, positively, an alternate-*Odyssey*, one that replaces the *Odyssey's* concluding triumvirate of Laertes–Odysseus–Telemachus[23] with a household run by, and for, women, including Penelope, Eurycleia, Melantho, and the handmaidens.

But the *Penelopiad* must follow its own rules: the backstory may *never* become story, and the dead maidens never achieve a proper revenge, whether fictional or metafictional. Indeed, in the novel's *Envoi*, the maidens complain "we had no voice/we had no name" as they morph into owls: exactly the type of nocturnal, spooky bird that calls to Lavinia in Le Guin's version of the *Aeneid*. Ultimately, the *Penelopiad*, like *Lavinia*, reifies its *own* type of marginalization: neither work could (or can) exist independently from the male-authored epic that spawned it. Indeed, both *Penelopiad* and *Lavinia* are *senseless* without the enduring works of Virgil and Homer: the novels are, at best, complementary to the ancient epics, and, at worst, dependent on them in exactly the same ways that their original heroines—Penelope and Lavinia—are dependent on their husbands. In hewing so strictly to the plot lines of the original epics, both novelists expose the obnoxious male-bias of the original texts—in that sense, mission accomplished!—but paradoxically create novels that inhabit the margins of the texts they critique. The novels thereby reflect in metaliterary terms the problematic gender relations of the original myths.

In some ways, perhaps, attacks from the margins work better when compacted into smaller form: as hand-grenades rather than howitzers. Carol Ann Duffy's delightful *The World's Wife* rewrites a number of male-centered Western narratives through the eyes of neglected women —for instance, "Mrs. Rip Van Winkle," "Frau Freud," "Mrs. Lazarus," *et aliae*. Unsurprisingly, about half of the poems are receptions of classical myth, especially from Ovid's *Metamorphoses*, a particularly problematic text from the point of view of gender relations. (As Amy Richlin succinctly

---

[23] Laertes himself notes the amazing establishment of the triumvirate, when he remarks how fortunate he is to see his son and grandson vying in excellence (*Od.* 24.515).

puts it: "A woman reading Ovid faces difficulties."[24]) Duffy is especially keen on emphasizing women's knowledge: a knowledge largely impossible for any of the male authors of antiquity to comprehend, or even to recognize. In Ovid's myth of Teiresias, for example, the seer changes gender—from man to woman and back again—through a pair of miracles: these metamorphoses grant him knowledge of the sexual pleasure known to each gender (3.323: *Venus huic erat utraque nota*). In Duffy's hilarious version of the myth, Teiresias' newfound understanding isn't just of inter-course, but of a rather more mundane—but still essential—matter: menstrual cramps. "... [H]e started his period. / One week in bed. / Two doctors in. / Three painkillers four times a day. / And later / a letter / to the powers that be / demanding full-paid menstrual leave twelve weeks per year" (15–16). The passage has sting because it implicitly comments on Ovid's version—i.e. even a metamorphosed man is still only interested in sex—while pointing out Ovid's glaring blind spot: in a woman's world, sex may be an attractive option but *menses* are ineluctable. (And Teiresias' outrage is neatly gendered: it's an appeal to power to rectify the obligations of the female body.) For other Ovidian myths, Duffy likewise emphasizes the elided women's perspective, whether of the frazzled *hausfrau* Mrs. Midas ("I locked the cat in the cellar. / I moved the phone. / The toilet I didn't mind," 12) or the disappointed Mrs. Icarus ("[Mr. Icarus] is a total, utter, absolute, Grade A pillock," she sighs, 54).[25] The title of the collection, however, refers to Penelope, who, while waiting for Odysseus to return, begins to weave (and unravel) a death-shroud for Laertes, just as in Homer's original poem. But Duffy's Penelope takes pains to weave the smiling image of a non-Homeric, non-Odyssean wife, a woman "self-contained, absorbed, content, / most certainly not waiting" (71). That is to say, Duffy's Penelope, in her backstory of the *Odyssey*, weaves the *idea* of a *non-waiting*, independent Penelope—but this *non-waiting* Penelope only remains viable within the backstory of Duffy's slender poem. At the end of the sentence—and at the end of the poem—Homer's master narrative again intrudes: "I heard a far-too-late familiar tread outside the door" (71). In Duffy's version, Penelope, instead of rushing to a recognition scene with her long-last husband, instead licks her thread: she has discovered her

---

[24] Richlin 1992: 158.

[25] See Braund 2012: 196–202 for a complex reading of *The World's Wife* in which Duffy's female narrators—far from being simply foils for a feminist authorial voice—reveal a range of sometimes unsavory attributes, including selfishness and nastiness. Duffy thus forces the modern reader to judge each narrator on her merits.

vocation as an artist, as Duffy explained in a later interview.[26] So, if not exactly subverting the master narrative of the *Odyssey*, Duffy's version nonetheless locates within the original text an opportunity for destabilization, as the "feminist" Duffy torpedoes the hackneyed idea of an ever-waiting, ontologically incomplete Penelope.

Another spin: in her lovely poem "Letter to Artemis" (1999), Teresa Cader juxtaposes the profundity of Ancient Greece with the frivolity of contemporary Los Angeles:[27]

> You would find Los Angeles distasteful, dear A.,
> so please don't consider it. . . .
> Prey and arrow in the same animal?
> The huntress who showers golden arrows on herself?
> They don't like paradox. They'll whisk you off to a shrink,
> or a sun lamp parlor. You won't be invited to dine.
> And why go if you won't be radiant, adored?
> Remember Euripides? "Once I felt this thrill of pain
> in my womb. I cried out to Artemis in heaven,
> who loves the hunt and whose care relieves those
> giving birth." That moment of surrender,
> when the mind won't do, when the body takes over,
> is a bit like the D-word, and no one in L.A.
> talks about the D-word. When the Great Above
> meets the Great Below they run for cover. . ..
> Dear Artemis, you will be miserable
> in a place where the Great Below can mean
> anything above the age of 3o.

Here Cader quotes—exactly—a famous section of Euripides' *Hippolytus* (ll. 165–168), in which a chorus of female servants ruminates on the collision of *eros*, 'desire,' and the female body: how the conjunction of the two can only end with a womb "opened up" to the breeze, in the painful process of childbirth. It's one of the most explicit references in ancient fictional literature to this moment of greatest (and dangerous) liminality: from maiden to mother during the arduous journey through pregnancy to labor. The woman therefore cries out to the hunter goddess Artemis, who is also a goddess of initiatory rites: at once a protector of life during successful childbirth—and a bringer of death when that a birth goes disastrously

---

[26] www.sheerpoetry.co.uk/advanced/interviews/carol-ann-duffy-the-world-s-wife. Accessed Sept. 10, 2012.
[27] DeNicola 1999: 242–3.

wrong (Callimachus, *Hymn to Artemis*, 3.126).[28] Cader, like Euripides, makes explicit the connection between birth and death: in labor, a woman's corporal distress is so terrible that the mind vanishes, leaving the body in a state something like the "D-word": dying. In L.A., of course, no one dies, or rather, no one *admits* to dying; dying (like birthing) is what those over thirty do. Artemis, who embodies the complexities of femininity, death, and pain, would be miserable and ignored in e.g. Malibu. Instead, the narrator implores Artemis to

> . . .. Come to Boston
> where drab is a political virtue. . .
> Besides, if I give birth,
> or die anytime soon, I'll need your counsel:
> I can't fathom that ancient wisdom
> about controlling one's mind by letting go of it.
> Skip L.A. They're not your kind of angels.
> Ours are metaphorically correct, although
> anatomically not as beautiful as theirs.
> Please arrive by tomorrow. Yours devoted, T.

Now, Los Angeles may *look* inviting, the narrator argues, but the citizens there shun paradox, the complexities of women's bodies as figured in our Greek texts, particularly women's *dustropos harmonia*, 'discordant harmony.'[29] Los Angeles is thus the *antithesis* of Euripides' Athens: sex has no consequences; life has no death. Boston, an intellectual *polis* that eschews the glamour and the superficiality of its Californian counterpart, is a happier fit: if not exactly Athens, it still tries to fathom the ancient (Dionysian) wisdom of attaining self-control (*sophrosyne*) through letting go.[30] Like Athens, Boston admires a good metaphor: it understands that life can only be comprehended abstractly. So Los Angeles—city of cinema and cheap entertainment, of parties and fast cars—can't and won't understand women, in the sense that the Greeks, and Euripides, understood women and their sometimes scary *rites de passage*. Los Angeles is thus a lost cause; if only Artemis, moon goddess and protector of mothers, would arrive in Boston by tomorrow.

---

[28] Halleran 1995: 165. "Just as [Artemis] regulates hunting, bring both protection and death to wild animals, so can both she both ease childbirth and bring death during it." See Barrett 1964: 193 for the ritual connotations of Artemis' epithets.

[29] Zeitlin 1996: 237 for women's bodies, in the Greek mind, as a "'natural' oxymoron of conflict and ambiguity."

[30] The *Hippolytus* features more instances of the Greek term *sophrosyne*, 'self-control' (lit. 'sound mindedness') than any other tragedy as both Hippolytus and his incestuous stepmother Phaedra demonstrate their impotence in this regard. See Halleran 1995: 45–6.

Classics and the environment

In the previous section, we saw how one marginalized voice—that of women—can be (and on some views, *must* be) reinscribed into the classical canon. But what of viewpoints and identities that may not have existed in the ancient world itself? For instance, ecological approaches to literature and the environment—sometimes known as eco-criticism—have, at long last, made their way to classical studies, and indeed, some individual classical works (such as Virgil's *Bucolics*) would seem a natural, so to speak, for modern eco-critical methodologies.[31] Larger-scale ecocriticism is still more controversial. For instance, the fundamental premise of Horden and Purcell's massive *The Corrupting Sea: A Study of Mediterranean History* is this: that orthodox and narrative-driven histories of the ancient world have largely constructed "an extended Arcadia, a place born entirely of the classicizing imagination" (30). In other words, most textbook versions of Greece and Rome emphasize a fairy-tale version of antiquity that, however improved at the level of detail, largely rehearses the same periods, epochs, rulers, and régimes of previous narrative constructions of the Mediterranean. Such metanarratives of Greek and Roman history privilege systems of government over systems of ecology (if ecology is to be mentioned at all), and thus represent a skewed understanding of the geographical considerations of Mediterranean civilization. Horden and Purcell thus skip the "dazzle" (5) of the great cities of the West in favor of more meaningful "microregions" that litter the sea, including Cefalù, Melos, and Albufera. Indeed, their project envisions an historical metanarrative built on "microfoundations" (54): the shortest distance between points. For Horden and Purcell, the easy interaction by sea between many microregions lent itself to (among other things) political instability, and the sea was accused even in antiquity of being a corrupting influence: hence the volume's title (5). Subsequent analyses treat such "modern" topics as deforestation, land reclamation, and food storage; the geomorphological peculiarities of the Mediterranean (including caves, springs, and particularly dense glades) were "readily assimilable to the world of the divine" (412), and thus account, at least partially, for the complex interaction of religion and topography in the Mediterranean mind. Some reviewers of *The Corrupting Sea* raised epistemological concerns about such an eco-friendly approach: "What microecological interactionism sacrifices

---

[31] See for instance Timothy Saunders' chapter "'Using Green Words' or 'Abusing Bucolic Ground'" in Skoie and Velázquez 2006.

is the possibility of confronting the Mediterranean's own categorical knowledge of itself."[32] That is to say, if one takes social institutions out of history, one also excises the types of anthropological structures that Mediterranean peoples *themselves* used to structure existence: kinship, inheritance, and social hierarchy. It's traditional historiography turned inside out.

Volume One of the already gigantic *Corrupting Sea* promises a Volume Two that treats climate, disease, demography, and comparative geography (4); in essence, it applies the tools of modern environmental science to the ancient world. The reverse approach is more challenging: it takes true ingenuity to apply classical wisdom to contemporary environmental concerns like oil production and light bulbs. Indeed, that's the primary thrust of Melissa Lane's provocative take on Plato, her book-length *Eco-Republic: What the Ancients Can Teach Us about Ethics, Virtue, and Sustainable Living* (2010). For Lane, a professor of politics at Princeton, it's not a problem, per se, that Plato doesn't explicitly address e.g. carbon capping, big-game hunting, or plastic bags. Rather, Plato's significance as an environmental philosopher derives from his take on ethics—the proper behavior of the individual within larger social institutions—and particularly from Plato's use of myth and metaphor in the pursuit of the greater good (and better argument). Indeed, Lane's most stimulating arguments "spin" Platonic metaphors so that they comment on current environmental problems and perils. For instance, the myth of the cave—in which the benighted masses, seduced by the shadows, remain happily in the dark— demonstrates the dangers of complacency about climate change, and the need to step out of the cave and examine matters anew (4–5). The fable of the Ring of Gyges points out the dangers of isolationism (*Republic* 359e– 360b): in it, the shepherd Gyges, stumbling across a recently riven tomb, acquires a ring that allows him to turn invisible, thereby allowing him to act with impunity. The humble Gyges uses the ring's power to seduce the queen and murder the king, which, on a purely personal level, is an excellent return on investment. At the level of *society*, however, Gyges' actions constitute an ethical problem: why should an individual refrain from societally unjust actions that would benefit him personally, if there were otherwise no negative repercussions? Lane reframes this questions in terms of pressing environmental concerns: "[T]here is a modern version of the ring of Gyges which has exercised a pernicious effect on contemporary thought. This is the idea that the effect of individual action is negligible in

---

[32] James Fentress and Elizabeth Fentress 2001: 217.

its effect on many social outcomes, and, in particular, on many actions designed to achieve sustainability, for example by reducing greenhouse gas emissions" (48). For Lane, a huge stumbling block in the quest for environmental sustainability is the Gygean mindset that an action without perceptible individual repercussions—such as individual's fossil fuel consumption —is negligible at the *societal* level. To continue the reasoning of the Greek even further than Lane did: an individual's private, unregulated use of greenhouse-gas-fostering lightbulbs is, ethically, the equivalent of Gyges' regicide: an expression of unchecked power (*dynamis*) rather than justice (*dikē*). Though Plato doesn't directly speak to the environment, he does speak *about* the environment, insofar as environmental sustainability is an ethical and political concern.[33]

But ecological treatments of antiquity need not concern themselves with the actual *facts* of e.g. microregions or the philosophy of the well-regulated state. Novelist and poet James Lasdun's surprising take on Ovid's tale of Erysichthon, for instance, weds an ancient morality tale to contemporary environmental concerns, thereby providing a fascinating example of an ideological reception of antiquity through the *un*-ancient filter of ecological sustainability. (In this respect, Lasdun mimics the artistic technique of Le Guin and Atwood by retelling an epic story through a completely new sensibility.) Throughout the poem—an English, multi-stanzaic version of *Metamorphoses* 8.738–878, anthologized in *After Ovid*—Lasdun playfully combines epic tropes with modern environmental horrors, including landfill, toxins, and deforestation.[34] By transplanting the Greco-Roman tale of Erysichthon to (apparently) the American Pacific Northwest, Lasdun continues the centuries-long tradition of allegorizing Ovid's epic—in this case as a cautionary tale of capitalistic excess, checked only by the wrath of Mother Nature herself. This, then, is the "greening" of antiquity.

In some senses, the tale of Erysichthon has always been ripe for such a greening. As related by Callimachus in the *Hymn to Demeter* (and later adapted by Ovid), the prince Erysichthon's trespass has traditionally centered on environmental outrage, though an outrage that is *religious* rather than wasteful. With scandalously little motivation, Erysichthon, abetted by a posse of similarly maleficent souls, proposes to chop down a grove of Demeter, including a mighty poplar beloved by nearby, cavorting

---

[33] For an overview of America's escalating greenhouse gas emissions, see the alarming statistics at the Environmental Protection Agency's website: www.epa.gov/climatechange/ghgemissions/usinventoryreport.html

[34] Hofmann and Lasdun 1995.

nymphs. At the first blow, the poplar (horrifically) cries out in pain and summons the goddess Demeter, disguised as the priestess Nicippe. Nicippe warns Erysichthon of Demeter's certain wrath, but the prince shrugs off her warning: "Step back, or else I'll fix my mighty axe in your flesh! These trees will make a water-tight mess hall for my companions—where we will always eat hearty!" (ll. 53–55). Demeter-as-Nicippe then enjoins Erysichthon to enjoy his new mess hall—and also his hearty banquets, for she curses him with never-ending famine through the power of Nemesis. Eventually Erysichthon literally eats himself out of house and home— even the family feline ends up in his gullet—and he concludes his life as a roadside beggar. Besides providing a spectacular example of an Aristotelian reversal of fortune—the perfect tragic turn from loftiness to destitution—the frame of the poem (as a religious hymn to Demeter) makes clear the narrator's ultimately didactic purpose: to remind the reader of Demeter's power, she who has the power to save, as well as destroy, her people (134).

Ovid's version trans-plants (so to speak) the fairy-tale atmosphere of Callimachus' version into the epic Roman hexameter, thereby "Virgilian-izing" the story, as Brooks Otis neatly put it.[35] Indeed, Ovid's retelling is even more baroque than Callimachus', as he exaggerates both the crime, and tellingly, the punishment.[36] In Ovid's version, Erysichthon's attack is all the more reprehensible because it's the work of a mature king, rather than of a thoughtless lad; thus, in Ovid's version, Erysichthon's attack on Ceres' favorite oak-tree results in a cascading torrent of blood (mere sap just doesn't have the Grand Guignol touch that Ovid adores) as well as a hair-raising curse from a dying nymph. Likewise, Ovid transforms Erysichthon's hunger into a tour de force set piece of wit and invention, as the goddess *Fames* (Hunger)—who has, for starters, just a hole where a belly should be—infects Erysichthon with unquenchable hunger. Having exhausted his own resources, the king next pimps his daughter for funds, only to discover that she possess the gift of shape-shifting (and is thus easily re-prostituted). Eventually his daughter escapes, and Erysichthon is left with just one source of nutrition: himself. As Ovid puts it: "Erysichthon began to tear at his own limbs and champ on them with his teeth. Little by little the unlucky man nourished his body by consuming it" (*Met.* 8.877–878). A tale that begins with a tree ends with autophagy.

---

[35] Otis 1970: 414.

[36] See Thomas 1988 for the ways in which Virgil consciously re-writes episodes of tree violation to comment on the general *failure* of "automatic" retribution in the world of the *Aeneid*.

Lasdun's version—first published in 1994—is tendentious, even didactic, as it re-weaves the episode in a distinctly modern vein. The poem opens in a dystopic near-future (or, perhaps more alarmingly, a dystopic present), crowded with abandoned, leaking chemical plants, shopping malls, and fast-food chains (198). Lasdun's political concerns make themselves clear from the get-go: these are "post-colonial" factory outlets, remnants of America's manifest destiny, its imperial drive towards the Pacific West. Erysichthon is no longer a mere king but mogul, an "ex-boxer, entrepreneur, ex-con," with a speculator's penchant for rebranding real estate from "Grade A Conservation" to "Grade E"—suitable for land-grabbing schemes (198). For himself, plumped by delusions of grandeur, Erysichthon erects an estate of "shoddy brickwork" and "cheap timbers warping"; he convinces his fellow townspeople to support a similarly doomed chemical plant, whose "fissured concrete floor" allows "PCBs and toxic potions" to leach into nearby streams. (In a remarkable coincidence, Lasdun's story was published the same year as the class action lawsuit against Pacific Gas & Electric was filed, the basis for the film *Erin Brockovich*.) Though the woods soon fill with such monstrosities as "web-footed mice" and "snakes with fur" (200), Erysichthon hatches his grandest scheme yet: a resort village entitled *Cascade*, powered by "windmills and solar panels" and populated not with houses but with an "ideal/ carved in organic forms/ from eco-friendly natural materials" (201). (The quasi-Platonic use of "ideal" here is a nice touch: *Cascade* as a philosophical wonder, a heavenly notion brought to earth.) In a word, Erysichthon promises *Cascade* will be "green" (202).

As Lasdun has intuited, the poetics of landscapes loom large in Ovid's *Metamorphoses*; indeed, Charles Segal devoted an entire monograph to exploring the complex relationship of Ovidian landscape to narrative.[37] Ovid's tale embodies the literary critical conceit of the *pathetic fallacy*: the emotions and stresses of the human-centered narrative "spill over" into the landscape, which then take on metaphysical characteristics. In Ovid's original tale, the world surrounding the goddess Hunger appropriately takes on the characteristics of Hunger: a sterile, desolate, tree-less landscape covered in frost and gravel (8.788ff). In Lasdun's eco-fable, the outraged local priestess Gendenwitha—Iroquois for 'Day Star'—is ordered by Ceres to traipse to the land of Hunger to seek help in avenging Erysichthon's crimes. At first, Gendenwitha encounters a landscape that

---

[37] C.P. Segal: 1969.

mirrors the blighted America of the poem's opening: "stockyards and junkyards, strip-mines, foundries, factories," the detritus of America's industrial boom. But as she approaches Lasdun's version of Hunger, the landscape becomes even bleaker, a trail of "spilt oil,/ solvents, pesticides, slurries, lead" leading to "exhausted farmland," "rusting silos," "crooked-chimneyed huts," and at last a single "cinderblock shack" (206–207). In essence, Gendenwitha journeys to America's polluted heartland, where unchecked industrial expansion has poisoned the local natural resources. Hunger's subsequent attack on Erysichthon is similarly loaded with American imagery, this time of heartland excess (and heart disease): the mogul dreams immediately of "pies, pastries, ripe cheeses," next orders up the even less heart-healthy trio of "homefries, bacon, and eggs," and concludes (after a round of extraordinary bingeing) with "Big Macs and cheese-steaks": the nadir of American commercial cuisine. In Lasdun's reimagining, Erysichthon becomes himself a type of machine or factory: always eating, "breaking off only to breathe and defecate" (209), and steadily turning "gold to shit" in a perversion of medieval alchemy. His initial punishment, then, is a reversal of the economic prosperity that he unlawfully accrued at the beginning of the poem: Erysichthon is his own financial downfall.

In Ovid's *Metamorphoses*, Erysichthon concludes his punishment by eating himself: how, then, to tackle this ending from a modern angle? Lasdun, in keeping with his sociopolitical commentary on capitalistic excess, extends his environmental concerns to one last, appropriately epic simile, as Erysichthon, bleeding from self-inflicted bites, staggers back to the scene of the crime:

> And here
> His mutilated shape began to alter
> Into its own double-orificed
> Essence of greed and waste;
> Mouth and rear end opening
> To two huge O's; stomach and barrel chest
> Hallowing out from rim to rim
> Hardening as his limbs disappeared
> And nothing was left of him but a yard
> Of concrete pipe.
>
>   (210)

In one sense, the image is humorously grotesque, as in Mikhail Bakhtin's formulation of the phenomenon of grotesquerie:[38] the orifices of ingestion

---

[38] Bakhtin 1968: 18–19.

and expulsion are exaggerated for comic effect, even as Lasdun juggles multiple puns (barrels and rims, among others). In another sense, the image is deeply tragic: Erysichthon ends his life as yet another pollutant of *Cascade*, spilling forth waste endlessly into the (formerly beautiful) grove. And then a twist: Lasdun leaves antiquity far, far, behind in a breathless, non-Ovidian epilogue that jettisons the morality tale, and that celebrates the beauty and mutability of nature; the "red and yellow mosaic" of fall; the sparkling trees of winter; and, with a touch of wistfulness, the arrival of a springtime that even in spring seems "autumnal" (212). Lasdun's elegiac take on Callimachus and Ovid comes full circle: what began as a sorry panorama of the American landscape ends with the possibility—and only the possibility—of reclaiming nature from man's endless appetite for lumber, and wealth, and the engorgement of itself.[39]

In *Lavinia*, *Penelopiad*, and *The World's Wife*, we see epic narratives from an unusual—that is female—point of view, as the "receiving" narrative focalizes the plot through the sensibilities of an otherwise marginalized or elided voice. Lasdun's "Eryischthon"—similarly passionate—takes that tactic even further by retelling a tale from Ovid from the point of view of contemporary environmentalism, thereby grafting Callimachus' original poplar onto the novel landscape of (North) American conservation. In each case, a contemporary social force intrudes upon—or, more charitably, improves upon!—the original text, as authors use the classical world as a springboard for contemporary social agitation, particularly for otherwise powerless or underrepresented voices. In the next section, we see how a text that already concerns Power—in fact, that's actually a character *in* the text—spawns receptions that covet that power, as various social movements use the play *Prometheus Bound* as a type of megaphone: in Aeschylus, they have found their voice. As we near the end of *Antiquity Now*, we see more than ever how individual myths can spawn a tug-of-war between subsequent ideological camps—a tug-of-war that might even end (as we will see in this book's conclusion) in an interpretative breaking point.

---

[39] Not every critic is dazzled by Lasdun's eco-friendly take on Ovid. In a review of *Woman Police Officer in Elevator* (1997), in which "Erysichthon" is collected, Rochelle Ratner complains that the poem "does little more than trivialize its subject, presenting inanities such as the Iroquois woman who prays to 'Demeter, Ishtar, Ceres.'" (Review in *Library Journal*, Jan. 1997, pp. 103–4).

The unexpected voices of *Prometheus Bound*

Though only occasionally produced, Aeschylus' *Prometheus Bound* is fertile ground for ideologically charged receptions of antiquity, and it's little wonder that Prometheus figures as the inspirational myth for fire-breathing Marxists.[40] Indeed, nothing could be more natural—though, most probably, erroneous—than reading *Prometheus Bound* as an allegory of class struggle, of the desperate fight for social justice against a backdrop of tyranny and oppression. In Aeschylus' original play, the Titan Prometheus has stolen fire from heaven in direct defiance of Zeus, king of the Gods; the Titan thus lends his aid to poor, downtrodden humans at considerable risk to himself.[41] Zeus, enraged, sends the allegorically named *Force* and *Power* to teach Prometheus a lesson, and the insolent Titan is bound to a rock in the play's very first scene. Various personages, including Hermes, Oceanus, and a gaggle of nymphs, alternately ply Prometheus with succor or temptation, even as Zeus manipulates matters off-stage. (A bravura cameo by the mortal Io, raped by Zeus, provides ample evidence of Zeus' injustices elsewhere in the world of the play.) Yet Prometheus, defiant and stubborn, refuses to renounce his theft, or to spill the beans concerning Zeus' so-called "marriage secret." As befitting his name ('Forethought'), Prometheus alone comprehends that Zeus' impending nuptials to the nymph Thetis will produce a child greater than the father: in effect, there will be a new Zeus, after a new power struggle and a violent toppling of the previous, corrupt régime. Though the Prometheus myth has a few awkward details for advocates of pure Marxism—there's certainly no guarantee that this new Zeus will be any less tyrannical or oppressive than the old Zeus—there's still a fine sense of Marxist dialectic at work: of a corrupt ruling class overthrown by the oppressed proletariat, in the pursuit of a new, and more just, government.[42]

For a classicist, there are—to put it mildly—problems with this interpretation. In the original trilogy—as reconstructed by M. L. West—

---

[40] Eagleton 2011: 226. "Critics of Marx have sometimes noted a so-called Promethean strain in his work—a belief in Man's sovereignty over Nature, along with a faith in limitless human progress." For Marx's own metaphor of the worker-as-Prometheus, chained to the rock of capitalist production, see *Das Kapital* I.25.

[41] There is considerable scholarly controversy over the authorship of the *Prometheus Bound*: see Griffith 1977 for a detailed, and persuasive, examination of the evidence *against* Aeschylean authorship. For ease of reference, however, I will refer to the *Prometheus Bound* as by Aeschylus; the disputed authorship does not seem to have materially affected later receptions.

[42] See Foley 2012: 154–8 for a brief overview of American versions of *Prometheus Bound*, including the Bethlehem, Pennsylvania production of *Steelbound*.

Prometheus Bound most likely figured as the *middle* play, with the Titan Prometheus stealing fire in the first play (*Prometheus the Fire-Bringer*); enduring bondage in the second (extant) play; and escaping his chains in the surprisingly chipper finale (*Prometheus Unbound*).[43] As a *trilogy*, then, *Prometheus* cannot represent any *cycle* of dialectical materialism, but, in fact, gestures towards the *opposite*: it's a self-contained, and extremely Hegelian, triad of thesis–antithesis–synthesis, culminating in a static, peaceful, even joyous conclusion.[44] Indeed, Prometheus and Zeus, who begin the drama as hated rivals, appear to reach a heartwarming détente, which is rather like Trotsky and the Czar shaking hands instead of fists. Thus left-of-center interpretations of *Prometheus Bound* only work when interpreting—or *mis*-interpreting—the play as an independent artwork, divorced from the (probable) plot of its surrounding trilogy.

But that misinterpretation can be powerful in and of itself, and even a force for good. In the spring of 2011, the American Repertory Theater in Cambridge, Massachusetts—the theater connected to Harvard University—mounted a musical production of Aeschylus' *Prometheus Bound* that was intended not to (vaguely) "explore" or (even more vaguely) "interrogate" social forces—both buzzwords of the academy—but to actively and immediately provoke social change. (In other words: revolution.)

To that end, the production was co-sponsored by Amnesty International, an organization dedicated to the revelation and redress of human rights abuses against the powerless, particularly in authoritarian states (see Figure 6.1). As the program flyer from Amnesty International indicates, the so-called "Prometheus Project" thus works to "free prisoners of conscience and aid individuals at risk all over the world." After each performance of *Prometheus Bound*, "postcards [are] collected, petitions signed and opportunities provided to engage with Amnesty and human rights advocates." At the March 2011 performance that I attended, the audience was exhorted to agitate for the un-binding of Dhondup Wangchen, a Tibetan dissident imprisoned by Chinese authorities for an unflattering documentary concerning Chinese politics and the treatment of the Dalai Lama. Other performances were dedicated to prisoners in such global locales as Guatemala, Uganda, Iran, and Vietnam; their so-called "crimes" included

---

[43] West 1979: 130–48.

[44] Scully and Herington 1975: 16 argues that the final play likely represented a "synthesis" between the antithetical constructions of Zeus as tyrant and savior, resulting in the "reconciliation of the almighty power of Zeus with the civilizing intelligence of Prometheus."

Figure 6.1. Production photo from the American Repertory Theater's *Prometheus Bound*.

"propaganda against the state," "subversion of state power," "promot[ing] the right of workers and farmers," and "abusing democracy and freedom rights."

Two of the Amnesty appeals call for especial comment since they map onto the textual world of *Prometheus Bound* in unexpected ways. The March 7–9 performances were dedicated, for instance, to the (female) survivors of sexual violence in the Democratic Republic of the Congo: as the program declares, "the perpetual cycle of violence against women in the DRC must end." For those performances, then, the Prometheus Project is implicitly tied to the tribulations and suffering of the female *Io*, not the male Prometheus: it's the same text, different emphasis. For that performance, Zeus is not then just a metaphor for authoritarian rule, but for sexual violence against women. Likewise, the inclusion of America's Reggie Clemons—on death row in Missouri—"illustrates the flaws inherent in the U.S. death penalty system." Clemons is thus included in an Amnesty appeal not as a prisoner of conscience per se, but as an illustration of another parallel: like Prometheus, he's a victim of a flawed and biased juridical system, with a confession coerced by means of (alleged) police brutality during interrogation.[45] Again, this compels a rereading of the original text. The strangely abstract characters *Force* and *Violence* in Aeschylus' play now find a concrete parallel in contemporary America: the officers of the St. Louis Police Department.

Further contemporary versions of *Prometheus Bound* include the fulminating version by Tom Paulin ("Seize the Fire," 1990), with its impassioned diatribe against the military–industrial complex: "The gods of our new mythology are all generals and politicians" (29), Prometheus laments, before renewing a call for "democratic light" (65). The filmed version of *Seize the Fire*—which includes a blackout to pinpoints of light—has been compared to the candle-holding protestors in Wenceslas Square during Czechoslovakia's "Velvet Revolution" in 1989.[46] A new version (2005) by James Kerr transferred from London to New York with the black actor David Oyelowo in the title role, a decision clearly made to emphasize the West's shameful colonial slave trade. (From Mark Blankenship's *Variety* review of the New York production: "Kerr deserves praise for showing us a black man, dressed only in a loincloth and trying to escape shackles,

[45] www.justiceforreggie.com/wp-content/uploads/2009/05/2009-postexecution-fact-sheet-edit.pdf
[46] Hardwick 1999, "Placing Prometheus." The ending "creates an unforgettable resonance with the candle-carrying protesters in Wenceslas Square before the fall of the Soviet-dominated regime in the former Czechoslovakia."

without overselling the obvious connection to slavery."[47]) Each of the aforementioned versions of Prometheus "spin" the political undertones of the middle play—*Prometheus Bound*—in order to highlight the role of oppression and to agitate on behalf of the unfairly disenfranchised. This list could be extended almost indefinitely: Tony Harrison's film version (1998) tackles (among other things) the rights of coal miners in post-WWII Britain, an adaptation with a strongly socialist slant.[48]

There's at least one political reception of *Prometheus Bound* that's likely to catch the unwary (or Greek-less) reader off-guard, but worthy of attention because it shows the complex interrelation between nascent social movements and classical reception.[49] In 1978, the team of Harold and Ruth Birnbaum crafted a theatrical reconstruction of the entire Prometheus trilogy, a project that seems, on its surface, a particularly noble undertaking. Scholarly reconstructions of ancient trilogies, such as Ruth Scodel's painstaking reconstruction of Euripides' *Trojan Trilogy*, tend to piece together extant papyrus fragments along with evidence from later quotations, summaries, and "influenced" texts: this is philological detective work, cast in the form of essay or book.[50] It's exhausting labor, requiring a host of technical skills, including an excellent working knowledge of Ancient Greek grammar as well as Greek tragic meter and conventions. Birnbaum and Birnbaum *seem* to be following a similarly conservative route in their artistic adaptation/translation of the Prometheus trilogy. Indeed, the first play—*Prometheus Bound*—is fairly literal, even pedestrian, in its translation of the original Greek. The second play, *Prometheus Unbound*, is "guided in part by the eleven extant fragments" from various classical sources, with the parts glued together by the Birnbaums' new text. For the last play, however, there's a surprise: the authors admit that

---

[47] www.variety.com/review/VE1117933141

[48] For a passionate appreciation of this film, see Hall 2002.

[49] This particular version was published in the eclectic Coronado Press, of Lawrence, Kansas. A search of Coronado Press volumes of the 1970s reveals an odd assortment of books on classical literature, American religious thought, and social policy. Indeed, another Coronado Press product of the year 1978—*Fluoridation: The Great Dilemma* by George L. Waldbott— argued vehemently against the burgeoning (and progressive) fluoridation movement in the United States; in a sharply critical review, G. Neil Jenkins worries that laymen will be "oblivious of the omissions and obsolete presuppositions upon which much of [Waldbott's argument] is based." (June 28, 1979) "Review of Fluoridation: The Great Dilemma," *New Scientist*: 1108.

[50] See, for instance, Scodel 1980: 64–79 for an interpretation of Euripides' *Troades* and the fragmentary *Alexander* and *Palamedes* as a "Trojan Trilogy," involving a thematic through-line of the Trojan War (and its aftermath); the complex character of Odysseus; and the murder of the innocent, on both sides of the Trojan War. Scodel introduces her task with the necessary disclaimer, "This is a highly speculative book" (7).

Prometheus Firebearer "should have portrayed the reconciliation of Zeus and Prometheus through the intermediation of some other god," along with the apotheosis of Hercules and the institution of a ritual torch-race (9). The authors then include the startling segue "Instead ..." (*Why* "instead"? That question is never quite answered) "... we undertook to portray further development in the character of Prometheus by putting him in direct contact with mortals ..." Even more intriguingly, further plot developments are suggested by "the meeting in 1972 between President Nixon and Chairman Mao Tze-Tung." Thus the Birnbaums jettison the intermediary gods suggested by parallels with other classical texts, and model the final, climactic meeting of Prometheus and Zeus on the leaders of the China and the United States, respectively.

This is a startling development. One might expect, then, a thoroughly political conclusion to the *Prometheus Trilogy*, a heady brew of capitalism, communism, and the struggle for social justice. It might even mirror, in its way, the American Repertory Theater/Amnesty International version, especially the emphasis on Communist political dissidents. Not so. For the Birnbaums also throw into the mix the impassioned musings of Nobel Prize winning biologist Jacques Monod, whose thundering *Chance and Necessity: An Essay on the Natural Philosophy of Modern Biology* (1971) tackles nothing less than the origins of species and the (im)possibilities of God. Judeo-Christianity, wherein man evolves in the image of "God," is an especial target; Monod urges instead a properly implemented *knowledge of ethics*, one that confronts "the animal in man," and that recognizes that man belongs both to the animal kingdom *and* the kingdom of ideas. For Monod, animist systems—in other words, religions—prefer to "ignore, to denigrate, or bully biological man," and "to instill in him an abhorrence or terror of certain traits inherent in his animal nature" (178).[51] In addition to the writings of Monod, the Birnbaums reflect on a particularly philosophical speech given to Congress by American Senator Sam J. Ervin on Sept. 20, 1966, in which the Senator waxes rhapsodic about the sundry beauties of nature, including dogwoods, marigolds, and twinkling stars (11). He concludes: "On the basis of these things, I affirm with complete conviction that the universe and man are not the haphazard products of

---

[51] For Monod, animisms have attempted to hijack ethical concerns that more properly originate in biology, a natural system ruled by chance and necessity (and not perforce by god). The resulting mishmash of science and religion in the twentieth century (in particular) has muddied the West's approach to ethics and rights: "For their moral bases, the 'liberal' societies of the West still teach—or pay lip-service to—a disgusting farrago of Judeo-Christian religiosity, scientific progressivism, belief in the 'natural' rights of man, and utilitarian pragmatism" (171).

blind atoms wandering aimlessly about in chaos, but, on the contrary are the creations of God, the Maker of the universe and man" (12).

To recap: for the final play of the trilogy, the Birnbaums have adopted the *form* of the Nixon/Tze-Tung political summit, but have filled the drama with the *content* of a dialectic between biologist Jacques Monod and American Senator Sam J. Ervin. So Prometheus/Monod and Zeus/Ervin meet not to discuss trade agreements, or political détente, but the unsettled question of the origin of the cosmos and the existence of God. Of course, Zeus *is* a god, which would rather seem to settle matters; but things take a surprising turn after Zeus and Prometheus agree that their conflict resulted not from the will of Fate (a common excuse) but from the employment of free will itself (110). Each god chose his own path—the one of theft, the other of vengeance—and was brought to this (literally) pretty pass. Prometheus then argues that the gods, then, are not beholden to Fate; but Zeus disabuses him of this notion, and argues that there is indeed a power that is greater than the gods themselves. The gods, after all, are not timeless: as Zeus confesses, "I did not live at the beginning of Time, nor did I create the Universe, of which the Earth is but part" (110). Instead, there must be something greater than the gods, and that entity is ... the Almighty. Just as Senator Ervin observed that the ordered beauty of nature proves the existence of a transcendental creator, so too does Zeus wax poetic about the *improbable* splendor of the cosmos:

> I look upon a tiny flower, I see its shape, its many parts, its color; and I smell its scent ... and I ask, who taught the seed to develop in that manner? I see a myriad of flowers, of divergent and varied shape, size, and hue; this multiplies my wonder, how all of this was ordered and arranged ... I look at animals—each different kind—and birds and insects, too ... I ask, does all this happen by chance alone? If I say that everything is possible, is it not also possible that patterns were established, by which each object in the Universe was made and shaped, in their invariant and also in their evolving and mutant forms? The answer seems to me to be a choice between the two, a choice between Chance and Plan. I cannot believe that all I see can result from Chance alone. I believe that each developed according to a Plan, although the Plan allows chance variations from the Plan which the Plan prescribes. A Plan requires a Planner, and in my belief that Planner is some part or all of that which I call God. (113)

Zeus doesn't explicitly demonize Darwin—that would be anachronistic, I suppose—but, clearly, the King of the Gods is no great fan of *On the Origin of Species* or of evolutionary theory in general. The overarching

"Plan" of the universe isn't dictated by Darwin's dispassionate system of scientific principles—of mutation and selection—but by a design that can only be described as intelligent. Indeed, the Birnbaums' 1978 *The Prometheus Trilogy* eerily prefigures the renewed attacks on evolution during the Reagan-era culture wars in America: just four year later, the Louisiana legislature will pass in 1982 the jawbreakingly-titled "Balanced Treatment for Creation-Science and Evolution-Science in Public School Instruction Act," which mandated equal public school class time for creationism and evolution.[52] After the Supreme Court found that Act unconstitutional (as establishment of religion), creation science morphed into the more constitutionally viable "Intelligent Design" movement, a philosophy that nevertheless attempts to "replace materialistic explanations with the theistic understanding that nature and human beings are created by God."[53] Even if the Supreme Court was ultimately unmoved, creation science finds its latest convert in the Titan Prometheus, who is wowed by Zeus' penetrating analysis of the mysteries of the universe: "And still I claim that I am wise, because I have the wisdom to know that you are wiser than I. . .. You say that there are things which you do not understand, that there are questions for which you do not know the answers. You thus leave me with problems which are still unsolved. . .. I look only for the means by which I can make a closer approach to Truth" (115). Zeus, triumphant, gives Prometheus a burning torch by which "men may see the Light of Reason to illuminate their Faith" (116). The curtain falls.

This is *very* different from the revolutionary Prometheus envisioned by the American Repertory Theater, a titan who brandishes a torch in one hand and a pitchfork in the other. In their section entitled *Annotations*, the Birnbaums note that this final play, *Prometheus Firebearer*, attacks not political tyranny, but "the tyranny of the absolute," and that "we have said our say in the Monologue of Zeus which ends the play" (2). It's a remarkably forthright admission of ideological bias: the American Repertory Theater argues that its "social justice" interpretation is true to the original play, while the Birnbaums—agitating for a flavor of creation-science—at least acknowledge some level of sheer invention. Yet the original text's themes of creation-and-evolution—Prometheus even catalogues the

[52] For the Supreme Court Decision based on this law, see Edwards v. Aguillard, 482 U.S. 578 (1987) at http://caselaw.lp.findlaw.com/scripts/getcase.pl?navby=CASE&court=US&vol=482&page=578
[53] From the Discovery Institute's "The Wedge Document: So What?," produced in the aftermath of a leaked internal memo (1999). www.discovery.org/scripts/viewDB/filesDB-download.php?id=349

evolution of civilization at ll. 436–468—might indeed invite reflections on how the universe is created, ordered, and operated. And with opportunities to expound on creation largely hijacked by discussions of e.g. The Gospel According to St. John 1.1–5,[54] the Birnbaums saw in Aeschylus a tantalizing opportunity to insert a novel voice: to construct a Supreme Judeo-Christian "Planner" from the fragments of a *pagan* author, using the form of a modern political summit, and the rhetoric of a Platonic dialogue. By recasting Aeschylus' play as an inquiry into cosmological truth, the Birnbaums steer the "immanent" meaning of the original text from political revolution to theological revolution, as god and god realize that an even greater God, if not a greater Good, guides us all.

---

[54] John's emphasis (John 1.1) on the literal primacy of *logos*, 'reason,' would seem to be perfect for Zeus' creation science argument concerning the importance, and existence, of a Plan and a Planner: Ἐν ἀρχῇ ἦν ὁ λόγος, καὶ ὁ λόγος ἦν πρὸς τὸν θεόν, καὶ θεὸς ἦν ὁ λόγος.

7 | In conclusion: On fractures and fracturing

To conclude this book-length survey of a host of classical receptions, I wish to propose a thought experiment. Let us imagine that in the year 4015—when enterprising Martians make planetfall on a barren, post-apocalyptic Earth—that the only passably relevant record of Earthling history between the Bronze Age and the Fall of Rome is this book: *Antiquity Now*. That is to say, nothing else exists: no texts, no artifacts, no monuments (not even the Parthenon, which was sadly evaporated in the 7th World War). Nothing. Fortunately, our Martians are as well versed in philology as they are in warp-drive technology, and are able to bring to bear on this text their superhuman powers of literary and historical deduction; still, even if they were to tease every possible "fact" about antiquity from this book, their narrative of Greece and Rome would look very, *very* different from the master-narratives, of, say, Christopher Kelley's *The Roman Empire: A Very Short Introduction* (Oxford, 2006) or Oxford's co-written collection *Ancient Greece: A Political, Social, and Cultural History* (1998). Indeed, a Martian dissertation on *Antiquity Now*—one of many dissecting its language, historical evidence, and curious footnoting conventions—could likely draw only a few tentative conclusions about human society in the ancient Mediterranean. That dissertation could say something generally true, or at least plausible, about ancient governments (tyrannical, democratic, oligarchic); something intriguing about the condition of women and civic minorities; and perhaps something rather more coherent about patterns of art and literature, and why ancient Earthlings ever bothered with *mimesis*. (This last might excite the Martians most of all. I should hope so.)

But what would be missing—conspicuously—is a comprehensive, temporal, "march" of history, as well as the ancient social institutions that usually figure so prominently in Earthling narratives of themselves. In *Antiquity Now*, a Martian searches in vain for such standard contours of classical narrative as The Rise of Christianity; or The Fall of Rome; or The Triumph of Art in the Age of Perikles—to say nothing of the technical terminology that most often accompanies such narratives. (A Martian would miss, for instance, the crucial term *princeps*, 'Emperor,' appropriated by Augustus to end-run around the problematic connotations of *rex*, 'king.' She would also miss the succession of emperors at least occasionally drilled into the brains of school children.) The Martian wouldn't, then, have recourse to the attempts by the classics profession to explain the Greek and Roman world as any sort of *unified* narrative, a sequence of events that we might happily (or unhappily) term ancient history, crammed with betrayals, and prayers, and wars, and fishing, and revolution, and sex, and death. Stuff, in other words, happened. But our industrious Martian couldn't possibly create any story of this period from the tidbits gleaned from *Antiquity Now*: the Rome of playwright Richard Nelson looks little like the Rome of novelist Ursula Le Guin; Oliver Stone's big-screen Macedonia—with its destiny manifestly Eastward—bears little resemblance to the Bronze Age, comic-book Greece of Eric Shanower. Hedwig's eight-limbed hermaphrodites gibe uneasily with the hairy-chested he-men of Frank Miller's *300*. This story—or, to wax more poetic, this mirror—of "our" past would seem irredeemably fractured.

And "fracturing" is exactly the right term, one now used by theorists of modern popular culture to describe certain trends in contemporary discourse. (*Antiquity Now* could as well be re-titled *Antiquity Shattered*, perhaps even *Pulverized*.) For some, such "fracturing" has deep economic roots: iconoclastic British historian Eric Hobsbawm sees in post-1960s globalization the fracturing of a previously cohesive "European bourgeois civilization," one that "lost its bearings" when it unwittingly—or, perhaps in a Marxist framework, ineluctably—produced advances in technology so impressive that it eventually demolished, through mass media, its own bourgeois underpinnings.[1] Suddenly, the "stories" of the European elites—as well as their art, literature, and narratives—held far less mindshare: high culture was out, and new, mass-media art forms (like comics and the blockbuster film!) were *in*. For Hobsbawm, the overriding metaphor of this new, post-60s world is "fracturing." High bourgeois culture had been unified, architectural, consistent. Mass culture, by contrast, is all slivers and shards.

Rana Emerson, working specifically on American television, emphasizes the hermeneutic ramifications of this new, postmodern phenomenon: "[Fragmentation] describes the ways that American culture has become split up into so very many specific pieces that a group that consumes one type of culture can be completely unaware of what is consumed by another."[2] Thus "fracturing" can describe the sorts of discourses now propagated by modern fanboy subcultures, in which passionate individuals

---

[1] Hobsbawm 2013: 1–2.
[2] www.popmatters.com/feature/138794-dollhouse-fox-television-and-cultural-fragmentation/

can easily locate—usually through the internet—like-minded fans, and thereby form a novel (and sometimes influential) interpretative community, a community that doesn't necessarily engage in wider considerations of context or applicability. (We saw a particularly good example of this in the introduction, in which fans of *Buffy the Vampire Slayer* worked feverishly to explicate Sappho's poem "Hymn to Aphrodite" in the episode "Restless"—but that explication was, for them, to further a penetrating analysis of *Buffy*'s themes, not Sappho's.) The subcultures analyzed by *Antiquity Now* unsurprisingly run the gamut of contemporary life, from fanboys of sci-fi and animated television, to environmentally conscious authors and critics (such as James Lasdun and his eco-friendly "Erysichthon"), to the earnest, Intelligent Design creators of a new *Prometheus* trilogy. Contemporary social communities thus "consume" antiquity in ways that are often mutually unintelligible, but which makes sense within the context, and ideological framework, of that specific consuming culture. (For instance, only dedicated fans of the animated children's show *My Little Pony: Friendship Is Magic* could fathom the stakes of its Icarus-inflected episode "Sonic Rainboom," eventually unpacked by enthusiasts at http://mlp.wikia.com/wiki/Sonic%5FRainboom.[3])

Just as often, *Antiquity Now* has examined receptions of the classical world by artists concerned with—for lack of a better word—"identity," such as Chicano identities (as in the case of Luis Alfaro and his Greek trilogy), or GLBT identities (such as Andrew Calimach and his *Gay Greek Myths*), or feminist identities (such as Margaret Atwood and her *Penelopiad*). In these cases, the ancient world has been used as a springboard for investigation of the contemporary self: the ancient world as a catalyst in the quest for self-definition. The traumatizing events of 9/11 pose a special case: in the aftermath of the attacks, the French paper *Le Monde* famously declared "Nous sommes tous Américains," a headline that indicates not only a crisis for *American* self-definition—who are Americans?—but demonstrates the wider, absolutely global implications of any answer.[4] Thus the chapter on the "classical reception" of 9/11 demonstrates how ancient tensions between East and West—already encoded in such texts as *The Bacchae* and Herodotus' *Histories*—are easily co-opted into contemporary debates over Western and (Middle) Eastern culture.

---

[3] Male fans of *My Little Pony* are known as Bronies; the phenomenon has been recently explored in the film documentary "Bronies: The Extremely Unexpected Adult Fans of *My Little Pony*" (2013).

[4] Reprinted at www.lemonde.fr/idees/article/2007/05/23/nous-sommes-tous-americains_913706_3232.html

For contemporary artists, adapters, and thinkers, then, the ancient world is not generally approached as a system, or even as a complete story. *Specific* works, themes, and events are adapted by *specific* authors, groups, and societies for *specific* arguments, objectives, and policies: reception is goal-oriented. There are, of course, artists who aim to translate into modernity the essence of a classical text, and whose goals are primarily aesthetic; to the extent that translation is a type of reception, we can perhaps allow an exception to the general rule. But a glance at the multifarious receptions in *Antiquity Now*—from calls for gay equality to examinations of gang violence to passionate pleas for peace (or war)—reveals a "classical antiquity" that reconfigures itself daily, as modernity explains itself to itself through ever-expanding technologies and media. In other words, modernity conducts surgical strikes on the art, history, and science of the ancient world, a realm charged with especial value in the imagination of modernity.

The response by the academy has been the creation of an entirely new subfield, "Classical Reception Studies," such as at Northwestern University in Evanston, Illinois, and at University College London. This field analyzes not Classical Antiquity per se—a geography bounded by time and space and material culture—but the diachronic *idea* of "Classical Antiquity," a type of narrative fractal. If the form of *Antiquity Now* seems ultimately kaleidoscopic, it's because form matches content: our fractured modernity has spawned necessarily—perhaps even beautifully—a similarly fractured antiquity.

At its best this fracturing of antiquity allows for a progressive dialogue between antiquity and modernity, between constructions of the past and our ever-morphing aspirations for the future. For instance, the recent block-buster film *Superman: Man of Steel* (2013) is, on the one hand, a perfect "popcorn" film—suitable for the consumption of America's favorite buttery snack. But it's also perfect for the consumption of Plato, similarly slippery but considerably less fattening. The film "reboots" the comic book series by imagining the infant Superman's escape from the doomed planet Krypton, as well as Superman's subsequent upbringing in Kansas, for a century now the bell-wether of sweeping political movements in the United States.[5] Superman's adolescence—under his adopted name Clark Kent—is a trau-matic one, since Clark needs to keep his pesky superpowers under wraps. In a pivotal flashback, our hero is bullied by scoundrels at school, even as he clutches his apparently cherished copy of Plato's *Republic* (see Figure 7.1).

---

[5] See especially Thomas Frank's witty and insightful *What's the Matter with Kansas?* (2005), which traces Kansas' tilt from leftist politics to extreme conservatism.

Figure 7.1. The young Superman clutches a copy of Plato's *Republic*.

What is Plato—of all texts—doing in the middle of a popcorn film? It turns out that just as there is nothing more American than *Superman*, there's nothing more American than classical reception in *Superman*. And the inclusion of the *Republic* isn't a throwaway gesture, nor an accident: Clark isn't working his way through, say, *Timaeus* (or, even better, *The Catcher in the Rye*) but through classical antiquity's most famous meditation on utopian society. Of course, Plato's ideal society—in which citizens are channeled into three general "castes" based on childhood talent (415a–415c)—has seemed to many an unfortunate precursor to fascism and/or totalitarianism, or in any case to dystopia. Indeed, Superman's home planet of Krypton seems to have operated on Platonic principles, as each Kryptonian baby—artificially conceived in the so-called Genesis chamber—must have its DNA decoded by a Codex, which then dictates its future role in society, including the military. (The film's arch villain Zod was born to be a soldier, for instance, or the "silver" caste in Plato's original framework. For Plato, philosophers naturally receive the metaphor of gold; workers, iron or copper.) Through the machinations of his surprisingly open-minded parents, Kal-El (*aka* Clark Kent) is the first baby in generations to be born *outside* of this Platonic framework; in other words, he's the first baby in modern Kryptonian history to *choose* his, or her, own destiny.

Superman's childhood consumption of Plato's *Republic* has been itself variously consumed by critics and fans in the blogosphere.[6] Peter Lawler, professor of government at Berry College and a former member of President Bush's council on bioethics, published a right-leaning column that stresses the film's valorization of personal choice, a buzzword of the contemporary American right (in healthcare and the market, especially): "The Greek and Roman efforts to make citizens through education sometimes failed, and it's the not-so-secret teaching of the *Republic* that it's contrary to nature—or both undesirable and impossible—to eradicate personal choice through some comprehensive and highly intrusive process of political socialization, one that abolishes privacy and the family and chains even sexual behavior to the requirements of the just city."[7] Nicholas Clairmont, a philosopher "shocked" at Lawler's reading, crafted an entire blogpost decrying the film's misguided philosophical underpinnings, in

---

[6] For an impressive list of Platonic parallels in *Man of Steel*, see Keith Wayne Brown's blog post "The Platonic Superman" at http://keithwaynebrown.com/2013/06/26/the-platonic-superman/. Accessed Apr. 14, 2014.

[7] "Reading Plato with the Man of Steel." http://bigthink.com/rightly-understood/reading-plato-with-the-man-of-steel. Accessed Apr. 15, 2014.

"Superman Should Not Study Philosophy." He proposes a more likely, more authentically Superman-esque reading of Plato:

> So, what reading would a scared and isolated teenage boy who is demonstrably, objectively superior to everyone around him take from the *Republic*?
>
> Clark Kent would be inspired by Plato to claim and take a superior position on Earth. When he met resistance, he would feel like he had humanity's permission to overcome that resistance with force. He would feel duty-bound to create and manage a race of superior beings.
>
> It just so happens that the above paragraph describes the motivation and agenda of *Man of Steel's* villain perfectly.
>
> In short, the producers of *Man of Steel* are guilty of pseudo-intellectualism and sheer hack-ery. They have managed to, at once, insult both human history's most important intellectual discipline and the message of their own movie.[8]

Now this is likely a more accurate reading of *The Republic* than Lawler's, but it falters a bit in equating the ideology of Plato with the ideology of the *film*. It posits that the young Clark Kent, in merely *reading* Plato, would *follow* Plato, which very few in human history have done, and fewer still in Kansas. (Even *Aristotle* doesn't follow Plato.)

What the narrative proposes is far more sophisticated than what Clairmont allows: it first offers up Planet Krypton as a Platonic Republic, and next introduces a liminal character—part-American, part Kryptonian—who investigates the ancient, philosophical underpinnings of that society and who must make a painful choice between the Platonic society of his birth land and his new, adopted American homeland. The Kryptonian villain Zod, both monosyllabic and monomaniacal, never had that choice, and has become a ruthlessly efficient Platonic guardian of his beleaguered *polis*: a superman (but not Superman) ready to soldier for his planet, and eager to terraform America (and for good measure, the rest of the planet) into Plato's *Republic*. Superman, by contrast, is a model *immigrant*, who, having *read* Plato's *Republic*, then *rejects* Plato's *Republic*, and instead adopts the prevailing ideology of America, with its enduring fascination with liberty, self-determination, and personal choice, both in the political sphere, and in the economic.[9] When, at the end of the film, an American

---

[8] http://bigthink.com/think-tank/superman-should-not-study-philosophy

[9] In his blog "Christ and Pulp Culture," Geoffrey Reiter likewise concludes that the film generally repudiates Plato's *Republic*; Reiter, however, concentrates on Superman's personal moral choices—exemplified by the Ring of Gyges myth from the *Republic*—and explores possible overlaps with the film's other overriding metaphor, that of Christ. www.patheos.com/blogs/christandpopculture/2013/07/superman-not-just-a-man-but-a-just-man/. Accessed Apr. 14, 2014.

general is worried that perhaps Superman is the enemy of America—a new, Platonic Zod?—the naturalized Superman rushes to reassure him: "I grew up in Kansas, you can't get more American than that." As an "ideal"—the word used to describe Superman by his father, Jor-El—Superman indeed represents a model American: strong, manly, impressively coiffed, and skeptical of freedom-squelching Platonic philosophy. In crafting this particular reception of antiquity, the screenwriters thus *juxtapose* one particular geography of antiquity—Plato's fictional Republic—with the political landscape of heartland America, whose narrative—or, rather, fiction of itself—is still being written.

And as various communities and consumers fall to fisticuffs over Plato—theologians and philosophers and classicists and bioethicists and *Superman* fans[10]—it's time that we bolt from the fracas, and from yet another fractured (and equally fractious) reception of the classical world. In other words, Superman's playground reading exemplifies the creative, meaningful use of antiquity, transplanted into the here and (especially) *now*.

---

[10] The forum "Fan Theories" continues the analysis of the Platonic underpinnings of *Man of Steel* with an especially thoughtful round-table discussion of possible allusions to Plato's Myth of the Cave. www.reddit.com/r/FanTheories/comments/1gw5ux/anonymous_on_man_of_steel/

References

Alfaro, Luis (2006) "Electricidad: A Chicano Take on the Tragedy of 'Electra.'" *American Theatre* 23: 63–85.

(2011). *Oedipus El Rey*. Washington, DC: Woolly Mammoth Theater Company.

(2013) *Bruja*. Unpublished.

Allan, William (2002) *Euripides: Medea*. London: Duckworth.

(2008) *Euripides: Helen*. Cambridge. Cambridge University Press.

Alvarez, R. (2009) *The Wire: Truth Be Told*. New York: Grove Press.

Anderson, Elijah (1999). *Code of the Street: Decency, Violence, and the Moral Life of the Inner City*. New York: W. W. Norton

Armstrong, David (1989) *Horace*. New Haven, CT: Yale University Press.

Armstrong, R. H. (2005) *A Compulsion for Antiquity: Freud and the Ancient World*. Ithaca, NY: Cornell University Press.

Bakhtin, M. M. (1968) *Rabelais and his World*. Cambridge, MA: MIT Press.

Barrett, W. S. (1964) *Hippolytus*. Oxford: Clarendon Press.

Barrow, Rosemary (2000) "'Mad about the boy': Mythological models and Victorian painting." *Dialogus. Hellenic Studies Review* 7: 124–42.

Bartel, Heike and Anne Simon (2010) *Unbinding Medea: Interdisciplinary Approaches to a Classical Myth from Antiquity to the 21st Century*. Oxford: Legenda.

Baswell, Christopher (1995) *Virgil in Medieval England: Figuring the Aeneid from the Twelfth Century to Chaucer*. Cambridge: Cambridge University Press.

Behlman, Lee (2003) "From ancient to Victorian cultural studies: Assessing Foucault." *Victorian Poetry* 41: 453–63.

Berkoff, S. (1983). *Decadence; and, Greek*. London: J. Calder.

Berlioz, Hector (1966). *Memoirs*. Trans. Rachel and Eleanor Holmes, revised Ernest Newman. New York: Dover.

Bernal, M. (1987) *Black Athena: The Afroasiatic Roots of Classical Civilization*. New Brunswick, NJ: Rutgers University Press.

Bloom, Allan (1987) *The Closing of the American Mind*. New York: Simon & Schuster.

Bowersock, G. W. (1994) *Fiction as History: Nero to Julian*. Berkeley, CA: University of California Press.

Braund, Susanna (2012) "'We're here too, the ones without names.' A study of female voices as imagined by Margaret Atwood, Carol Ann Duffy, and Marguerite Yourcenar." *Classical Receptions Journal* 4(2): 190–208.

Bravmann, Scott (1997) *Queer Fictions of the Past: History, Culture and Difference*. Cambridge: Cambridge University Press.

Broadhead, H. D. (1960) *The Persae of Aeschylus*. Cambridge: Cambridge University Press.

Cahill, Thomas (2003) *Sailing the Wine-dark Sea: Why the Greeks Matter*. New York: Doubleday.

Cairns, Francis (1989) *Virgil's Augustan Epic*. Cambridge: Cambridge University Press.

Caldwell, Tanya M. (2008). *Virgil Made English: The Decline of Classical Authority*. New York: Palgrave.

Calimach, Andrew (2002) *Lovers' Legends: The Gay Greek Myths*. New Rochelle, NY: Haiduk Press.

Chantraine, Pierre (1968–1980) *Dictionnaire étymologique de la langue grecque*. Paris: Klincksieck.

Chapman, John Jay (1931) *Lucian, Plato, and Greek Morals*. Boston, MA: Houghton Mifflin.

Conte, Gian Biago (1994) *Latin Literature. A History*. Trans. Joseph B. Solodow, revised by Don Fowler and Glenn W. Most. Baltimore, MD: Johns Hopkins University Press.

Cook, Erwin (2009) "Active and passive heroics in the *Odyssey*." In *Oxford Readings in the 'Odyssey,'* ed. L. Doherty. Oxford: Oxford University Press. Pp. 111–34.

Cyrino, M. S. (2005) *Big Screen Rome*. Malden, MA: Blackwell.

Dale, A. M. (1967) *Helen*. Oxford: Clarendon Press.

Davidson, James (2007) *The Greeks and Greek Love: A Radical Reappraisal of Homosexuality in Ancient Greece*. London: Weidenfeld & Nicolson.

D'Emelio, John (1983) *Sexual Politics, Sexual Communities: The Making of a Homosexual Minority in the United States, 1940–1970*. Chicago, IL: University of Chicago Press.

Demetriou, Kyriacos N. (2001) "Historians on Macedonian imperialism and Alexander the Great." *Journal of Modern Greek Studies* 19: 23–60.

DeNicola, D. (1999) *Orpheus & Company: Contemporary Poems on Greek Mythology*. Hanover, NH: University Press of New England.

Denton, Martin (2006) *Playing with Canons: Explosive New Works from Great Literature by America's Indie Playwrights*. New York: The New York Theatre Experience, Inc.

Derrida, Jacques (1985) *Margins of Philosophy*. Trans. Alan Bass. Chicago, IL: University of Chicago Press.

Devereux, George (1967) "Greek pseudo-homosexuality and the 'Greek Miracle.'" *Symbolae Osloenses* 42: 69–92.

(1970) "The nature of Sappho's seizure in Fr. 31 LP as evidence of her inversion." *The Classical Quarterly* NS 20, No. (1): 17–31.

(1985) *The Character of the Euripidean Hippolytus: An Ethno-psychoanalytical Study*. Chico, CA: Scholars Press.

DiLullo, Tara (2007) *300: The Art of the Film*. Milwaukie, OR: Dark Horse Comics.

Dodds, E. R. (1960) *Euripides. Bacchae*, 2nd edn. Oxford: Oxford University Press.

(1966) "On misunderstanding the 'Oedipus Rex'." *Greece & Rome* Second Series 13(1): 37–49.

Drake, Robert (1998) *The Gay Canon: Great Books Every Gay Man Should Read.* New York: Anchor Books.

Driver, Susan (2007) *Queer Girls and Popular Culture: Reading, Resisting, and Creating Media.* New York: Peter Lang.

Duckworth, George Eckel (1994) *The Nature of Roman Comedy: A Study in Popular Entertainment,* 2nd edn. Norman, OK: University of Oklahoma Press.

Dué, Casey (2006) *The Captive Woman's Lament in Greek Tragedy.* Austin, TX: University of Texas Press.

Dutch, Dorota (2010) "From hip hop to Homer: Practicing translation in central Los Angeles." *Classical World* 103(2): 246–50.

Dyson, Julia T. (1999) "Lilies and violence: Lavinia's blush in the Song of Orpheus," *Classical Philology* 94(3): 281–8.

Eagleton, T. (2011). *Why Marx Was Right.* New Haven, CT: Yale University Press.

Ebbott, Mary (2000) "The List of the War Dead in Aeschylus' *Persians*." *Harvard Studies in Classical Philology* 100: 83–96.

Eco, Umberto (1986) *Travels in Hyperreality.* San Diego, CA: Harvest Books.

Eisner, Robert (1987) *The Road to Daulis: Psychoanalysis, Psychology, and Classical Mythology.* Syracuse, NY: Syracuse University Press.

Eliot, T. S. (1975, orig. 1944) *"What Is a Classic?" Selected Prose of T.S. Eliot.* San Diego, CA: Harvest Books. Pp. 115–31.

Fagles, Robert (2006) *The Aeneid.* New York: Viking.

Fairey, Emily (2011) "Persians in Frank Miller's *300* and Greek vase painting." In *Classics and Comics,* eds. George Kovacs and C. W. Marshall. Oxford: Oxford University Press. Pp. 158–72.

Fantham, Elaine (1979) "Ovid's Ceyx and Alcyone: The metamorphosis of a myth." *Phoenix* 33(4): 330–45.

Faraone, Christopher A. (1999) *Ancient Greek Love Magic.* Cambridge, MA: Harvard University Press.

Farrell, Joseph (2002) "'Metamorphoses': A play by Mary Zimmerman." *American Journal of Philology* 123(4): 623–7.

Feldman, Allen (2001) "Philoktetes revisited: White public space and the political geography of public safety." *Social Text 68* 19(3): 57–89.

Fentress, James and Elizabeth Fentress (2001) "'The hole in the doughnut,' a review of *The Corrupting Sea: A Study of Mediterranean History* by Peregrine Horden and Nicholas Purcell." *Past and Present* 173: 203–19.

Fleischman, Paul, Gwen Frankfeldt, and Glenn Morrow (2006) *Dateline: Troy,* 2nd edn. Cambridge, MA: Candlewick..

Foley, Helene (1994) *The Homeric Hymn to Demeter: Translation, Commentary, and Interpretative Essays.* Princeton, NJ: Princeton University Press.

(2012) *Re-imagining Greek Tragedy on the American Stage.* Berkeley, CA: University of California Press.

Fordyce, C. J. (1961) *Catullus. A Commentary.* Oxford: Oxford University Press.

Formicula, Crescenzo (2006) "Dark visibility: Lavinia in the *Aeneid*." *Vergilius* 52: 76–95.

Foucault, Michel (1979) *Discipline and Punish: The Birth of the Prison.* Trans. Alan Sheridan. New York: Vintage.

(1980) *The History of Sexuality,* vol. 1, *An Introduction.* Trans. Robert Hurley. New York: Vintage.

Fowler, D. P. (1992) "Postscript: Images of Horace in twentieth-century scholarship." In *Horace Made New,* eds. David Hopkins and Charles Martindale. Cambridge: Cambridge University Press. Pp. 268–76.

Frank, Richard I. (1975) "Augustus' legislation on marriage and children." *California Studies in Classical Antiquity.*8: 41–52.

Frank, Thomas (2005) *What's the Matter with Kansas?* Dumfries, NC: Holt McDougal.

Freud, Sigmund (1967) *The Interpretation of Dreams.* Trans. James Strachey. New York: Basic Books.

Fulkerson, Laurel (2002) "Epic ways of killing a woman: Gender and transgression in *Odyssey* 22.465–72." *The Classical Journal* 97(4): 335–50.

Gagarin, M. (1976). *Æschylean Drama.* Berkeley, CA: University of California Press.

Galinsky, Karl (1996) *Augustan Culture: An Interpretive Introduction.* Princeton, NJ: Princeton University Press.

Gantz, Timothy (1993) *Early Greek Myth: A Guide to Literary and Artistic Sources.* Baltimore, MD: Johns Hopkins University Press.

Garwood, Deborah (2003) "Myth as public dream: The metamorphosis of Mary Zimmerman's *Metamorphoses*." *PAJ: A Journal of Performance and Art* 25(1): 69–78.

Gide, André (1925, 1983) *Corydon.* Trans. Richard Howard. New York: Farrar, Straus, & Giroux.

Gildenhard, Ingo (2007) *Paideia Romana: Cicero's Tusculan Disputations.* Cambridge: Cambridge Philological Society.

Goldhill, S. (2002). *Who Needs Greek? Contests in the Cultural History of Hellenism.* Cambridge: Cambridge University Press.

(2006) "The touch of Sappho." In *Classics and the Uses of Reception,* eds. Charles Martindale and Richard F. Thomas. Oxford: Blackwell. Pp. 250–73.

Golding, William (1961) *The Hot Gates and other Occasional Pieces.* New York: Harcourt, Brace.

Graf, Fritz (1997) *Magic in the Ancient World.* Trans. F. Philip. Cambridge, MA: Harvard University Press.

Gratwick, A. S. (1993). *Menaechmi.* Cambridge: Cambridge University Press.

Gresseth, Gerald K. (1964) "The myth of Alcyone." *Transactions and Proceedings of the American Philological Association* 95: 88–98.

Griffith, M. (1977). *The Authenticity of "Prometheus Bound."* Cambridge: Cambridge University Press.

Gruen, Erich S. (2011) *Rethinking the Other in Antiquity*. Princeton, NJ: Princeton University Press.

Hall, Edith (1989) *Inventing the Barbarian*. Oxford: Oxford University Press.

  (2002) "Tony Harrison's 'Prometheus': A view from the left." *Arion* 10: 129–40.

Halleran, M. R. (1995). *Hippolytus*. Warminster, UK: Aris & Phillips.

Halperin, David (1995) *Saint Foucault: Towards a Gay Hagiography*. Oxford: Oxford University Press.

  (2002) *How to Do the History of Homosexuality*. Chicago, IL: University of Chicago Press.

Hanson, Victor Davis (2002) *An Autumn of War: What America Learned from September 11 and the War on Terrorism*. New York: Anchor.

Hardwick, Lorna (1999) "Placing Prometheus." In *Tony Harrison's Poetry, Drama and Film: The Classical Dimension*, ed. L. Hardwick. Milton Keynes, UK: The Open University, and atwww2.open.ac.uk/ClassicalStudies/GreekPlays/Colq99/colq99.htm

  (2003) *Reception Studies*. Greece and Rome New Surveys in the Classics No. 33. Oxford: Oxford University Press.

  (2006) "Murmurs in the Cathedral: The impact of translations from Greek poetry and drama on modern work in English by Michael Longley and Seamus Heaney." *Yearbook of English Studies* 36(1): 204–15.

Harris, Stephen L. and Gloria Platzner (2004) *Classical Mythology: Images and Insights*, 4th edn. New York: McGraw Hill.

Harrison, Thomas (2000) *The Emptiness of Asia: Aeschylus' Persians and the History of the Fifth Century*. London: Duckworth.

Hawkins, Harriet (1990) *Classics and Trash: Traditions and Taboos in High Literature and Popular Modern Genres*. Toronto: University of Toronto Press.

Heaney, Seamus, and Sophocles (2004a) *The Burial at Thebes: A Version of Sophocles' Antigone*. New York: Farrar, Straus, & Giroux.

  (2004b) "Title deeds: Translating a classic." *Proceedings of the American Philosophical Society* 148(4): 411–26.

Heitman, Richard (2005) *Taking Her Seriously: Penelope and the Plot of Homer's Odyssey*. Ann Arbor, MI: University of Michigan Press.

Herrick, Marvin T. (1966) "Hyrcanian tigers in Renaissance tragedy." In *The Classical Tradition: Literary and Historical Studies in Honor of Harry Caplan*, ed. L. Wallach. Ithaca, NY: Cornell University Press. Pp. 559–71.

Highet, Gilbert (1949) *The Classical Tradition: Greek and Roman Influences on the Western Literature*. Oxford: Oxford University Press.

Hillman, A. L., and Charles Cullen (1928) *Lucian: Mimes of the Courtesans*. New York: Press of Classic Lore.

Hobsbawm, Eric (2013) *Fractured Times: Culture and Society in the Twentieth Century*. Boston, MA: Little, Brown.

Hofmann, M., and J. Lasdun (1995). *After Ovid: New Metamorphoses*. New York: Farrar, Straus, & Giroux.

Holoka, James P. (ed.) (2003) *Simone Weil's The Iliad or the Poem of Force: A Critical Edition.* New York: Peter Lang.

Hopkins, David, and Tom Kurzanski (2006) *Antigone.* Arlington, TX: Silent Devil.

Horden, Peregrine, and Nicholas Purcell (2000) *The Corrupting Sea: A Study of Mediterranean History.* Oxford: Oxford University Press.

Housman, A. E. (1972). *The Classical Papers of A. E. Housman.* Edited by J. Diggle and F. R. D. Goodyear. Cambridge: Cambridge University Press.

Hubbard, Thomas (2003) "The architecture of Sophocles' (Ajax.)" *Hermes* 131(2): 158–71.

(2009) H-Net Book Review of Davidson. February 2009. Main URL: h-net.msu.edu

Hubert, Susan J. (1999) "What's wrong with this picture? The politics of *Ellen's* coming out party." *Journal of Popular Culture* 33: 31–6.

Hunter, Richard (2004) *Plato's Symposium.* Oxford: Oxford University Press.

Hutchinson, G. O. (2002) "The publication and individuality of Horace's *Odes* Book 1–3." *Classical Quarterly* 52: 517–37.

Isaac, Dan (1970) "Review of Performance Group 1970." *Educational Theatre Journal* 22(4): 432–6.

Jauss, Hans Robert (1982) *Toward an Aesthetic of Reception.* Trans. Timothy Bahti. Minneapolis, MN: University of Minnesota Press.

Jenkins, Thomas E. (2005) "An American 'Classic': Hillman and Cullen's *Mimes of the Courtesans.*" *Arethusa* 38: 387–414.

(2010) "X-rated Sophocles: Alice Tuan's *Ajax (por nobody).*" *Helios* 38: 181–91.

Jenkyns, Richard (2002) "Slaying Buffy." *Prospect Magazine Online* Issue 71, Feb. 2002.

Jowett, Lorna (2005) *Sex and the Slayer: A Gender Studies Primer for the "Buffy" Fan.* Middletown, CT: Wesleyan University Press.

Kallendorf, Craig (2007) *The Other Virgil: "Pessimistic" Readings of the Aeneid in Early Modern Culture.* Oxford: Oxford University Press.

Kane, Sarah (2001) *Complete Plays.* London: Methuen.

Karras, R. M. (2000) "Active/passive: Greek and Roman sexualities." *American Historical Review*, Oct. 2000: 1250–65.

Katz, M. A. (1991) *Penelope's Renown: Meaning and Indeterminacy in the Odyssey.* Princeton, NJ: Princeton University Press.

Kauffmann, Stanley (1966) "Homosexual drama and its disguises." *New York Times*, Jan. 23, 1966, sec. 2, p. 1

Kiefer, Otto (1934) *Sexual Life in Ancient Rome.* Trans. Gilbert and Helen Highet. London: George Routledge & Sons.

Kirk, G. S. (1990) *The Iliad: A Commentary,* vol. 2, *Books 5–8.* Oxford: Oxford University Press.

Kirkwood, Gordon M. (1952) "Thucydides' words for 'cause.'" *American Journal of Philology* 73(1): 37–61.

Knox, Bernard (1957) *Oedipus at Thebes.* New Haven, CT: Yale University Press.

(1961) "The Ajax of Sophocles." *Harvard Studies in Classical Philology* 65: 1–37.

(1993) *The Oldest Dead White European Males and other Reflections on the Classics.* New York: W. W. Norton.

Knox, Peter E. (1995) *Ovid: Select Epistles.* Cambridge: Cambridge University Press.

Koestenbaum, Wayne (1993) *The Queen's Throat: Opera, Homosexuality, and the Mystery of Desire.* New York: Poseidon Press.

Kostelanetz, Richard (1989) "The discovery of alternative theater: Notes on art performances in New York City in the 1960s and 1970s." *Perspectives of New Music* 27(1): 128–72.

LaBute, Neil (2007). *Wrecks and Other Plays.* New York: Faber & Faber.

Lane Fox, Robin (2004) *The Making of "Alexander."* Oxford: R&L.

Larson, Jennifer (2001) *Greek Nymphs: Myth, Cult, Lore.* Oxford: Oxford University Press.

Latacz, Joachim (1996) *Homer: His Art and His World.* Trans. James P. Holoka. Ann Arbor, MI: University of Michigan Press.

Lawrence, John Shelton (2010) "*Star Trek* as American monomyth." In *Star Trek as Myth: Essays on Symbol and Archetype at the Final Frontier,* ed. Matthew Wilhelm Kapell. Jefferson, NC: McFarland & Co. Pp. 93–111.

Lefkowitz, M. R. (1996). *Not out of Africa: How Afrocentrism Became an Excuse to Teach Myth as History.* New York: Basic Books.

Le Guin, Ursula (2008) *Lavinia.* Orlando, FL: Harcourt.

Leinieks, Valdis (1996) *The City of Dionysos. A Study of Euripides' Bakchai.* Stuttgart: Teubner.

Leonard, Miriam (2005) *Athens in Paris: Ancient Greece and the Political in Post-War French Thought.* Oxford: Oxford University Press.

Lesher, James (2006) "Some notable afterimages of Plato's *Symposium.*" In *Plato's Symposium: Issues in Interpretation and Reception,* eds. J. H. Lesher, D. Nails, and F. C. C. Sheffield. Cambridge, MA: Harvard University Press. Pp. 313–40.

Levine, Elana (2007) "*Buffy* and the 'New Girl Order': Defining feminism and femininity." In *Undead TV: Essays on Buffy the Vampire Slayer,* eds. E. Levine and L. A. Parks. Durham, NC: Duke University Press. Pp. 168–89.

Loraux, N. (1987) *Tragic Ways of Killing a Woman.* Trans. Anthony Forster. Cambridge, MA: Harvard University Press.

Lucas, C. (2005) *Small Tragedy.* New York: Samuel French.

Lyne, R. O. A. M. (1983) "Lavinia's Blush: Vergil, 'Aeneid' 12.64–70." *Greece & Rome* Second Series 30(1): 55–64.

MacLeish, Archibald (1967) *A Continuing Journey.* Boston, MA: Houghton Mifflin.

Marshall, C. W. (2003) "Aeneas the Vampire Slayer: A Roman model for why Giles kills Ben." *Slayage* 3.1. http://www.slayage.tv/essays/slayage9/Marshall.htm

Martindale, Charles (1993) *Redeeming the Text: Latin Poetry and the Hermeneutics of Reception.* Cambridge: Cambridge University Press.

(2006) "Thinking through Reception." In *Classics and the Uses of Reception,* eds. C. Martindale and R. F. Thomas. Malden, MA: Blackwell. Pp. 1–13.

McCarthy, K. (2000) *Slaves, Masters, and the Art of Authority in Plautine Comedy.* Princeton, NJ: Princeton University Press.

McClatchy, J. D. (2001) *Love Speaks Its Name: Gay and Lesbian Love Poems.* London: Everyman's Library.

McDermott, Emily (1989) *Euripides' Medea: The Incarnation of Disorder.* University Park, PA: Penn State University Press.

McDonald, Marianne (2001) "Eye of the camera, eye of the victim: *Iphigenia* in Euripides and Cacoyannis." In Winkler 2001. Pp. 90–101.

McLaughlin, Ellen (2005) *The Greek Plays.* New York: Theatre Communications Group.

Meineck, Peter (2008) "Talking the talk at Tusculum." *Arion* 16: 177–86.

Mendlesohn, Farah (2002) "Surpassing the love of vampires: Or, why (and how) a queer reading of the Buffy/Willow relationship is denied." In *Fighting the Forces: What's at Stake in Buffy the Vampire Slayer,* eds. R. V. Wilcox and D. Lavery. Lanham, MD: Rowman & Littlefield. Pp. 45–60.

Merlis, Mark (1999) *An Arrow's Flight.* New York: Stonewall Inn Editions.

Mezey, Robert (2000) *Collected Poems 1952–1999.* Fayetteville, AR: University of Arkansas Press.

Michelakis, Pantelis (2006) *Euripides: Iphigenia at Aulis.* London: Duckworth.

Michelini, Ann N. (1982) *Tradition and Dramatic Form in the Persians of Aeschylus.* Leiden: Brill.

Miller, Henry (1941) *The Colossus of Maroussi.* New York: New Directions.

Moddelmog, Debra A. (1993) *Readers and Mythic Signs: The Oedipus Myth in Twentieth-Century Fiction.* Carbondale, IL: Southern Illinois University Press.

Monod, J. (1971) *Chance and Necessity: An Essay on the Natural Philosophy of Modern Biology.* New York: Knopf.

Morris, Gay. (1996) "'Styles of the flesh': Gender in the dances of Mark Morris." In *Moving Words: Re-Writing Dance, ed. G. Morris.* London: Routledge. Pp. 124–38.

Morrison, Conall (2009) "The future of Greek tragedy." In *The Dreaming Body: Contemporary Irish Theatre,* eds. Melissa Sihra and Paul Murphy. Gerrards Cross, UK: Colin Smythe. Pp. 151–2.

Nelson, E. S. (2003) *Contemporary Gay American Poets and Playwrights: An A-to-Z Guide.* Westport, CT: Greenwood Press.

Nisbet, Gideon (2006) *Ancient Greece in Film and Popular Culture.* Exeter, UK: Bristol Phoenix Press.

Nisbet, R. G. M., and Niall Rudd (2004) *A Commentary on Horace: Odes Book III.* Oxford: Oxford University Press.

Nussbaum, Martha (1990) "Therapeutic arguments and structures of desire." In *Sexuality in Greek and Roman Society.* eds. D. Konstan and M. Nussbaum. Providence, RI: Brown University Press. Pp. 46–66.

Olson, S. Douglas (1990) "The stories of Agamemnon in Homer's *Odyssey.*" *Transactions of the American Philological Association* 120: 57–71.

Orwell, George (1949) *Nineteen Eighty-Four.* London: Secker & Warburg.

Otis, Brooks (1970) *Ovid as an Epic Poet,* 2nd edn. London: Cambridge University Press.

Parker, Holt (1993) "Sappho Schoolmistress." *Transactions of the American Philological Association* 123: 309–51.

(1997) "The teratogenic grid." In *Roman Sexualities*, eds. Judith P. Hallett and Marilyn Skinner. Princeton, NJ: Princeton University Press. Pp. 47–66.

Paulin, Tom (1990) *Seize the Fire.* London: Faber & Faber.

Pearson, Lionel (1952) "Prophasis and Aitia." *Transactions of the American Philological Association* 83: 205–23. = *Selected Papers* (1983, eds. D. Lateiner and S.A. Stephens) pp. 91–109.

Peraino, Judith (2005) *Listening to the Sirens: Musical Technologies of Queer Identity from Homer to Hedwig.* Berkeley, CA: University of California Press.

Performance Group (1970) *Dionysus in 69.* Edited by Richard Schechner. Photos by Frederick Eberstadt. New York: Farrar, Straus, & Giroux.

Podlecki, Anthony J. (1966) "The political significance of the Athenian 'tyrannicide'-cult." *Historia: Zeitschrift für Alte Geschichte* 15(2) 129–41.

Pollitt, J. J. (1972) *Art and Experience in Classical Greece.* Cambridge: Cambridge University Press.

Powell, Neil (1997) *Gay Love Poetry.* New York: Carroll & Graf.

Powers, Melinda (2009) "Unveiling Euripides." *Journal of Dramatic Theory and Criticism* Spring 2009: 5–20.

(2011) "Syncretic sites in Luis Alfaro's *Electricidad.*" *Helios* 38: 193–206.

Prins, Yopie (1999) *Victorian Sappho.* Princeton, NJ: Princeton University Press.

Pucci, Pietro (1980) *The Violence of Pity in Euripides' Medea.* Ithaca, NY: Cornell University Press.

(1992) *Oedipus and the Fabrication of the Father: Oedipus Tyrannus in Modern Criticism and Philosophy.* Baltimore, MD: Johns Hopkins University Press.

Rabinowitz, Nancy Sorkin (1993) *Anxiety Veiled: Euripides and the Traffic in Women.* Ithaca, NY: Cornell University Press.

Rankin, A. Vannan (1962) "Penelope's dreams in Books XIX and XX of the Odyssey." *Helikon* 2: 617–24.

Rea, J. (2010) "*Pietas* and post-colonialism in Ursula K. Le Guin's *Lavinia.*" *Classical Outlook* 87(4): 26–31.

Rees, B. R. (1972) "'Pathos' in the 'Poetics' of Aristotle." *Greece & Rome* Second Series 19(1): 1–11.

Rees, Roger (2004) *Romane Memento: Vergil in the Fourth Century.* London: Duckworth.

Richlin, Amy (1991) "Zeus and Metis: Foucault, feminism, classics." *Helios* 18(2): 160–80.

(1992) "Reading Ovid's rapes. In *Pornography and Representation in Greece and Rome*, ed. A. Richlin. Oxford: Oxford University Press. Pp. 158–79.

(1993) "Not before homosexuality: The materiality of the Cinaedus and the Roman law against love between men." *Journal of the History of Sexuality* 3: 523–73.

(2005) "Eros underground: Greece and Rome in gay print culture, 1953–65." *Journal of Homosexuality* 49(3–4): 421–61. Special issue on Classics, eds. Beert C. Verstraete and Vernon Provencal.

Robinson, Mary (1796) *Sappho and Phaon in a Series of Legitimate Sonnets, with Thoughts on Poetical Subjects and Anecdotes of the Grecian Poetess.* London: S. Gosnell.

Roisman, Hanna M. (2001) "The ever-present Odysseus: Eavesdropping and disguise in Sophocles' *Philoctetes.*" *Eranos* 99: 38–53.

(2005) *Sophocles: Philoctetes.* London: Duckworth.

Rosen, Stanley (1968) *Plato's Symposium.* New Haven, CT: Yale University Press.

Rozokoki, Alexandra (2001) "Penelope's dream in book 19 of the *Odyssey.*" *The Classical Quarterly* NS 51(1): 1–6.

Rudd, Niall (2006) "Reception: Some caveats (with special reference to the *Aeneid.*)" *Arion* 14(2): 1–20.

Ruden, Sarah (2008) *The Aeneid.* New Haven, CT: Yale University Press.

Russo, J. (1992) *A Commentary on Homer's Odyssey.* Oxford: Clarendon Press.

Said, Edward W. (1978) *Orientalism.* New York: Pantheon.

Schechner, Richard (1988) *Performance Theory*, 2nd edn. London: Routledge.

Schenker, David J. (1993) "Poetic voices in Horace's Roman odes." *The Classical Journal* 88(2): 147–66.

Schleiner, Winfried (1975) "Aeneas' flight from Troy." *Comparative Literature* 27 (2): 97–112.

Scodel, R. (1980) *The Trojan Trilogy of Euripides.* Göttingen: Vandenhoeck und Ruprecht.

Scully, J., and C. J. Herington (1975). *Prometheus Bound.* Oxford: Oxford University Press.

Seaford, Richard (1996) *Euripides: Bacchae.* Warminster, UK: Aris & Phillips.

Segal, C. P. (1969) *Landscape in Ovid's Metamorphoses: A Study in the Transformations of a Literary Symbol.* Weisbaden: Franz Steiner.

(1971) "The two worlds of Euripides' *Helen.*" *Transactions of the American Philological Association* 102: 553–614.

(1974) "Eros and incantation: Sappho and oral poetry." *Arethusa* 7: 139–60.

(1981) *Tragedy and Civilization: An Interpretation of Sophocles.* Cambridge, MA: Published for Oberlin College by Harvard University Press.

(1993) *Oedipus Tyrannus: Tragic Heroism and the Limits of Knowledge.* New York: Twayne.

(1997) *Dionysiac Poetics and Euripides' Bacchae*, expanded edn. Princeton, NJ: Princeton University Press.

Segal, Erich (1983) "Euripides: Poet of paradox." In *Oxford Readings in Greek Tragedy*, ed. E. Segal. Oxford: Oxford University Press. Pp. 244–53.

Shanley, John Patrick (2005) *Doubt.* New York: Theatre Communications Group.

Shanower, Eric (2002) *Age of Bronze, vol. 1, Behind the Scenes.* Orange, CA: Image Comics.

(2005) *Age of Bronze*, vol. 2, *Sacrifice*. Orange, CA: Image Comics.

Shein, Seth L. (2013) *Philoctetes*. Cambridge: Cambridge University Press.

Shogan, Colleen J. (2007) "Anti-intellectualism in the modern presidency: A Republican populism." *Perspectives on Politics* 5(2): 295–303.

Skoie, Mathilde,and Sonia Bjørnstad Velázquez (2006) *Pastoral and the Humanities: Arcadia Re-inscribed*. Exeter, UK: Bristol Phoenix Press.

Stanford, W. B. (1963) *Ajax*. London: Macmillan.

Starr, Chester (1960) "The history of the Roman Empire 1911–1960." *Journal of Roman Studies* 50(1–2): 149–60.

Steuter, Erin, and Deborah Wills (2008) *At War with Metaphor: Media, Propaganda, and Racism in the War on Terror*. Lanham, MD: Lexington Books.

Stevenson, Jonathan (1995) *Losing Mogadishu: Testing U.S. Policy in Somalia*. Annapolis, MD: Naval Institute Press.

Storrs, Ronald (1959) *Ad Pyrrham: A Polyglot Collection of Translations of Horace's Ode to Pyrrha (Book 1, Ode 5)*. Oxford: Oxford University Press.

Suzuki, M. (2007) "Rewriting the Odyssey in the twenty-first century: Mary Zimmerman's Odyssey and Margaret Atwood's Penelopiad." *College Literature* 34(2): 263–78.

Swarns, R. L. (2012) *American Tapestry: The Story of the Black, White, and Multiracial Ancestors of Michelle Obama*. New York: Amistad.

Sypniewski, Holly (2008) "The pursuit of Eros in Plato's *Symposium* and 'Hedwig and the Angry Inch,'" *International Journal of the Classical Tradition* 15(4): 558–86.

Taylor, Don (1990) *The War Plays: Iphigenia at Aulis, The Women of Troy, Helen*. London: Methuen.

Thomas, Richard (1988a) "Tree violation and ambivalence in Virgil." *Transactions of the American Philological Association* 118: 261–73.

(1988b) *Virgil, Georgics*. Cambridge: Cambridge University Press.

(2001) *Virgil and the Augustan Reception*. Cambridge: Cambridge University Press.

Thorp, John (1992) "The social construction of homosexuality." *Phoenix* 46: 54–65.

Tomasso, Vincent (2011) "Hard-boiled hot gates: Making the classical past other in Frank Miller's *Sin City*." In *Classics and Comics*, eds. George Kovacs and C. W. Marshall. Oxford: Oxford University Press. Pp. 145–58.

Treggiari, Susan (1991) *Roman Marriage: Iusti Coniuges from the Time of Cicero to the Time of Ulpian*. Oxford: Clarendon Press.

Tuan, Alice (2004) *Ajax (por nobody)*. In *Play: A Journal of Plays* 2: 35–86.

Unsworth, Barry (2002) *The Songs of the Kings*. London: Hamish Hamilton.

Walton, J. Michael (2009) *Euripides Our Contemporary*. Berkeley, CA: University of California Press.

Weber, Wilhelm (1936) "Commodus." In *The Cambridge Ancient History*, vol. XI. Cambridge: Cambridge University Press. Pp. 325–91.

Wells, Colin (1995) *The Roman Empire*, 2nd edn. Cambridge, MA: Harvard University Press.

West, David (2002) *Horace Odes III: Dulce Periculum.* Oxford: Oxford University Press.

West, M. L. (1979) "The Prometheus Trilogy." *Journal of Hellenic Studies* 99: 130–48.

Wiles, David (2005) "Sophoclean diptychs: Modern translations of dramatic poetry." *Arion: A Journal of Humanities and the Classics* Third Series 13(1): 9–26.

Wilkinson. L. P. (1978) *Classical Attitudes to Modern Issues.* London: William Kimber.

Williamson, David (2004) *Flatfoot: Incorporating the Comedy The Swaggering Soldier by Titus Maccius Plautus.* Sydney: Currency Press.

Wills, Garry (1984) *Cincinnatus: George Washington and the Enlightenment.* Garden City, NY: Doubleday.

Wiltshire, Susan Ford (1992) *Greece, Rome, and the Bill of Rights.* Norman, OK: University of Oklahoma Press.

Winkler, Martin M. (2001) *Classical Myth & Culture in the Cinema.* Oxford: Oxford University Press.

Witke, Charles (1983) *Horace's Roman Odes. Mnemosyne* Supplement vol. 77. Leiden: Brill.

Wood, Elizabeth (1994) "Sapphonics." in *Queering the Pitch: The New Gay and Lesbian Musicology*, eds. Philip Brett, Elizabeth Wood, and Gary C. Thomas. Routledge: New York. Pp. 27–66.

Wyke, Maria (1978) "Written women: Propertius' Scripta Puella." *Journal of Roman Studies* 77: 47–61.

Yatromanolakis, Dimitrios (2007) *Sappho in the Making: The Early Reception.* Cambridge, MA: Harvard University Press.

Zeitlin, F. (1978) "The dynamics of misogyny: Myth and mythmaking in the *Oresteia.*" *Arethusa* 11: 149–81.

    (1996) *Playing the Other: Gender and Society in Classical Greek Literature.* Chicago, IL: University of Chicago Press.

Ziolkowski, Jan (2007) "Middle Ages." In *A Companion to the Classical Tradition*, ed. Craig W. Kallendorf. Oxford: Blackwell. Pp. 17–29.

Ziolkowski, Theodore (2005) "Uses and abuses of Horace: His reception since 1935 in Germany and Anglo-America." *International Journal of the Classical Tradition* 12(2): 183–215.

Index

241

Printed in the United States
By Bookmasters